Damaged Goods

Damaged Goods

*The Inside Story of Sir Philip Green, the Collapse
of BHS and the Death of the High Street*

OLIVER SHAH

PORTFOLIO
PENGUIN

PORTFOLIO

UK | USA | Canada | Ireland | Australia
India | New Zealand | South Africa

Portfolio is part of the Penguin Random House group of companies whose
addresses can be found at global.penguinrandomhouse.com.

First published 2018
002

Set in 12/14.75 pt Dante MT Std
Typeset by Jouve (UK), Milton Keynes
Printed in Great Britain by Clays Ltd, Elcograf S.p.A.

A CIP catalogue record for this book is available from the British Library

HARDBACK ISBN: 978–0–241–34118–6
TRADE PAPERBACK ISBN: 978–0–241–34121–6

www.greenpenguin.co.uk

For Henry Hector, Melissa Tarrant, George Vallossian and all the sources who made this story possible

Contents

A word of thanks

With special thanks to Toby Mundy, my agent; Lydia Yadi, my editor at Penguin Random House; Eric Musgrave, for his painstaking archive research; Pia Sarma and the legal team at the *Sunday Times*, for all their help with the original BHS stories; and to Judi Bevan, John Jay and Richard Hyman, for their forensic reading of the draft manuscript.

The protagonists

The following descriptions indicate the positions occupied by the main characters, some of whom have since moved on or retired, at the time of the events set out in this book. They also include any titles held at the time of writing, although some of these were not awarded until after the events described, and so are not used in the text.

Ros Altmann	Pensions minister
Mike Ashley	Founder of Sports Direct
Ted Ball	Founder of Landhurst Leasing
Sir David and Sir Frederick Barclay	Backers of Sir Philip Green's takeover bid for Sears
David Barraclough	Managing director at HSBC
Neil Bennett	PR adviser to Sir Philip Green and chief executive of Maitland
Tony Berry	Executive chairman of Blue Arrow
George Bingham	Neighbour of Dominic Chappell in Dorset
Chris Blackhurst	City editor of the *Evening Standard*
Andy Bond	Former chief executive of Asda
Stephen Bourne	Former head of corporate finance at BDO Stoy Hayward and adviser to Retail Acquisitions
Baroness Karren Brady	Chair of Taveta Investments, Arcadia Group's holding company, since 2017
Robert Breare	Founder of Snoozebox and associate of Paul Sutton
Rebekah Brooks	Chief executive of News UK
Henry Broughton	Son of Lord and Lady Fairhaven
James Broughton	Son of Lord and Lady Fairhaven

The protagonists

Alex Brummer	City editor of the *Daily Mail*
Karen Buck	Labour MP and member of the BHS select committee
Paul Budge	Finance director of Arcadia Group
Neil Burns	Brother-in-law of Paul Sutton
Jackie Caring (née Stead)	Wife of Richard Caring between 1971 and 2016
Richard Caring	Hong Kong-based clothing supplier; later owner of Annabel's and other fashionable London venues
Simon Cawkwell	Short seller known as Evil Knievel
Dominic Chandler	Barrister and legal adviser to Retail Acquisitions
Damon Chappell	Brother of Dominic Chappell
Dominic Chappell	Serial bankrupt and 90 per cent owner of Retail Acquisitions
Joe Chappell	Father of Dominic Chappell
Rebecca Chappell	Wife of Dominic Chappell
Owen Clay	Partner at Linklaters and adviser to Sir Philip Green
Sir Charles Clore	Pioneer of the hostile takeover
Paul Coackley	Finance director of Sears after Sir Philip Green's takeover; later finance director and chief operating officer of BHS between 2000 and 2010
Graham Coles	Finance director of Amber Day
Jean Costello	Shop worker at BHS in South Shields
Jack Cotton	Business partner of Sir Charles Clore
Simon Cowell	Creator of *The X Factor* and *Britain's Got Talent*
Geoff Cruickshank	Head of intelligence at the Pensions Regulator
Peter Cummings	Head of corporate lending at Bank of Scotland, later HBOS

The protagonists

Paul Dacre	Editor of the *Daily Mail*
Malcolm Dalgleish	Property agent and adviser to Sir Philip Green; later European chairman of retail at CBRE
John Danhakl	Joint managing partner of Leonard Green & Partners
Alex Dellal	Property trader and grandson of 'Black Jack' Dellal
Steve Denison	Partner at PwC and auditor to Arcadia Group
Dr Margaret Downes	Chair of the BHS pension trustees between 2000 and the end of 2013
Joseph Dryer	Head of capital markets at RiverRock and adviser to Retail Acquisitions
Phil Duffy	Managing director of Duff & Phelps; appointed as administrator to BHS
Robert Earl	Founder of Planet Hollywood and Everton FC stakeholder
Panos Eliades	Schoolfriend of Sir Philip Green; later an insolvency professional
Jimmy Evans	Violent criminal and protection man for Tony Schneider
Lord and Lady Fairhaven	Owners of the Kirtling estate near Newmarket and victims of Paul Sutton
Frank Field	Labour MP and joint chairman of the BHS select committee
Steve Frankham	Building contractor who bankrupted Dominic Chappell over the Island Harbour property development
Richard Fuller	Conservative MP and member of the BHS select committee
Sir David Garrard	Chairman of Minerva, parent company of Allders
Rodney Geminder	Shoe importer and Sir Philip Green's first employer

Rory Godson	Business editor of the *Sunday Times* between 2001 and 2002
Adam Goldman	Company secretary of Arcadia Group
Ian Grabiner	Senior employee at What Everyone Wants; later chief executive of Arcadia Group
Lord Tony Grabiner	Chairman of Taveta Investments, Arcadia Group's holding company, between 2002 and 2017
Peter Graf	Former chief executive of Charles Vögele
Alma Green (née Bull)	Mother of Sir Philip Green
Brandon Green	Son of Lady Cristina Green and Sir Philip Green
Chloe Green	Daughter of Lady Cristina Green and Sir Philip Green
Lady Cristina Green (née Stuart)	Wife of Sir Philip Green
Elizabeth Green	Sister of Sir Philip Green
Sir Philip Green	Chairman of Arcadia Group
Simon Green (originally Terkeltaub)	Father of Sir Philip Green
Terry Green	Chief executive of Debenhams; later chief executive of BHS (no relation to Sir Philip Green)
Sir Rick Greenbury	Executive chairman of Marks & Spencer between 1991 and 1999
Prince Albert Grimaldi II	Reigning monarch of Monaco
Anthony Gutman	Co-head of UK investment banking at Goldman Sachs
Chris Harris	Property director of Arcadia Group
Jonathan Hawker	PR adviser to BHS

The protagonists

Henry Hector	Harbourmaster for Dominic Chappell's Island Harbour property development
Lennart Henningson	Friend of Joe Chappell and member of Retail Acquisitions
Aida Dellal Hersham	Close friend of Sir Philip Green in the late 1990s
Brian Hill	Head of menswear at BHS at the time of Sir Philip Green's takeover
Michael Hitchcock	Interim finance director of BHS between 2015 and 2016
Roger Holmes	Chief executive of Marks & Spencer between 2002 and 2004
Sir Tom Hunter	Founder of Sports Division
Eddie Irvine	Retired racing driver and friend of Dominic Chappell
Martin Ivens	Editor of the *Sunday Times* since 2013
John Jay	*Sunday Telegraph* City editor; later managing editor for business news at the *Sunday Times* between 1995 and 2001
Jón Ásgeir Jóhannesson	Chief executive of Baugur Group
Jilly Johnson	Member of Blonde on Blonde and Page Three model
Neville Kahn	Managing partner at Deloitte and adviser to Sir Philip Green
Stephen Kay	Owner of video wholesaler Intervision
Bill Kenwright	Theatre producer and owner of Everton FC
Morris Keston	Tottenham Hotspur superfan
Vimla Lalvani	Yoga guru and girlfriend of Sir Philip Green in the mid-1980s
Madeleine Legwinski	Ex-wife of footballer Sylvain Legwinski and victim of Paul Sutton

Allan Leighton	Chief executive of Asda; later serial non-executive director
Roger Levitt	Disgraced insurance salesman and boxing promoter
Will Lewis	Business editor of the *Sunday Times* between 2002 and 2005
John Lovering	Finance director at Sears; later serial private equity investor
Sir Laurie Magnus	Investment banker at Samuel Montagu and later Donaldson, Lufkin and Jenrette
Chris Martin	Chairman of the BHS pension trustees since January 2014
Paul Martin	Partner at Grant Thornton and adviser to Retail Acquisitions
David Mayhew	Chairman of Cazenove
Paul McGowan	Chief executive of Hilco UK
Patricia Mondinni	Partner of Richard Caring since 2016
Philip Monjack	Insolvency professional at Leonard Curtis and associate of Sir Philip Green
Kate Moss	Supermodel
Rupert Murdoch	Ultimate owner of newspapers including the *Sunday Times*
Lord Myners	Chairman of Marks & Spencer between 2004 and 2006
Andrew Neil	Editor of the *Sunday Times* between 1983 and 1994
Simon Neville	Nephew of Sir Philip Green
Sir David Norgrove	Chairman of the Marks & Spencer pension trustees
Richard North	Finance director of Bass
Katie O'Brien	PA to Sir Philip Green
Dominic O'Connell	Business editor of the *Sunday Times* between 2010 and 2016

Brett Palos	Stepson of Sir Philip Green
Stasha Palos	Stepdaughter of Sir Philip Green
Eddie Parladorio	Legal director of Retail Acquisitions
Chai Patel	Care homes boss and prospective Labour peer
Jeremy Quin	Conservative MP and member of the BHS select committee
Jeff Randall	City and then business editor of the *Sunday Times* between 1989 and 1995; later business editor of the BBC and business presenter for Sky News
Richard 'Ratty' Ratner	City analyst
Sir Bob Reid	Chairman of Sears between 1995 and 1999
David and Simon Reuben	Aluminium trader brothers; later property tycoons and sometime associates of Sir Philip Green
John Richards	Analyst at NatWest Securities; later Deutsche Bank financier
Bruce Ritchie	Founder of Residential Land and friend of Sir Philip Green
David Roberts	Partner at Olswang and adviser to Retail Acquisitions
Nick Robertson	Founder of Asos
Steve Rodger	Former business partner of Dominic Chappell in Spain
Gerald Ronson	Property tycoon jailed for his role in the Guinness share-support scandal; later developer of the Heron Tower in the City
Lord Stuart Rose	Chief executive of Arcadia Group and later Marks & Spencer between 2004 and 2010, the last two years as executive chairman
Andrew Rosenfeld	Chief executive of Minerva, parent company of Allders

The protagonists

Alan Rubenstein	Chief executive of the Pension Protection Fund
Peter Salsbury	Chief executive of Marks & Spencer between 1998 and 2000
Robin Saunders	Head of securitization and then principal finance at WestLB; later founder of Clearbrook Capital
Peter de Savary	Property developer and friend of Blue Arrow boss Tony Berry
Tony Schneider	Loan shark
Irvine Sellar	Founder of Mates fashion chain; later property developer
Jane Shepherdson	Brand director of Topshop between 1998 and 2006
Mark Sherwood	Partner at Vail Williams and property director of Retail Acquisitions
Mike Sherwood	Star bond trader at Goldman Sachs; later joint head of Goldman Sachs in Europe
Keith Smith	Dominic Chappell's uncle and chairman of Retail Acquisitions
Jon Sokoloff	Joint managing partner of Leonard Green & Partners
David Stamler	Sir Philip Green's headmaster at Carmel College
Lord Dennis Stevenson	Non-executive director of Blue Arrow; later chairman of HBOS
Liam Strong	Chief executive of Sears between 1992 and 1997
Ian Stuart	Head of commercial banking in Europe at HSBC; later UK chief executive
Lord Alan Sugar	Founder of Amstrad and majority shareholder in Tottenham Hotspur FC between 1991 and 2001
Paul Sutton	Convicted fraudster

Nicola Tarrant	Girlfriend of Paul Sutton
Mark Tasker	Head of commercial department at Bates Wells Braithwaite and adviser to Retail Acquisitions
Wesley Taylor	Brand director of Burton
Robert Tchenguiz	Iranian-born property tycoon; friend of Sir Philip Green
David Thompson	Sir Philip Green's successor at Amber Day; later Green's business partner at Owen Owen
Kenny Tibber	Job buyer and friend of Sir Philip Green
Harold Tillman	Chairman of Honorbilt menswear chain and friend of Sir Philip Green
Lesley Titcomb	Chief executive of the Pensions Regulator
Darren Topp	Chief executive of BHS between 2015 and 2016
Aidan Treacy	Finance director of Retail Acquisitions
George Vallossian	Hairdresser based in Knightsbridge and husband of Melissa Tarrant
Melissa Vallossian (née Tarrant)	Sister of Paul Sutton's girlfriend, Nicola Tarrant
Luc Vandevelde	Chairman of Marks & Spencer between 2000 and 2004
Terry Venables	Manager and later part-owner of Tottenham Hotspur FC
Paul Wareham	Dominic Chappell's best man and project manager for Retail Acquisitions
Leslie Warman	Non-executive director of Amber Day
Frank Warren	Boxing promoter
Malcolm Weir	Head of restructuring at the Pension Protection Fund
Gerald and Vera Weisfeld	Founders of What Everyone Wants
Christo Wiese	South African retail tycoon

The protagonists

Bob Wigley European chairman of Merrill Lynch

Charles Wilson Right-hand man to Lord Stuart Rose at Marks & Spencer between 2004 and 2005; later chief executive of Booker and UK chief executive of Tesco

Robert Winnett Investigative journalist at the *Sunday Times* and later the *Daily Telegraph*

John Witherow Editor of the *Sunday Times* between 1995 and 2013

Virginia and Dick Withers Farmers and victims of Paul Sutton

Iain Wright Labour MP and joint chairman of the BHS select committee

Michelle Young (née Orwell) Wife of Scot Young

Scot Young Associate of Tony Schneider; later property developer

Defenestration

Envy and jealousy, my doctor told me, are two incurable diseases.
I have done nothing wrong.

Sir Philip Green to the BHS select committee, 15 June 2016

There are times as a journalist when you step back and think: *Is this really happening?*

The morning of 23 April 2016 was one of those moments. It was a bright spring Saturday, and the king of the high street was threatening to kill me.

I was a thirty-two-year-old reporter on the *Sunday Times*. I had spent the past year pursuing Sir Philip Green, the billionaire owner of brands such as Topshop, asking awkward questions about his sale of the department-store chain BHS, once known as British Home Stores. For the token sum of £1, Green had passed the tired high-street institution and its 164 shops – heavily loss-making, riddled with asbestos and struggling to support a huge pension liability – to a charlatan with no real business experience. Dominic Chappell, the buyer, had turned out to be a serial bankrupt and a fantasist. From the start, I had suspected Green was trying to distance himself from BHS's inevitable collapse and the whopping £571 million pension bill that would land on his desk if it happened under his watch. With an estimated family fortune of £3.2 billion, he could easily have afforded to make good his debt to BHS's 20,000 pension-fund members. Now, little more than a year on from the sale, I caught wind that BHS was about to file for administration. The previous evening, one of my best contacts had called me as I travelled home from work. 'Monday's going to be a big day for the retail industry,' he teased. I hurried home, rang him back and pleaded for the full story. Green still held BHS's strings like a puppet master because he was its biggest lender and had the power to call in his loan. 'Philip's had enough,' my source confided. 'He's going to put BHS under.'

That Saturday morning, I sat at my desk on the ninth floor of the *Sunday Times* building in London Bridge and looked out at the springtime light glowing over Southwark. Swallowing the knot of fear that always preceded a call to Green, I dialled his number. We both knew that BHS's demise would bring the pension scandal out into the open.

The tycoon answered on the first ring.

'You know I'm not going to talk to you, don't you,' he said, his voice gravelly yet nasal. This was the latest in a series of skirmishes we had fought. I told Green that I was working on a new story about BHS. 'What a shock!' he replied, not missing a beat.

I put it to him that a firm of insolvency specialists based in Manchester, Duff & Phelps, had been lined up to place the department store into administration. This time there was a pause. 'Incorrect,' Green said. 'OK? All of it incorrect. OK? So be careful what you're writing. I'm not going to engage with you, I'm going to engage with your editor. Whatever answers you get, you write what the fuck you like. You don't give a fuck about the consequences.'

I told Green that I would write what I thought was the truth. That provoked a volcanic eruption. 'If you want to come and call me a liar, come round to my office on Monday, call me a liar to my face and face the consequences,' he shouted. 'How's that, if you're such a big fucking boy? Because you will get thrown through the fucking window. You're not a nice individual. You couldn't give a fuck what trouble you cause. I find it pretty sad that the *Sunday Times* can't find anything better to put on their front page than BHS.'

This was the king of the high street as the public never heard him. Mr Toad-like in appearance, with a bulging belly and a mischievous grin, Green was a business celebrity, often spotted on the front row of fashion shows between Kate Moss and Anna Wintour. Nut-brown from the Monaco sun, his silver hair slicked back into a rat's tail, he relished the role he had carved out for himself as the retail industry's roguish uncle. Bankers from Goldman Sachs and HSBC fell over themselves to offer him money and advice. Simon Cowell and Ronnie Wood attended his parties. He had paid his wife almost £2 billion of offshore dividends from his high-street empire and made two headline-grabbing hostile takeover attempts for Marks & Spencer. He had been knighted by Tony Blair despite his family's address in a tax haven – a striking example of New Labour's intensely relaxed attitude to the filthy rich – and been made a special adviser to David Cameron.

Green loved to manipulate the media, and the *Sunday Times* had previously been his favourite newspaper. Just nine months before that expletive-laden phone call, relations had been good enough for Green to invite me and the business editor to the tenth anniversary party of his Fashion Retail Academy, the not-for-profit venture that earned him his knighthood. The event, held at the grand Freemasons' Hall in Covent Garden, was classic Green. The ornate interior was transformed into a kind of nightclub, with turquoise lights flashing and dance music pounding. The main hall was packed with the crème de la crème of both business and politics. The Topshop boss sat in a prime position, wearing an open-necked shirt, flanked by Marc Bolland, then chief executive of M&S, and Tony Blair. Vernon Kay, the TV presenter, sashayed onstage with a mock catwalk strut to present the evening's entertainment. Blair gave the first speech, recalling how civil servants had warned him the larger-than-life businessman could be 'quite direct' in a briefing before Green visited Number Ten to discuss his idea for the academy – 'which indeed he was . . '. Philip never graduated from the school of diplomacy, he graduated from the school of life,' the former prime minister said. He recounted how he had asked Green, 'What do you want me to do?' And Green had quipped, 'You're a politician – I don't expect you to do anything.' Blair praised him as 'the person who thought up the dream and dreamt the dream into reality'.

Green was uncharacteristically modest when he took to the podium, his market trader's voice somehow softer at the edges. 'Ten years seem to have gone by in a flash,' he said, fiddling with his reading glasses. 'I don't want to spend the next year thanking all the people who have been involved in making this happen, but it's taken more than just me.'

Paloma Faith closed the party with an acoustic performance of the pop drum 'n' bass hit 'Changing'. It was unintentionally apt. That evening in 2015 was the end of an era – the last time Green would be able to attract grand guests and lord it over the retail industry. Beneath the event's glitzy surface, insiders were already murmuring about the dubious deal he had done on BHS. Those who looked closely saw he was unshaven and had dark rings under his eyes. He seemed tired and shifty when he gave an interview to the editor of a trade magazine at the end of the night. The journalist suggested that Green had originally contacted Blair to ask for his support for the academy. 'No, no, he called me,' Green snapped, his eyes flicking to the camera.

On 24 April 2016 – despite his denials – the *Sunday Times* broke the news that changed everything. The article, headlined 'BHS on the Brink as Rescue Talks Fail', exposed a behind-the-scenes power struggle between Green and Chappell. It said the row was 'likely to tip BHS into administration' the next morning, putting 11,000 jobs at risk, and it noted that Green and his partners had taken out more than £400 million of dividends before the enormous pension deficit emerged. As the BBC picked up the report on Sunday morning, Green called the *Sunday Times'* business editor, Dominic O'Connell, to complain. He ranted about how unfair the coverage had been. Exasperated after a year of heavy-handed lobbying from the billionaire, O'Connell declared that BHS's failure was Green's own fault and hung up. As their relationship disintegrated over the following weeks, Green threatened O'Connell, advising him, 'Be careful next time you're walking down a dark alley on your way home.' '*Really*, Philip?' asked the incredulous editor.

Green told business associates he thought the press would quickly tire of BHS's collapse. Clearly, he underestimated the strength of public feeling. On Monday 25th, the crisis made the front pages of

The Guardian and the *Daily Mirror*. On Tuesday 26th, the *Daily Mail* splashed with the headline, 'Sharks Who Bled BHS Dry'. The *Mail* story said that 'Sir Philip Green pocketed £400 million from the 164-store chain before presiding over its decline and selling it for just £1'. Richard Fuller, a Conservative MP, revived the 'unacceptable face of capitalism' slogan first applied in the 1970s to Tiny Rowland, the Lonrho tycoon who was accused of bribing African leaders and violating international sanctions on Rhodesia, as Zimbabwe was then known. By Wednesday morning, Green was showing signs of strain. Duff & Phelps, which had been appointed early on Monday, organized a round-table meeting for the various parties involved at the headquarters of Green's Arcadia Group behind Oxford Street in London. The professionals were brought in by a back door to avoid any journalists lurking at the front. Green waited for them at the end of a plush-carpeted corridor leading to the boardroom on the sixth floor, greeting each in turn. When it came to a property agent from Savills who had been appointed to review BHS's store portfolio, he suddenly let rip. 'Fucking Savills, you fucking cunts!' he exploded at the bewildered agent, who assumed Green must have had some previous beef with the firm. 'Your valuations always come in fucking millions below where they should be!' The diatribe continued as the assembled cast took their seats around the boardroom table. Green then stopped and levelled a finger at an experienced lawyer from DLA Piper, who was sitting in stunned silence. 'Who are you?' he asked abruptly. The lawyer was so terrified he suffered what one onlooker described as a 'complete meltdown'. 'M-M-M,' he stuttered, unable to get his name out. Phil Duffy, a bluff Mancunian who was running the administration for Duff & Phelps, had to intervene and make the introduction. From that point on, everyone spoke slowly and carefully, their eyes fixed on the table as if it held an autocue.

Green might have been able to control rooms filled with insolvency practitioners and lawyers, but he was unable to manage the media circus. Over the coming weeks, as thousands of mostly low-paid BHS staff lost their jobs and its pension-fund members were thrown into limbo, the Topshop boss became engulfed in his own personal Alamo.

On 10 June, as the outcry became deafening, the *Mail* demanded the previously unthinkable on its front page, 'Strip Sir Shifty of His Title!' Five days later, he was hauled snarling before a special committee of MPs and accused of trying to duck his obligation to BHS's pensioners. He promised Parliament that he would 'sort it', but not before putting on a display of remarkable petulance. Green barked at Richard Fuller, the Tory member who had deployed the Tiny Rowland barb, to stop 'looking at me like that all the time'. He then made clear who he saw as the real victim. 'I could be a murderer, the way they're writing about me,' Green complained. 'I haven't got any guns, but the stuff that's getting written every day is pretty outrageous.'

Despite being in the middle of a firestorm, Green still found time to give me his frank views on the *Sunday Times'* coverage of BHS's collapse. 'You think you're being a fucking smartarse,' he ranted down the phone, 'writing this, that and the other. But let's see the end of the movie. OK? When you've got to write across your front page an apology. Because that's what the end of the movie will be.'

With no end in sight to the pension crisis, the tycoon thumbed his nose at public opinion and escaped for a two-month cruise around the Greek islands on his new £100 million superyacht, *Lionheart*, a 300ft floating village with its own helipad and swimming pool. Jean Costello, a BHS shop worker who had lost her job at the South Shields branch, went on ITV to give her opinion. 'I could sit and cry, when I look at what he's got, and I was coming down here with corned beef sandwiches on the train,' she said. Throughout a long, torrid summer when the only other big news was the Brexit vote, tabloid reporters and paparazzi hired speedboats to pursue Green around the Mediterranean. Confronted by a Sky News crew on a morning constitutional walk around the harbour of Ithaca, he tussled with the cameraman, shouting, 'That's going to go in the fucking sea.' Green's wife, Tina, was unimpressed – both by her husband's behaviour and by his treatment at the hands of a media that had built him up for so long. She texted a relative to say the events had been 'devastating for our family'.

Attitudes towards brashness and wealth had shifted like tectonic plates since Green's heyday in the mid-2000s – imperceptibly at first, then with unstoppable force. Two years on from that summer, Green still did not seem to understand. 'If you want to make a fucking career out of Philip Green, don't get it wrong,' he warned when I approached him about this project. 'Because I will sue your arse off if you write one word in that book that's wrong.' BHS may have disappeared, but his problems are far from over. Topshop's sales are declining at an alarming rate and Arcadia has disclosed a pension deficit bigger than the shortfall that toppled BHS. The most famous retail tycoon of his generation faces the dilemma of a lifetime as he decides whether to stand and fight or extricate himself from his crumbling empire.

Green's rise and fall is a story with profound implications for the way we live.

It is a tale of an exceptionally determined middle-class boy from north London who shunned a privileged education to learn business the hard way. It is about learning to detest the establishment while simultaneously craving its recognition. It is the story of the long post-war consumption boom that powered the expansion of property-heavy high-street chains, and the go-go years of cheap debt and weak corporate governance in the 1990s and 2000s, when some of those brands surrendered to takeover bids and were broken up. It is an indictment of the media and the political class, both of which were quick to venerate celebrity and wealth while turning a blind eye to bullying and threats. It is the story of how rag traders with quick minds and an instinct for the public's desire to consume were over-taken by university graduates with cloud computers full of big data. Since Blair's landslide election victory in 1997, online retail sales have gone from almost nothing to more than £60 billion a year, with com-petition becoming fiercer and smartphone shopping proliferating. BHS withered and died partly because of the shift in consumer spend-ing. With former giants like Debenhams, M&S and Tesco struggling to adapt, BHS will not be the last household name to disappear.

Most of all, Green's story is one of intense ambition undone by old-fashioned greed. In other words, it is the story of life in the early twenty-first century.

2.

Wapping Stories

The *Sunday Times* is renowned as one of the toughest national papers in Britain. Its red meat are exclusives and scoops, which are fiendishly difficult to find and even harder to stand up. When I first joined, aged twenty-six, it was still based in Fortress Wapping, the warehouse complex in east London where Rupert Murdoch's titles moved when he broke the print unions in 1986. Entry was via a pillbox-style security post emblazoned with the logos of *The Times*, the *Sunday Times*, *The Sun* and the *News of the World*. I arrived for my junior reporter's interview in August 2010 jangling with nerves, eager to move on from *City AM*, the daily freesheet where I had been churning out ten articles a day. To my immense relief, I was summarily told by the business editor, Dominic O'Connell, 'The job's yours if you want it.'

The *Sunday Times* was based in a hulking old printing plant in the middle of the Wapping site. There was a strange water feature in the foyer, perhaps installed as a token effort to make it feel more like an office, which gave off a smell of stale chlorine. An antique typesetting machine sat in the corridor by the lifts and a portrait of Murdoch looked down on everyone entering and leaving. The newsroom on the fifth floor was a drab place, dominated by stacks of yellowing newspapers and ancient desktop PCs. One of the few sources of daylight was a tiny moss-encrusted skylight. To my beginner's eyes, the temperature seemed to rise relentlessly throughout the week until it reached boiling point on press day – Saturday. The front-page headline on the Sunday of my first week, 26 September 2010, was 'Victorious Ed Miliband Begs David Not to Quit' – a reference to the younger Miliband's surprise win over his more plausible brother for the Labour leadership. The paper has since moved to its modern offices in London Bridge, but the culture has stayed the same: sweat, stress and occasionally tears are poured into every edition.

The DNA of the *Sunday Times* is part broadsheet and part tabloid, and its history is an equal mix of landmark investigations – Thalidomide, Cambridge spies, cash for questions, the Qatari World Cup scandal – and high jinks. There were moments of farce that would not have been out of place at a tabloid: in 1995, the newsroom was occupied by an action group known as The Lesbian Avengers after a reporter, Maurice Chittenden, wrote an article claiming that lesbians were 'on the warpath and their unlikely target is Britain's gay men'. Chittenden happened to be sitting there as they stormed in. 'Where's Maurice Chittenden?' one Avenger asked him. 'Maurice Chittenden?' Chittenden mumbled, standing up. 'No, he's out.' The Lesbian Avengers were eventually removed after the new editor, John Witherow, emerged from his office scowling and called the police. The next day's *News of the World* carried the headline, 'The Editor, Sixty Coppers, Eight Lesbians (and Four Pairs of Handcuffs!)'.

The business desk perfectly embodied the paper's irreverent side. Almost every *Sunday Times* business editor since the late 1980s has been state schooled and educated outside Oxbridge, an unusually consistent exception to the elitism still rife in journalism, including in the main part of the paper. Whereas in the 1990s and 2000s the *Sunday Telegraph* may have had better contacts among blue-chip companies like British Airways, M&S and Rolls-Royce, the *Sunday Times* championed up-and-coming new-money entrepreneurs who often used debt and white-knuckle tactics to wrest control of companies. There was Mohammed Al-Fayed, who fought an epic battle with the *Observer* owner Tiny Rowland for control of Harrods, leading to Al-Fayed's censure by the Department of Trade and Industry; Gerald Ronson, who emerged from a six-month prison sentence for his involvement in the Guinness share-support scandal and rebuilt his Heron property empire with help from Bill Gates and Rupert Murdoch, among others;

Sir David and Sir Frederick Barclay, painters and decorators who were accused of asset-stripping but went on to buy trophy properties such as the Ritz and the *Telegraph* newspapers; Sir Tom Hunter, a green-grocer's son from a small town in East Ayrshire who ploughed the fortune he made from selling Sports Division into several takeovers; David and Simon Reuben, Indian-born brothers who made more than £1 billion trading aluminium in Russia after the break-up of the Soviet Union; and there was Sir Philip Green. These buccaneering newcomers, unconstrained by corporate structures or PR advisers, were often fantastic sources of information.

Those of us who worked on the business section would regularly pick up the phone to hear Green's staccato voice dispensing tips and requesting favours. Green had an insider's understanding of newspapers. He grasped the impact of a direct call from a billionaire to a journalist, and he knew how a well-timed leak could sometimes nudge a deal or dispute in his favour. At one point, when he was trying to think of a title for an authorized biography that eventually never materialized, Green came up with *Lucky 5766*. As a circle of trusted contacts knew, 5766 was the extension number of the *Sunday Times'* business editor.

I was something of an anomaly among my colleagues. Bespectacled, Cambridge-educated and initially fairly shy, I was far from the typical *Sunday Times* business-desk recruit of the 2000s. When I arrived, I was seated between a hardened mergers and acquisitions reporter from Grimsby and a City news veteran known as the Yorkshire Terrier. At the end of my first day, a small group went for a drink in west London, where a business editor from a rival paper was having her leaving party. The night ended with one of my new colleagues rolling around on the floor of the pub fighting a reporter from another paper, fists flying and – allegedly – an ear being bitten. I slipped into work late the next morning feeling awful, unable to believe I had allowed myself to come in hungover on the second day of my dream job. I felt better when my errant colleague came in at 4 p.m., looking like death. He barely spoke to anyone and left after an hour.

The *Sunday Times* was different from anywhere I had worked

before. Its weekly circulation of 1.1 million copies meant it had real power. Corporate leaders suddenly wanted to take my calls. My boss, Dominic O'Connell, was a diminutive Kiwi with a viperish wit who had worked his way up through trade magazines and the now-defunct *Sunday Business* paper. I was usually referred to as 'the posh one', and there were plenty of jokes about not being able to learn shorthand in a punt. Nonetheless, after three years fishing for stories in the backwater of the property industry, I was given the chance to prove myself by covering retail – a prime beat. In line with more than a decade of tradition, I made my first call to Sir Philip Green.

Britain's best-selling broadsheet and the barrel-shaped billionaire had a very special relationship. It had begun in the days of Jeff Randall, a grammar-school boy from Essex who was City and then business editor between 1989 and 1995. Randall's parents had been market traders in east London, and he obviously felt an affinity with Green. In 1992, Green was forced to resign from a stock market-listed discount retailer, Amber Day, over a litany of corporate governance breaches and a missed financial target – the first big humiliation of his career. Against the tide of negative newspaper coverage, Randall waded to Green's defence. 'It is a depressing reminder for those whose fathers were not vicars, librarians or building-society managers,' he wrote. 'They carry the baggage of their backgrounds forever.' As Green progressed onwards and upwards, he developed and embellished this portrait of himself as a barrow boy fighting back against the snobbery of faceless City cliques.

Private Eye magazine mocked Randall as Green's faithful Boswell, the biographer who trailed after the eighteenth-century essayist Samuel Johnson. Some of Randall's colleagues also thought he was unhealthily close to Green. They heard rumours of parties on Green's yacht in Marbella and suspected the scrappy outsider was the source of some of Randall's best stories, including his stunning scoop about the publishing tycoon Robert Maxwell's secret plan to take control of Tottenham Hotspur in 1990. Andrew Neil, the paper's editor between 1983 and 1994, was said to have come across Green as part of a crowd that went to Barbados every winter. Neil was reportedly irritated by Green's 'noisy' views on politics. A former colleague said, 'Andrew found him this bombastic guy – boasting and loud, and rather crude. Andrew asked Jeff to restrain himself – not in any nasty sense, because he had great respect for Jeff – but Andrew felt Green was a bit shady. We felt he was appearing rather more in the paper than he should have done, in the sense that he wasn't very important.'

In 1995, Randall was succeeded by John Jay, who had been educated at the fee-paying University College School in Hampstead and Magdalen College, Oxford. As they handed over, Randall remarked to Jay that there were 'two sorts of Jew: the trader and the intellectual. Philip is a trader and you're a completely different tribe. You'll never understand each other and there will be a huge prejudice between you.' Jay was married to Judi Bevan, a *Sunday Telegraph* journalist. In 1991, Bevan had written a profile of Green in which she described the living room of his house in St John's Wood as 'unremitting beige and not a book in sight'. Green called her when it came out. 'I'm phoning you from my holiday home because I'm having a library put in the one in London,' he said. True to Randall's prediction, there was no meeting of minds between Green and Jay. In his farewell column before he left the *Sunday Times* in 2001, Jay gave the retailer a special award 'for vulgarity and rudeness'. On the Saturday evening before publication, Jay and Bevan went to their weekend retreat in Seaford, on the East Sussex coast. They returned on Sunday evening to find the landline in their Rotherhithe house ringing off the hook. Jay picked it up and immediately received a torrent of abuse from Green. When he finally managed to interrupt, Jay asked, 'Philip, how's your ancient Greek?' There was another outburst of effing and blinding. 'Look up the phrase "gnōthi seauton",' Jay said. 'It means "know thyself".' He hung up.

Jay was replaced by Rory Godson, the former editor of the *Sunday Times'* Irish edition. To his predecessor's dismay, Godson vigorously renewed the paper's love affair with Green. 'I had a great breakfast on Friday with the irrepressible and apparently unstoppable Philip Green,' Godson wrote in September 2002, less than two years into the job. A month earlier, Godson had received a scoop about Green's intention to take over Topshop's parent company, Arcadia, in partnership with an Icelandic fund. Green had just sealed the deal for £850 million – without Icelandic help – when Godson wrote his column. 'The pair of us dined in his hotel suite as he waited for the official news that the board of Arcadia had recommended his bid for the company,' Godson said. 'The phone rang constantly as old pals and the great and good offered congratulations.' Arcadia's new owner, the business editor told his readers, was 'a self-made genius with extraordinary tactical nous, startling brainpower and memory, as well as great retailing instinct'. Godson said that Green would now need to prove himself as 'a team builder, not just a solo superstar'. He added, 'We are betting and hoping he can achieve this.' Godson was followed as business editor by Will Lewis and then John Waples, both of whom admired Green and benefited from his contacts and tips in return.

When Dominic O'Connell took over as business editor in 2010 he had few sources in retail, having spent most of his career covering aerospace and industry. Nonetheless, he and Green were soon on the phone every Saturday morning, shooting the breeze for up to an hour before the print deadline. Green would dispense his thoughts on everything from the yield on bonds issued by the mining giant BHP Billiton to the trading at Marks & Spencer.

A few hours into my first day as retail correspondent, I dialled Green's number with trepidation and tried to keep any plumminess out of my voice.

'You'd better come and see me,' he said gruffly.

A week or two later, I walked into the London headquarters of Green's Arcadia Group. A pretty blonde receptionist in the shiny black foyer showed me to the lift. I stepped out onto the sixth floor, where a prettier blonde receptionist in a shinier black foyer showed me into a meeting room. The only decorations were black-and-white photographs of Green and Kate Moss posing like a celebrity couple at events. I waited for ten minutes with increasing nervousness. Then Green burst in, all avuncular twinkle and one-liners, and quizzed me with affable irascibility about my background. He pulled out his battered mobile. 'So, who are you having trouble getting hold of?' he asked. The billionaire owner of Topshop was offering to act as my introducer. I threw out a few elusive names such as Don McCarthy, then chairman of House of Fraser, who disliked meeting journalists. Green gleefully scrolled through his contacts and clasped the discontinued Nokia 6310 to his ear. 'I've got the new *Sunday Times* retail man here,' he said again and again, looking at me intently with beady almond eyes. 'Better to know him than not to, if you know what I mean?' I scribbled down the numbers he gave me. The meeting was over in twenty minutes. 'Young Oliver,' Green pronounced as we shook hands. 'Call me if you need anything, OK?' I felt a ritual had been performed. Like so many of my *Sunday Times* predecessors, I had received Green's blessing and taken his shilling.

3.

The Bond Street Bandit

On 2 June 1953, thousands of people camped overnight in the wet to cheer and wave flags as Queen Elizabeth was drawn down The Mall in a state coach for her coronation. Many were wrapped in soaked newspapers or plastic raincoats, but they were jubilant at catching a glimpse of their twenty-seven-year-old monarch. The general excitement was enhanced by the news that a British team had just reached the summit of Mount Everest. The *Daily Express* captured the moment with the famous headline, 'All this – and Everest too!'

The coronation, that most traditional of events, carried with it the seeds of social change. As well as securing the national treasure status of Richard Dimbleby, who presented the BBC's coverage, it marked the real birth of television. Modernizers led by the Duke of Edinburgh won the argument for broadcasting, and more than 20 million people crowded around 2.5 million TV sets to watch. Within a year, licence numbers had increased to 3.5 million, and by 1960 there were 10 million TV sets in use, with half the population watching at peak time. The introduction of commercial TV in 1955, and programmes like ITV's *Double Your Money*, which featured a £1,000 'treasure trail' for contestants, horrified traditionalists but started to brush away some of the fustiness of post-war Britain. A new spirit of American-style consumerism blew in.

Philip Green, whose first birthday had been celebrated a few months earlier, was born at a unique economic tipping point. Years of post-war austerity were coming to an end, replaced by a new positivity. The British were tired of hardship. In 1951, the Labour government cut the weekly meat ration to its lowest ever level – 'not

bigger than a matchbox', according to the *Popular Pictorial*. Part of
the Conservatives' pitch to voters was a promise to do away with
rationing altogether. Churchill's party won the 1951 election despite
the *Daily Mirror*'s attempt to portray him as a warmonger with his
finger on the nuclear button. The new prime minister's assessment
of the situation that winter was grim. According to the historian
David Kynaston, Churchill asked his minister of food, Gwilym
Lloyd-George, to show him a person's rations. 'Not a bad meal, not
a bad meal,' the prime minister clucked as he examined the provisions. 'But these are not rations for a meal or for a day,' Lloyd-George
exclaimed. 'They are for a *week*.'

Ham and tea came off the ration in 1952, followed by chocolate
and sweets in 1953 – for some, an event just as momentous as the
coronation. Rationing of butter, cheese, cooking fat and margarine
ended in May 1954, followed by meat two months later. There was a
short-term spike in the price of bacon and steak as butchers struggled to cope with demand. The average person's weekly intake of
sugar, fresh fruit, bacon and ham soared. At the same time, food and
drink fell as an overall percentage of consumers' spending, with
proportionally more money going on cars and housing. The historian Peter Hennessy described the 1950s as 'a decade of easement
without previous parallel in British economic and social history'.

A shortage of working-age men after the war produced a tight-
ness in the labour market, and with full employment, wages started
to rise. Between the Conservatives' election victory in 1951 and the
next Labour government in 1964, the average weekly wage more
than doubled to £18 7s. – well ahead of inflation. The ending of hire-
purchase restrictions in 1958 meant that shoppers were suddenly
able to rush out and buy cars, fridges, furniture and TVs on credit.
A *Daily Mail* cartoon after Harold Macmillan's comprehensive Tory
election victory in 1959 showed the new prime minister sitting back
in his armchair, remarking to a collection of white goods, 'Well,
gentlemen, I think we all fought a good fight.'

This was the great consumer explosion that powered the growth
of chains like BHS, C&A, Dixons, Marks & Spencer, Tesco and

Woolworths. Simon Marks, the legendary M&S chairman, captured the spirit of the time when he told the company's 1954 annual meeting, 'With more abundant supplies at our disposal, and the lifting of restrictions which for so many years hampered our freedom of action, we have been able to take steps systematically to improve our values over a wide range of goods.' That year, the government scrapped building licences, a bureaucratic system of controls that gave government ministries first refusal to occupy new developments. Oliver Marriott, a former *Sunday Times* City editor and author of *The Property Boom*, told the story of an unlucky young trader who sold a building in London's Grafton Street a week before the announcement only to see its value shoot up by 70 per cent, literally overnight.

These were fertile conditions for Green's childhood hero, Sir Charles Clore. Clore was born in the East End of London in 1904, the son of Jewish immigrants who fled pogroms in Latvia in the late nineteenth century. His parents, Israel and Yetta Claw, had arrived at the docks in Liverpool with a few pounds and a sewing machine and made their way to the 'Mittel East', as the area around Shoreditch and Bethnal Green was jokingly known. It was described by the writer Emanuel Litvinoff as 'a district populated by persecuted Jews from the Russian empire and transformed into a crowded East European ghetto full of synagogues, backroom factories and little grocery stores reeking of pickled herring, garlic sausage and onion bread'. Clore's father, who quickly anglicized his name, ran a tailor's shop. His mother died in childbirth when Clore was five. Ten years later, his father's second wife committed suicide. According to Charles Gordon, one of his biographers, Clore had 'the force of granite' and 'cobalt eyes [that] made people cringe'. He grew up with what Gordon described as a 'cynical and melancholic view of life'. 'He expected the worst of people and was rarely surprised,' Gordon said.

Clore's nickname at school was 'Poppy', a slang word for money. He started out buying properties such as the Cricklewood skating rink in north-west London and the Prince of Wales theatre in

Piccadilly. Flat-footed and mildly diabetic, he escaped being drafted for the Second World War and instead made a fortune speculating on properties at depressed prices. But it was the rise of consumerism in the 1950s that turned the taciturn boy from Bethnal Green into the godfather of corporate raiders and the richest man in Britain. With employment at full capacity and the economy growing at 3 per cent a year, consumption boomed. Retailers' profits expanded on the back of the unprecedented high-street spending, but they also faced higher taxes to pay for the nascent welfare state, which the Tories had maintained. As a result, many were reluctant to increase their dividends to shareholders, who became frustrated. At the same time, some of those companies were conservative about the way they revalued their property portfolios, which in reality were soaring. In other words, the stock market was full of ripe fruit that could be plucked cheaply – if someone could only find a way to reach it.

In 1953, Clore pulled off a deal that revolutionized takeovers in Britain. He had already dabbled in retail companies such as Richard Shops when Douglas Tovey, a gregarious estate agent, visited him at home in Mayfair with an idea. Tovey pointed out that J. Sears & Co., famous owner of the shoe chains Freeman, Hardy & Willis and Trueform, was stuffed with property assets. The morning after their drink, Tovey sent Clore an Exchange Telegraph card setting out Sears' financial details. Its 920 shops were in the books at £6 million. Tovey estimated they would be worth at least £10 million on the open market. Clore gathered his closest advisers and laid a plan.

The problem was the City of the early 1950s. In size and social mores, it was still a Victorian village. Bankers wore bowler hats and shirts with detachable collars and cuffs. Messenger boys ran between buildings delivering notes. The principal characters all knew one another, often from school days, and deals were regularly done on a handshake. The gentlemanly way to take over a listed company was to approach its board of directors and agree a price. Hostile takeovers – where a bidder made an offer direct to a company's shareholders without the directors' approval – were almost unheard of. Yet that is what Clore had in mind for Sears. No British merchant bank would finance him, so he turned to Bank of America, which was familiar with contentious deals from the US. Out of the blue, in February 1953, Clore announced his takeover bid. Sears' management panicked and raised the dividend from 22.5 per cent to 66.5 per cent – a move that undermined their credibility, since shareholders then questioned why it had been kept so low in the first place. After a brief siege, Clore won control of Sears. According to David Clutterbuck and Marion Devine, two of Clore's biographers, the shell-shocked chairman spluttered, 'We never thought anything like this would happen to us.' Clore sent Tovey a letter thanking him for the tip and pointing out with deadpan humour that he had slightly overestimated the value of the property surplus.

The coup astonished both the City and Westminster. Pundits started to quip about an era known as 'Acquisitions BC' – Before Clore. One newspaper said that Sears' new boss was 'today the subject of discussion in every boardroom. In every company making fat profits he is pictured as a big bad wolf who might gobble them up.' Lord Bicester, of Morgan Grenfell, one of the oldest and most influential merchant banks, privately told the Bank of England that he was 'very agitated about further manoeuvres by Mr Clore'. The Bank's governor, Kim Cobbold, was forced to act that autumn when an emboldened Clore launched a hostile takeover bid for the Savoy Group, which included the Berkeley Hotel and Claridge's. Winston Churchill, an enthusiastic patron of Claridge's and the Savoy, made clear that he would not tolerate such impudence. The Savoy's chairman deployed complicated tactics to fend off Clore and his bidding partner, controversially transferring ownership of the properties to the staff pension fund, putting them in the hands of the trustees. After the raiders backed down, Cobbold urged all banks 'to use special caution in respect of any invitations coming before them which appear to be connected with these takeover operations'. There was a nasty smell of anti-Semitism as parts of Fleet Street branded Clore 'the notorious West End financier'.

Undeterred by the criticism, he turned Sears into an acquisition machine, buying assets as disparate as Furness shipyard, the Selfridges department store and the bookmaker William Hill. He and his wife led a rarefied life, dividing their time between a town-house behind Park Lane and a country home in Oxfordshire, but the Savoy controversy was the final straw for their troubled marriage. Francine Halphen, a beautiful war heroine who had won the Croix de Guerre as a Red Cross driver in the Battle of France, had met Clore at a friend's Christmas lunch. She represented everything he lacked – she was cultured and connected, counting Sassoons and Rothschilds among her relatives – and they married in 1943 despite an awkward courtship. Francine, an independent woman who knew her own mind, grew tired of his obsession with work. She left Clore in 1956, when he was fifty-two. They divorced a year later. According to Charles Gordon, Clore then embarked on 'a determined sexual rampage, never finding companionship, because he never sought it'. Christine Keeler, the call girl at the centre of the Profumo scandal, was believed to have been among his many mistresses. 'It was a gluttony of shameful proportions,' Gordon wrote.

It was a failed marriage of a different kind that ended Clore's career. In 1959, Douglas Tovey, the agent who had brokered the Sears takeover, persuaded Clore to merge his extensive property interests with those of Jack Cotton, a flamboyant property developer from Birmingham. Cotton was a genial man who wore a bow tie and had a suite at the Dorchester on Park Lane, where he hung Renoir's *La Pensée*. He turned out to be a terrible match for the hard, unforgiving Clore. The merger unravelled and Clore eventually pushed Cotton out. The ousted partner retired to the Bahamas in misery, drank himself into a stupor every night and died of a heart attack in 1964. Four years later, Clore and Cotton's company, City Centre, was bought by a rival, Land Securities. The *Daily Express* cartoon of the day said, 'I'm emigrating from this crazy, mixed-up country. Someone's taking over Charlie Clore.'

In 1971, Clore was knighted for charitable giving. He grumbled that it should have come far sooner. He had bought estates in Herefordshire and Wiltshire and hosted shooting parties for newfound aristocratic friends, enjoying the acceptance to polite society he had always craved. Yet in 1976, just when he should have been relaxing, he surprised even his closest allies by announcing his intention to resign as chairman of Sears and go into tax exile. Clore planned to become a resident of Monaco to shield his enormous fortune from death duties, but he found himself unable to resist regular trips back to London. The most feared businessman of his generation cut a lonely figure as he wandered around five-star hotels in Europe. He died from complications relating to a bowel cancer operation in Harley Street in 1979, aged seventy-four. The Inland Revenue challenged Clore's domicile. It won after a six-year legal battle and took £67 million of his £123 million estate. The High Court judge who delivered the verdict added a poignant personal note. 'In his last two or three years the pattern of his life was greatly altered,' Justice Nourse said. 'Able, restless, cerebral without being intellectual or cultured, dutiful in religion but not spiritual, sometimes on the edge of loneliness or boredom, the impression with which the evidence has left me is of a final period of unhappiness and doubts.'

The trail blazed by Clore was followed by a long line of corporate raiders in the 1970s and 1980s. There was Jim Slater of the financial conglomerate Slater Walker, who was forced into early retirement after being convicted of minor Companies Act offences, and who later declared that 'if a firm has its assets stripped it means they have not been properly used'; Lords Hanson and White, transatlantic playboys who built an empire ranging from Player's cigarettes to Seven Sea vitamins, and who enjoyed cosy Friday afternoon whiskies with Margaret Thatcher; Sir James Goldsmith, a prolific dealmaker and womanizer, who put some of his multibillion-pound fortune into an early campaign for Britain to renegotiate its relationship with Europe; and Tiny Rowland, the cold-blooded boss of Lonrho, Africa's biggest food producer, who used *The Observer* as his mouthpiece in the brutal fight with Al-Fayed over Harrods. But it was Sir Charles Clore – the flawed, ruthless retail and property tycoon from the East End of London – who captured the young Green's imagination.

Although the two never met, the similarities between Green and Clore go far beyond a fondness for pinstripe suits and slicked-back grey hair. Green's maternal great-grandparents, Mordekhai-Zev 'Max' Bull and Rivka 'Rebecca' Dimantstein, were Latvian refugees who came to Britain in the late nineteenth century and settled in Stoke Newington, north-east London. According to Chaim Freedman, a genealogist who has blogged about the Bull family, Mordekhai-Zev was a strict patriarch who cut 'an imposing figure, immaculately dressed in a frock coat and high black skullcap'. Rivka was deeply religious, but simultaneously strong-willed enough to rebel against wearing the *sheitel*, a modesty wig worn by married Orthodox Jewish women. She liked smoking a pipe and wearing lipstick. The family home on Evering Road was known as a centre of study for the Orthodox community. Mordekhai-Zev also ran a wholesale fur-cutting business, M. Bull and Sons, on Kingsland Road in Dalston, on the fringe of the Mittel East. Harry Blacker, a painter and writer, described the surrounding area as 'a conglomeration of narrow, cobbled streets, terraced houses, cat-smelling tenements and gas-lit cabinet-making workshops'. Stoke Newington was only slightly more salubrious.

The Bulls had ten children. One of their five sons, Ephraim, married Rose Ginsberg, who had mildly anglicized her surname from Gunzburg. In 1918, a month before the end of the First World War, Rose gave birth to a girl, Alma Constance Bull – Green's mother. Her birth certificate gave the family's address as Kings Road in Walton-on-Thames, a suburb in south-west London. The following year, they moved back to Stoke Newington and bought a house on Fountayne Road, a few minutes' walk from Ephraim's parents. Alma had two older brothers, Harold and Monty, and a younger sister, Annette. She went to the Skinners' Company School for Girls in Stamford Hill, run by the furriers' livery company. The main source of entertainment at weekends was the local synagogue, which put on afternoons of coffee and dancing. It was there that Alma, aged sixteen, met her future husband, Simon David Green. Simon lived on Osbaldeston Road, parallel to Fountayne Road.

Simon was four years older than Alma. He was born in 1914 as Simon David Terkeltaub, the son of Polish émigrés who moved to Britain. The address on his birth certificate was a maisonette on the main road running through Stamford Hill in north-east London. His father, Joseph Samuel Terkeltaub, was a greengrocer who did business from a shop in Finsbury Park and a stall on Thrawl Street, between Spitalfields market and Brick Lane in Shoreditch. Joseph went by the anglicized name Bernard Green, perhaps chosen for his profession. His wife, Sarah, looked after Simon and his four younger siblings – Annie, Jack, Bertie and Victor (born Avigidor).

A history of financial trauma ran through both Alma and Simon's families. According to the *London Gazette*, Bernard Green was made bankrupt in 1926, when Simon was eleven. He was released from bankruptcy two years later, after which the family moved to Stoke Newington. Alma's father, Ephraim, was also declared bankrupt in the *London Gazette* – in 1939, along with his brother, Emanuel, with whom he had been running M. Bull and Sons. Alma was twenty at the time. She went to work as a secretary for a lingerie company owned by Norman Feltz, nicknamed 'Norman the Knicker King' – father of the TV presenter Vanessa Feltz.

Simon applied to change his surname from Terkeltaub to Green by deed poll in April 1946, two months before he married Alma at the New Synagogue in Stamford Hill. Their families' financial woes had affected them in different ways, and they made an odd couple. Alma, a petite blonde, was hard and unemotional. She was determined never to face money problems again. Simon, round-faced and podgy, was depressive and lugubrious. A black-and-white photograph from their wedding day shows Alma holding a bunch of flowers, an ambiguous expression on her lips. Simon was in a top hat and round-rimmed glasses, looking serious.

The Greens moved from Stoke Newington to Tamworth Road in Croydon. Elizabeth Anne, their first child, was born on 17 July

1948. Philip Nigel Ross, their second, arrived on 15 March 1952. Simon ran a business repairing radios and renting out TV sets. Alma opened the first coin-operated launderette in the area, followed by the first self-service petrol station. She opened several more garages and built a buy-to-let property portfolio. In 1956, as the family's wealth grew, Alma and Simon decided to move to north London. They narrowed their search to Bancroft Avenue or Bishops Avenue, two of the best roads near Hampstead Garden Suburb. They picked Bancroft Avenue and bought a six-bedroom house at number 26.

The Greens' family life was materially comfortable. Elizabeth went to South Hampstead High, a girls' school with a mixture of fee-paying and direct-grant students. Philip went to Norfolk House, a private prep school where pupils had to wear bright orange blazers and matching caps. Simon drove an Armstrong Siddeley Sapphire, an upmarket car similar to a Rolls-Royce. They had a poodle called Coco and took family holidays at Birchington-on-Sea in Kent. Elizabeth and Philip's upbringing was emotionally barren, however. Alma nagged and terrorized Simon, who began to complain of migraines. He would often stay in bed until the late afternoon, getting dressed only when Elizabeth came home from school in order to give his daughter the impression he had been to work. He was prescribed opiate painkillers for his crippling headaches. At some point, he became addicted. A relative said that Simon lived 'like a functioning alcoholic', keeping his electricals business going but struggling through the fog of every day.

Alma grew frustrated by her husband's weakness. She starved her children of affection, relentlessly drilling into them the importance of making money above all else. The matriarch would play Elizabeth and Philip off against each other to toughen them up, making them compete for her approval. Conversations around the dinner table tended to take the form of arguments, with Elizabeth and Philip attacking each other, probing for soft spots. They developed similar personalities – aggressive, cocky and opinionated – and a strong mutual dislike festered. Their childhood was the beginning of a lifelong feud that was punctuated by occasional rapprochements at family events such as their mother's birthday.

At the age of nine, Philip left Norfolk House for Carmel College, a private boarding school in Oxfordshire described by *The Observer* as 'the Jewish Eton'. Carmel was founded in 1948 by Kopul Rosen, a charismatic rabbi who had a vision of combining the best parts of an English public-school education with an Orthodox religious induction. It went on to send a stream of bright Jewish boys to Oxford and Cambridge. Among its early governors and patrons were the philosopher Sir Isaiah Berlin, the M&S chairman Israel Sieff and the retail tycoon Sir Isaac Wolfson. Carmel opened on a site near Newbury in Berkshire with twenty-two pupils, but by 1953 it had moved to Mongewell Park, a former RAF base near Walling-ford. The main building was a grand Victorian house that inspired the mansion in Agatha Christie's play *The Mousetrap*.

When Green arrived in 1961, the school was still being built. Many of the lessons were held in prefabricated RAF huts. Corporal punishment was rare. There were daily prayers and Hebrew lessons. Shabbat – the period of rest between Friday night and Saturday night – was strictly observed. A former pupil said, 'You had religion thrown down your throat, and you were made to live it on such a high level that you either accepted it as your future way of life or you rejected it.' But Carmel also had a heated indoor swimming pool and generous playing fields. It was set in idyllic countryside: a trout stream ran from hatcheries to an overgrown lake that flowed over a small waterfall into the Thames, where the school's rowing teams practised.

In the 1960s, Carmel was one of only a few boarding schools to offer a backdrop of Jewish culture and religion, and its fees were more expensive than those charged by Eton. The purple uniform had to be purchased at Harrods. Some pupils were dropped off by chauffeur at the start of term, and one was driven to and from London every day. Another boy arrived by helicopter. 'You had to be pretty damn rich to go there, or very successful in terms of negotiating a grant or scholar-ship,' said Toni Rauch, a direct contemporary of Green's.

Rauch said that Green was 'not one of the Rolls-Royce brigade', but neither was he one of the hardest-up: Rauch remembered his peer from Hampstead Garden Suburb as 'just one of the guys'. 'There were one or two scraps, particularly when it came to a selection of ping-pong bats and who got the good-condition red one and who got the bad-condition green one,' he said. '[But] I don't remember Philip being good at anything, specifically. He wasn't a specifically high-calibre sportsman. I would never have dreamed in a pink month of Sundays that he would turn himself into the person he did. From the point of view of his business acumen, all credit to him. What he's grown into in terms of his total arrogance is a whole different ball game. He certainly wasn't that type of kid at school.'

Kopul Rosen died of leukaemia in 1962, aged forty-eight. With the passing of its idealistic founder, Carmel gradually lost its sense of direction. The school closed in 1997 after years of dwindling student numbers and mounting financial difficulties. Toni Rauch added that a group of twelve old boys from his year still met occasionally for a 'mini-reunion' lunch. 'We always talk about Philip, but Philip has not made any attempt to be in contact with any of us,' he said. 'One or two of us have invited him, but he's never responded at all.'

Matthew Engel, a *Financial Times* journalist who was in the year above Green, remembered him differently. 'The child was very much the father of the man,' he said. 'When I started seeing him in the newspapers years later, he was instantly recognizable. As I remember, he had chutzpah – but it was a petulant kind of chutzpah rather than an engagingly cheeky chutzpah.' Engel said that Green was 'certainly not considered a clever kid' at the intensely academic school. He added, 'A lot of my contemporaries either went into a family business or the professions, and he was very much an exception. There's certainly no one from Carmel who started with nothing and achieved what he achieved.'

Green was twelve when his father died suddenly of a heart attack. Simon Green was just forty-nine. His death certificate stated that he suffered from obesity and high blood pressure. According to a family story, Alma reacted with a characteristic lack of emotion. She is said to have telephoned one of Simon's siblings and told him, 'Your brother's lying here dead. You'd better come and deal with it.' Simon left an estate valued at £12,520 – the equivalent of about £240,000 in today's money. He bestowed annuities of £5 a week each on his mother, Sarah, and his father-in-law, Ephraim. The rest of his estate was put into a trust for his wife.

Alma was already driving to south London every day. She took over Simon's electricals shop on top of her own launderette, petrol stations and properties. Alma was a typical conservative, with both a small and a capital C. She read the *Daily Mail*, complained about immigration and loved cigarettes. After work, she liked to gamble – or 'spiel' – at Les Ambassadeurs casino on Park Lane, where she and a schoolfriend, Phyllis Gould, later became known as 'The Duracell Girls' for their ability to play roulette deep into the night. One of Green's early business associates, George Malde, estimated that Alma's buy-to-let portfolio comprised sixty or seventy houses in the Croydon area. He described driving her around on Fridays in the 1980s, collecting the rent in cash and emptying electricity and gas meters. 'She was tough,' said Malde. 'No-nonsense. All the guys paid up or she would get them out.' Alma employed two 'heavy' builders who doubled as bailiffs. 'If there was a problem with rent, they would throw them out,' Malde said. 'Different world in those days. You can't do that now.'

Green must have been embarrassed by his father's failure to provide for the family: he rarely spoke of Simon after his death, even to his closest associates. Now, before he was even a teenager, he was thrust into the role of patriarch. His mother had always been the dominant force in his life. Green was desperate to make money and win her approval. In an in-depth interview with *The Guardian* in 2004, the tycoon said he started coming home at weekends and working at Alma's petrol stations, topping up oil and wiping windscreens. Customers would tip him – sixpence, a shilling, sometimes half a crown. 'Half a crown,' he told the interviewer with a nostalgic smile. 'Remember them? Nice heavy coin, that.'

At Carmel, Green's behaviour deteriorated. He was placed in the lowest academic stream. To Alma's chagrin, her son left suddenly at fifteen. One of the Greens' neighbours saw him go off to Carmel as usual at the start of term. Three or four days later, he was surprised to spot Green back in Bancroft Avenue, 'skulking along, looking not very happy'. The neighbour asked one of Green's contemporaries at Carmel what had happened and was told he had been expelled. He asked why. There was a two-word answer, 'For fucking.' The neighbour joked that he 'didn't discover whether it was another boy, the matron, or a cat'. Toni Rauch said that Green was rumoured to have 'had some sexual experimentation' with one of his male friends. 'There was a limited amount of homosexual activity going on at the time, because we were all in our puberty and we were exclusively, at that point in time, a boys' school,' Rauch said. He added, 'I wouldn't have thought it was an expellable situation, from a pastoral point of view.' David Stamler, Green's old headmaster, said, 'I have no recollection of an expulsion. It was a sufficiently rare thing that I would certainly remember. I think there's no truth in that whatsoever.' Stamler described Green as 'a perfectly normal sort of schoolboy. Possibly better at sports than certain academic subjects, but nothing special comes to mind.'

For a short spell, Green transferred to Tollington grammar school in Muswell Hill. Panos Eliades, one of his friends there, said that Green never explained the reason for the move. Eliades added, 'You could see he was going to be a businessman. He was studying stocks and shares and movements, even at an early age. I was interested in chemistry and physics and he was interested in the markets.' Green left Tollington at sixteen with no O levels.

The question of how this restless and undistinguished young man became a multibillionaire tax exile is the enigma at the heart of this story. His dysfunctional upbringing and the overbearing influence of his mother must have contributed to his aggressiveness and resilience. His failure at school might have given him a chippy determination. But he was also the consummate baby boomer, born at the perfect time to surf the huge wave of post-war borrowing and spending. Green left school in 1968, the year the Beatles released the *White Album* and women at Ford's Dagenham plant went on strike for equal pay. Carnaby Street and King's Road in Chelsea were the twin fashion capitals of the world. Green shot into the business world with an intensity of ambition and energy his teachers at Carmel would have struggled to recognize. Within a year, Alma had arranged a job for him with Rodney Geminder, a family friend who ran a wholesale shoe-importing business in Old Street, east London.

The company was named after Rodney's father, Martin Geminder. It sourced cheap footwear from China, Hong Kong and Italy and supplied retail chains such as Dolcis. Green later told Robert Peston, the BBC's business editor, that he 'worked in the warehouse, humped the boxes, you know, did everything'. In contrast, a former colleague saw him as 'a sort of upmarket apprentice, with family connections to the boss'. In a 2016 blog post, Linda Wigzell Cress said her first impression was of a 'cocky youngster, a bit of a wide boy' – albeit an 'extremely well-heeled' wide boy. Green, then aged seventeen, drove an Opel Rekord Sport, had a 'mop of curly hair à la Leo Sayer' and wore 'expensive, smart and fashionable suits, which perfectly suited his then-slim frame'. Wigzell Cress said he had 'attractive features' and was 'likeable once you got the hang of him', although he was 'not too keen on putting his hand in his pocket' and was always the first to leave the pub, 'eager to be back at work, not wanting to miss any business. He loved it when the boss and his son were abroad on buying trips, and really lorded it over us then, or at least tried to. But no one could deny he worked hard.'

John Timpson, chairman of the Timpsons key-cutting and shoe-repair chain, was a ladies' footwear buyer working his way up the family business when he visited Martin Geminder's Old Street showroom in the late 1960s. 'I distinctly remember meeting this guy because he made me a cup of tea, which was nice,' he said. 'He was straight out of school and quite full of himself. He was clearly someone who thought he was going to go a long way, even at that stage.' Timpson next came across Green more than two decades later, when Green happened to become the landlord to one of

Timpsons' shops in Ilford, east London. 'He decided to boot me out, and I needed three or four weeks to find somewhere else,' Timpson said. 'The message came back, "Tell John to fuck off." That's the way he was, and probably is.'

After four years as a dogsbody, Green was allowed to man one of Martin Geminder's sale stands at a wholesale exhibition. 'In those days, they used to set up in hotels,' he told *The Guardian*. 'This was in the Mount Royal Hotel, above the Cumberland . . . I was standing there and this guy came in and picked up one of our shoes. Well, it was a clog, really, like a Scholl with a bit of a heel and a leather strip over the top. Liked it. How much is it? I said £1.99. What's the price of 40,000 pairs? I said I'd look into it, belted over to the boss.' Green pointed out the buyer to Rodney Geminder. 'No, he said, he's got long hair, he can't be serious. I knew the guy came from a big group so I said, right, I'm going to get that order. He bet me £5 that I couldn't and gave me a deadline. So off I went. They wanted them wrapped in a special way, special box, special this, special that, what didn't they want? I said yes, yes, I'd see to all that, and the weeks went by and the deadline was coming up, so I'm chasing, chasing, dadadada, and I get the order, on the nail.' Green said that he ran 'all the way up the five flights, up to the top of our building, slapped it down, said there's your order. And he got this old-fashioned leather wallet out of his back pocket, and every note was like it had been ironed. Got the note out, feeling it to make sure it was just the one and handed me the five quid. That was my first order.' Eight weeks later, the buyer cancelled. Rodney Geminder 'called me up and said, when you're passing, call in and give me my fiver back. Still, he trained me up.'

Green was more often on the right side of his early deals, however. While he was learning the shoe trade at Martin Geminder, one of his cousins took a job working in PR for Lotus, the sports car manufacturer. Green begged him to help get hold of a new Lotus Europa, which would usually have involved sitting on a lengthy waiting list. Green's cousin pulled a few strings with Lotus's sales director and procured one of the cars. To his amazement and indignation, Green flipped it for a profit a week or two later and never mentioned it again.

In 1973, Rodney Geminder's apprentice left and struck out on his own. Green dived into the job-buying scene, where a small group of wheeler-dealers picked up excess stock from badly run or bankrupt retail companies and tried to sell it on for a profit to independent shopkeepers or market-stall holders. A job buyer from that era explained, 'Say somebody imports 10,000 towels but they only sell 8,000? They want to get rid of the other 2,000, so they job 'em out cheap, because they've earned the money on the 8,000. Or, say, you could write to Pringle. Now, they might make a jumper but this winter it's not in fashion. They don't want it. They sell the jumper for £10 wholesale, but they job it out for £5 or £4.'

Buying 'parcels', as the consignments of discounted goods were known, required a gambler's instinct for what would sell and quick mathematical thinking. The hungrier job buyers also nurtured relationships with the insolvency practitioners who were appointed to liquidate failed companies. Job buying gave Green contacts in the insolvency industry and a lifelong understanding of the ways money could be wrung from the apparently lifeless corpses of retail chains. 'If you can get into the insolvency agencies, it's like everything else – it's the inside track,' said the job-buying veteran. 'If you get to know them, they mark your card and say, "This company's gone skint, do you want to buy this?" The job buyers tended to congregate in Fino's, a wine bar on Mount Street in Mayfair. They also met in the pubs north of Oxford Street, between Great Portland Street and Great Titchfield Street – a bustling area packed with clothing factories, fabric showrooms and tailors' shops.

In 1976, Green moved into making and importing garments. He and his mother set up a company called Tarbrook using £9,500 raised through a short-term loan. Tarbrook made a profit of £10,500 on sales of £175,000 in its first eighteen months, but it only ever filed one set of accounts. It was wound down six years later owing creditors £239,350. It had assets of just £436. Green's mother served as his guardian and mentor as he learned to duck and dive. A family friend who observed them working together in the mid-1970s said that Alma was 'like a lioness with him'. 'One of the biggest crimes you could commit then was to dishonour a bill of exchange, and Philip did it regularly,' he said. 'When the debt collector came, she was brilliant. She just fended the guy off and wouldn't let him anywhere near him.'

Green became a familiar figure in the area north of Oxford Street. He was often seen in the showroom of Nathaniel Williams, a wholesaler of printed dress fabrics run by Arnold Crook, a charming merchant whose parents had been market traders in High Wycombe. Crook was proud of his ability to turn around on-trend designs in two or three weeks using textile mills in Germany. He remembered Green as 'energetic, very hungry, a character'. By the mid-1970s, the economic boom of the 1950s and the pop-inspired optimism of the 1960s were puttering out. It was a time of industrial strife, political instability and soaring inflation. In April 1975, the *Wall Street Journal* published a famous editorial, 'Goodbye, Great Britain', pointing out that 20 per cent inflation, combined with the Labour government's tax rises, meant the average person would need a pay rise of 40 per cent just to maintain their purchasing power. But Crook, who went on to own the Theatre Royal on Haymarket, said, 'It didn't stop the fashion industry. Nothing stops the fashion industry if you've got something people want.' The cast of rag traders coming into his showroom reminded him of 'something like *Guys and Dolls*. They were all characters – quick-witted, fast-thinking and exciting. They would compete against one another but it was all friendly.'

On 14 November 1980, Green burst into the public consciousness with a front-page story in *Fashion Weekly*, one of the industry's trade magazines. Headlined 'Mark Down for Mark Up', it announced the opening of a new shop in Mayfair, 41 Conduit Street, which would sell 'designer merchandise at almost production-line prices'. It featured a photograph of a frizzy-haired Green smiling next to Viviane Ventura, a brunette actress and socialite who was said to be helping with the shop. Green had bought £35,000 worth of clothes by second-tier brands like Jacques Azagury for about £3,500 from liquidators to Originelle, a small chain that had gone bust that summer. Green told *The Guardian* that he took delivery of the stock, 'sent it all to the dry cleaners, got it put on nice satin hangers and polythened it up so it looked brand new'.

Alma was by her son's side as he opened the store. *Fashion Weekly* promised there would be 'startling' bargains, such as a Bruce Oldfield silk evening dress (usually sold for £285) priced at £99. However, it also reported the brands' warnings that 'some of the designs are two or three seasons old and not factory-bought'. Green responded, 'Designers are living on cloud nine. They work on enormous margins.' The article gave an early glimpse into Green's obsession with press coverage. It said the unknown twenty-eight-year-old was 'already dubbed the Freddie Laker of the rag trade' – a reference to the boyish entrepreneur who tried to disrupt the air-travel industry by offering £59 flights from London to New York in 1977. Soon afterwards, Green paid £950 at a Sotheby's auction for a dress worn by Marilyn Monroe and attracted more media attention by displaying it in the window of 41 Conduit Street.

He tried to tap into celebrity culture in a bigger way. In 1979, Gloria Vanderbilt, the American railroad heiress, had achieved remarkable success by putting her name to a pair of super-tight jeans at the age of fifty-four. A year after he opened 41 Conduit Street, Green tried to mimic the idea by persuading Joan Collins to collaborate on a denim range. Collins, who was forty-nine, had recently appeared in two low-budget erotic films, *The Stud* and *The Bitch*. She turned out to have less than the requisite star power. Green made the garments in Hong Kong and launched them with bombast. He held a lunch at which Collins cut a chocolate cake in the shape of a pair of jeans. He told the industry magazine *Drapers Record* there had been £250,000 of orders in the first four weeks and that he aimed to sell 1 million a year at £16.95 a pair. 'She has an affinity with the customers,' he said, from an office plastered with Joan Collins press cuttings. The reality turned out to be different. Joan Collins Jeans flopped. The stock had to be liquidated at heavily discounted prices and in 1982 the company was wound up after a creditor, a publisher called Viceroy Press, petitioned for the payment of just £6,666.

Green had another venture up and running on the side. In May 1981, he landed on the front page of *Fashion Weekly* for a second time, boasting about a designer haul he had sourced from a 'greatly overstocked' boutique in Italy. 'Philip Green has done it again,' the magazine chirped. 'Yves Saint Laurent, Georgio Armani [sic], Thierry Mugler, Sonia Rykiel, Christine Dior [sic], Chloe [sic] and Blue Marine [sic] will all be sold at less than half price.' Green said he had bought 2,500 items with a face value of £330,000. He hinted at plans for a second discount shop. A week later, *Fashion Weekly* reported, 'The word in Bond Street is that Lady Rendlesham, just back in the country, is not taking the situation lightly. She holds the Yves Saint Laurent franchise in England.' Clare Rendlesham, an aristocrat by marriage, was a fearsome former editor of *Vogue* who was described as 'thin as a rake and as hard as nails' by the fashion photographer Helmut Newton. Her solicitor wrote to Green threatening to seek an injunction unless he promised to stop trashing YSL's brand by discounting it. 'If Lady Rendlesham wants to sue, we'll certainly fight her,' he told the *Evening Standard*. 'If the worse comes to the worst, we'll have to cut the labels out.' Green won. In June, *Fashion Weekly* reported that Green 'reckons Lady Rendlesham . . . has lost her case to stop him selling cut-price YSL. He now plans to open another womenswear shop and is negotiating with new suppliers. Lady Rendlesham was not available for comment.'

Sure enough, Green launched Bond Street Bandit at number 100 on London's most prestigious shopping street in September 1981. 'We have enough customers to keep ten shops going,' he told the trade press. In June 1982, he announced the opening of another five Bond Street Bandits and a plan to offer the brand to franchisees – news that again made the front page of *Fashion Weekly*. A few weeks later, however, the magazine told readers it had been 'too good to be true'. Two of the five new shops had closed within six days of opening. 'I got the merchandise wrong,' Green admitted. 'Stock which sells in London doesn't sell in Leeds and Bournemouth.' *Fashion*

Weekly said that Bond Street Bandit's flagship store on Bond Street was also 'currently holding a closing-down sale and the company now says the shop will close'. In August, Crocodile, a partner chain that had provided the stores for Bond Street Bandit's expansion, went into receivership. Green was left out of pocket but said he was owed 'no great figure'. Beneath the hype, 41 Conduit Street and Bond Street Bandit made very little money. Accounts for Wearstyle, the company set up by Green and his mother to run the businesses, showed profits of just £3,740 on sales of more than £400,000 in the first twenty months. The auditors mentioned that they had been forced 'to rely upon representations from the directors where alternative confirmation of transactions was not available'.

Most of Green's early projects were, directly or indirectly, funded by his mother. At twenty-one, he had joined the board of her buy-to-let property company, Langley Road Investments. Alma had a relationship with Bank Leumi of Israel (two Bank Leumi directors happened to live next door to the Greens on Bancroft Avenue). When Green needed to raise money, his mother would allow him to use her properties as collateral for loans from the bank, which he then repaid as quickly as possible. In 1985, Alma helped her son leap into a bigger league. That July, stories appeared in *Drapers Record* and *Men's Wear* magazines about the collapse of a denim brand based in Devon. Bonanza Jeans was run by George Malde, a Kenyan Indian who had moved to London at thirteen and started out selling pre-washed Levi's from a stall in Kensington market in the days when unwashed 501s were 'like cardboard'. Bonanza had borrowed £4.5 million from Johnson Matthey bank, which had gone on a risky lending spree to compensate for falling profits in its gold trading division. Johnson Matthey went bust in 1984. Receivers from PricewaterhouseCoopers combed through its loan book and called in debts owed by clients, including Bonanza. The jeans brand was unable to find the money.

A desperate Malde was introduced to Green as his potential saviour by Kenny Tibber, a job buyer. Green summoned Malde for breakfast at Grosvenor House hotel on Park Lane. As Malde began to explain his problem, a waiter spilled scrambled eggs on his suit. Green demanded to see the manager and bellowed at him until he promised Malde a new suit from Savile Row and £500 compensation. 'From that day on, I thought he was a great man,' Malde said. 'Very forceful. Quite rude to some people. Within two hours I could see that he could really get things done.' They agreed that Green would buy Bonanza from the receivers and run it in partnership with Malde. To fund the purchase, Green negotiated a loan of up to £2 million from Bank Leumi, secured against some of Alma's rental properties. He knew Malde had 400,000 pairs of jeans in a warehouse and millions of pounds of debts that could be collected from retail customers, so Bonanza was potentially worth a lot more than the amount he planned to offer PwC. The next day, Green chartered a helicopter and flew to Bristol with a banker and a lawyer to close the deal. According to Malde, the Bank Leumi man was carrying £2 million of cash and bankers' drafts in a briefcase – and a gun for security. Green had cleverly asked the banker to make out most of the drafts in amounts of £50,000 so that he could haggle.

Malde sat in a separate room in PwC's Bristol office while Green rammed the deal home with two of the accountancy firm's partners. Finally, at 5 a.m., they agreed a price of £1.1 million – almost half the maximum £2 million Green had been willing to pay, and a fraction of the £4.5 million Johnson Matthey had lent Bonanza. Green recounted to *The Guardian* how he was unable to fly back to London because the helicopter would have been 'too noisy that time of the morning. Middle of nowhere, pitch black, police car comes by, gives us a lift to the station, quick kip on a bench, caught the milk train back to London. Monday morning we're up and running.'

As part of their arrangement, Malde had urged Green to arrange for his release from a personal guarantee he had given to the bank, 'but in all the negotiations he forgot about me, basically'. Green's oversight meant that PwC pursued Malde for the outstanding £3.4 million debt and made him bankrupt, taking his five-bedroom detached house in Harrow. Malde was 'upset', but Green offered him a deal. 'He said look, we're 50:50 in the new company unofficially, and whatever we make we'll share 50:50,' Malde said. 'We straight away went and collected all our debts and we got £2 million back in the company within three months. He was very good at collecting debts, I must say. Bloody hell.' Green repaid Bank Leumi's £1.1 million within a month and Malde soon had enough money to buy a new house in Knightsbridge. 'Philip said don't worry, I'll sort you out,' Malde said. 'And to be fair, he did.'

Green took out bullish ads in trade magazines to announce that 'business is back to normal at Bonanza'. Chris Astridge, the owner of *MAB News*, took a dim view of people using insolvencies to shed liabilities and buy businesses back. In September 1985, he mocked Bonanza with a spoof ad for Pond-é-Rosa Jeans – a play on the TV series *Bonanza*, which was set on the fictional Ponderosa ranch in the Sierra Nevada. 'Back in the market after the most spectacular financial disaster yet!' it said. 'Yes, we're back! After going bust last week for a mere £3 million and leaving all our suppliers, customers and bankers up the creek, we've secured another mug to back us with as much money as we can squeeze out of him.' It ran in a special edition of *MAB News* produced for a jeans trade fair at Earls Court. Astridge was setting up the *MAB* stand when Green thundered over, accompanied by two henchmen. 'Did you write that story about me?' he demanded. 'If you do that again, I'll take your kneecaps off.'

Green introduced Malde to a new way of working. Suppliers were routinely called into his office on Great Portland Street to be roasted. 'Some of them would leave crying, some would leave giving him a 50 per cent discount,' Malde said. 'He didn't take any nonsense from any suppliers.' After a brutal twelve-hour day, Bonanza's new owner would be chauffeur-driven to the Ritz casino in his Bentley. 'We'd have dinner there and he would gamble on the tables,' Malde said. 'He played either blackjack or roulette. They would close the table down and he was the only guy allowed to play. He had power, and all the girls would be impressed. There'd be loads of champagne, caviar, free food – whatever he wanted. On the roulette, he would only play number five and the corners around five. When he won, he won loads. When he lost, he lost loads. He'd thump the table and everybody would be watching him.'

Sometimes, Green's temper burst out at unexpected moments. Malde remembered flying first-class with his new partner from London to Rio de Janeiro via Geneva for supplier meetings in the days before there were direct flights from London. Green started off calling the German passengers on the plane 'Nazis'. Then, when the Swissair steward came down the aisle with food, Green shouted 'This is crap! You have it back!' and threw it over him. 'That's the thing I remember,' Malde said. 'The steward upsetting him and – boom!' Some of Bonanza's junior staff were less amused than Malde by Green's behaviour. A sales rep who was persuaded to join the company after Green took over said, 'He was a fucking pig – just tyrannical. He didn't want to hear anything you had to tell him anyway. He was effing and blinding at me one day and I just walked out, and that was the end of that.'

One of the suppliers Green and Malde chased to recover a debt was Jean Jeanie, which ran a chain of shops and owned the brand FU's Jeans. Jean Jeanie owed Bonanza £250,000. Green coerced ten postdated cheques for £25,000 each from its reluctant boss, Grant Casey. On the way out, Casey said that he wished he could get rid of his business. Intrigued, Green went to see him for a Chinese meal the next day in Slough, where Jean Jeanie was based.

Casey said he wanted £4 million. A few days' investigation revealed that Jean Jeanie was losing £70,000 a week. Green called Casey. 'The good news is I'll buy it,' he said. 'The bad news is you're broke.' Green told *The Guardian* he offered Casey £65,000 upfront, plus a further £435,000 'if I get round the bend in six months'. Casey accepted. In the era before H&M and Zara, the acquisition of Jean Jeanie and its sixty-five stores turned Green into one of the most powerful players in the denim industry. He wrestled it back into profit and in February 1986, less than six months after the deal, Lee Cooper Jeans offered to buy the combined group. Green asked for £10 million on the basis that 'I don't want to sell, so if you pay me what it's not worth I'll sell it.' The two sides settled on £7 million, with half to be deferred as a performance bonus. According to Malde, at that point Green forgot about their 50:50 arrangement. Malde said he received £750,000, with Casey and Kenny Tibber getting £1 million each. He estimated that Green personally banked 'between £4 million and £5m'. (Press reports at the time suggested it was closer to £3 million.) 'I did probably say to him I deserved a bit more,' Malde said, although he added, 'I was happy, to be honest with you. I had a new life and I was OK.'

Green signed a three-year contract to stay on at Lee Cooper. He garnered glowing write-ups in the trade press under headlines such as 'Green Genie?' and 'Stroke of Jeanius'. 'At the end of the day, there is no great mystique about retailing,' Green told *Men's Wear* magazine in one of the interviews. 'It's all about logic and common sense, and yet those are the two virtues that it is hardest to find these days.' But the honeymoon proved short lived. Green had a bust-up with his new boss, an urbane Frenchman called Pierre Pouillot, and in September 1987 *Fashion Weekly* reported that he had been 'edged out'. The magazine said that Green was refusing to comment 'until I have seen my lawyers'. After his exit, Lee Cooper, which was renamed Vivat, suffered severe indigestion from Bonanza and Jean Jeanie. The chairman, Lord Marsh, resigned in 1988 and the company booked a £12.7 million loss in 1989 – although to be fair it had plenty of problems other than Bonanza and Jean Jeanie. Green was later keen to present his departure as his own decision. A year after he left, he forced an apology from *Fashion Weekly* for suggesting that he was sacked. In 2006, he told the BBC's Robert Peston, 'In the end, one of my funny moments, left there, forfeited six million quid – had a contract for an earn-out and I just thought, "Fuck it."'

When he first met Malde in 1985, Green was a conspicuously wealthy thirtysomething with an expanding waistline and Spandau Ballet hair. A well-known figure on the London party circuit, Green had been seen with a number of attractive women on his arm. His past girlfriends included Juliette Owide, daughter of the Soho lap-dancing club owner Oscar Owide, and Viviane Ventura, the aspiring actress who was involved in 41 Conduit Street. According to Malde, at the time of their acquaintance, Green was dating Vimla Lalvani, a Hawaiian-Indian yoga guru. Vimla had just divorced from Gulu Lalvani, the Pakistani electronics tycoon who co-founded the Binatone telephone empire and was said to have given Alan Sugar his first break in business. 'Vimla and Philip were together for about three years,' Malde said. 'We went out for dinner, they slept together, they stayed together. She was obviously divorced from this other guy and she wouldn't marry Philip, and this was the girl Philip wanted to marry.' Malde described Lalvani as 'the love of Philip's life . . . He was very, very keen. He was in love with her, but it just didn't happen.' Lalvani, whose students included Jerry Hall and Olivia Newton-John, confirmed that she had been in a relationship with Green in the mid-1980s, but declined to comment further.

Malde said that when Lalvani 'rejected him and wouldn't marry him, Tina came onto the scene'. Tina Palos was born in 1949 as Cristina Stuart Paine, the daughter of a successful wine merchant. Her birth certificate gave the family's address as a house on Oxford Square, north of Hyde Park, although in a 2014 interview with the *Sunday Times*, she said her father's work took the family to Hong Kong, Japan and Thailand for long spells. At seventeen, Tina Paine met a South African jazz drummer in Hong Kong, Robert Palos. He was 'fourteen years older than me, 6ft 2in and divine'. They married in South Africa in 1967, a year after meeting. The couple opened a clothes shop in Johannesburg and had two children, Stasha and Brett. Tina was a party girl: Stasha later said that her mother was the first female DJ in Johannesburg and a go-go dancer who performed with the Beach Boys. In 1978, when Stasha was six and Brett was four, the family moved to London and Robert and Tina opened Harabels, a fashion boutique in Beauchamp Place, Knightsbridge. By the time she met Green, Tina was about to divorce from Palos, although she kept his surname and continued to run the shop.

Like Alma, Tina was a petite, tough blonde who knew how to get her own way. Like Philip, she had lost her father (Stuart

Marshall Paine died of a haemorrhage caused by a chronic ulcer in 1983, when his elder daughter was thirty-three). In Tina's version of the story, they were introduced by mutual friends in 1985, although she said the relationship took a while to develop. 'I thought he was dreadful, actually,' she told the *Daily Mail* in 2005. 'I remember him asking me who I was. I said I ran a boutique called Harabels and he said, rather dismissively, "Well, I've never heard of it." I thought, what an arrogant pig.' Tina said they saw each other the next evening at a friend's flat before a party. 'His bow tie was crooked and without thinking I went right up to him and straightened it. And that was it. It was the oddest thing. I thought, I'm in trouble here. I just fell in love with him at that moment.'

Malde remembered the genesis of the romance differently. He thought Alma had introduced Tina to her son, having got to know the younger woman by popping into Harabels to browse. 'His mother had gone in the shop – that's how they met,' he said. Trading at Harabels was becoming difficult, and Tina was in need of money and support. Malde said, 'They met and then he didn't want to date Tina. I was spending sixteen hours with Philip every day, and I know Tina would chase him, he wasn't chasing Tina . . . Tina was a bit like Philip – what she wanted, she tried very hard to get. She wanted Philip and she tried every which way to get him. In the end, I know the reason they got married was because she was pregnant.'

In her *Sunday Times* interview, Tina said it took them a while to make their relationship 'official'. 'I said to him, "Look, I will only tell everyone you are my boyfriend when I feel we can all handle it,"' she recounted. She moved into his house at 55 Avenue Road, St John's Wood – an address that featured Philip's lucky number twice. Some of Philip's relatives thought he began to change as Tina encouraged an appetite for celebrity and luxury goods. 'Unwrapping gifts under the tree in St John's Wood, it would be Hèrmes scarves, this, that and the other,' said one. 'He wouldn't know a Hèrmes scarf from a bar of soap.'

The two were soon inseparable, although Philip still refused to commit for as long as possible. Tina told the *Mail* the final straw came when she waved him off one morning in her dressing gown as he got into his Bentley. A newspaper ran a headline like 'Tycoon's Gal Waves Him Off'. 'I thought, I'm nobody's "gal",' she said. Tina proposed to Philip and ran off to Marbella until he said yes. They married on 13 September 1990 at Westminster register office, when he was thirty-eight and she was forty-one. Tina was already pregnant with their first child, Chloe. The simple ceremony was followed by a reception at the house on Avenue Road, where they served dinner for a hundred guests. Edwin Starr, the Motown singer famous for his hit 'War', performed live in the garden. Philip and Tina Green posed for photographs holding doves on their fingertips. From the look on their faces, they knew they were on the cusp of a remarkable journey.

4.

Uncle Tony and Amber Day

There was a single house among the flats on Titchfield Road, a turning on the edge of Regent's Park. Its loneliness was exaggerated by the metal bars its owner had installed across the front windows, which were also coated with blast-resistant film. In the early 1990s, 3 Titchfield Road was the address of a man called Tony Schneider and his wife, Vassiliki, known as Julie.

Schneider was a crook and a loan shark with connections to violent crime. Although he came from the East End, he looked and dressed like an Italian mob boss, his suits immaculately tailored and his dyed black hair slicked back from his forehead. Schneider had a small hump on his shoulder. He walked with a slight limp, which he claimed was the result of an injury he had sustained falling through a glass skylight while burgling a stocking factory in his teens. John O'Connor, a former head of Scotland Yard's Flying Squad, said, 'He had the blackest eyes I've ever seen on a human being. To me, he looked like a character out of Charles Dickens.'

Schneider sat at the intersection between the business community and the criminal underworld. Through money lending, he knew some of the most prominent City figures of the late 1980s, including Ted Ball, a brash financier whose leasing business counted Bob Geldof and Terry Venables as customers. Charging interest rates of 50 per cent or more also gave Schneider the need for edgier friends. One of his protection men was Jimmy Evans, an erratic villain who was infamous for having blasted a love rival in the testicles with a sawn-off shotgun. O'Connor, who came to know Schneider after he left Scotland Yard for the investigations agency Kroll in 1993, said, 'I would place him as untouchable, virtually. He had so many fingers in the pie that anybody that set up an action group to target him, he'd know about it. He was a manipulator and a user and a controller, and was held in the highest regard – and in some cases fear.'

Between the early 1970s and the early 1990s, Schneider was a significant figure in Philip Green's life. Schneider was born into a Russian émigré family on the Boundary estate in Shoreditch in 1923. His father was a cabinet maker. His mother looked after their three sons. Schneider was the 'black sheep', according to one of his closest former associates. He moved from Shoreditch to a bedsit in the basement of a hotel in Belsize Park, then to a flat in the Quadrangle building near Edgware Road, which was used to film the opening scenes of the 1971 Michael Caine gangster film *Get Carter*. In his teens and twenties, Schneider was a protégé of Jack 'Spot' Comer, one of the East End's most powerful crime bosses before the rise of Ronnie and Reggie Kray. Jack Spot, so called for the black mole on his left cheek, was best known as the suspected mastermind of a failed plot to steal £1.25 million's worth of gold and diamonds from a security depot at Heathrow airport in 1948. Perhaps because of his affiliation with Comer, who was a rival of the Krays in Hackney, Schneider had his jaw broken by the twins on one occasion. According to his old associate, the Krays arranged to meet Schneider at a snooker hall in Whitechapel. As he sat down, they offered him a cigarette. The loan shark leaned forward, his mouth relaxed and 'Ronnie Kray bashed him with a knuckle-duster'.

Green met Schneider through job buying. According to several people who knew them in the 1970s, Schneider used to lend Green money for parcel deals. 'He'd borrow maybe £5,000, £6,000, £7,000 – not hundreds,' said one. Green looked up to Schneider, whom he called 'Uncle Tony'. He tried to copy Schneider's menacing charm, rasping Cockney accent and withering one-liners. In return, the loan shark viewed the middle-class pretender with amusement and contempt. 'He wasn't bothered about Philip,' said Schneider's associate. 'He used to laugh at him. Tony would say, "Philip, stop it. I know who you are and where you come from. Kid the other people, don't kid me."' One of Schneider's neighbours asked why he disliked Green so much. 'If you're earning money out of him, what's the bloody problem?' he said. Schneider apparently replied, 'Well, he's a fat prick, and you don't know him.'

Schneider's day would start at 10 a.m., when he would get up and wander around in a dressing gown, waiting for the first borrower to arrive. Visitors would almost unfailingly be offered a ham sandwich and a cup of tea. Julie, who had met Schneider while working as a waitress in King's Cross, would clank around in the kitchen, swearing under her breath. 'All of a sudden you could have five or six people sitting there, and most of 'em knew one another,' said his former associate. Schneider's heavies, Jimmy Evans and Terry Plummer, a part-time film and TV extra, maintained a background presence. Evans, a professional bank robber and safe blower, wore his receding red hair long at the back. He could be unpredictable. A few days before Christmas 1964, he knocked on the door of a rival in south London, George Foreman, whom Evans suspected was sleeping with his wife. In his autobiography, *The Survivor*, Evans said he called out 'Happy Christmas, you cunt!' and fired a shotgun at Foreman's crotch. When the case came to trial, the prosecution put 279 of the shot's 280 pellets into a jar as evidence. 'They couldn't find the last one but they'd dug all the rest out of his groin and the wall behind him,' Evans wrote. (He was acquitted after Foreman declined to identify him as the gunman.)

At the end of his day, Schneider would often walk over to the Victoria Sporting Club on Edgware Road. It was illegal for casinos to lend gamblers money to keep playing, but as a third party Schneider would discreetly cash cheques for desperate punters. His links with gambling led some in Scotland Yard to believe he was connected to the murder of Andre Mizelas, a society hairdresser who was shot dead as he drove to work along the south side of Hyde Park on 9 November 1970. Mizelas was believed to be mired in gambling debts.

Schneider's flat in the Quadrangle, where he lived until he moved to Titchfield Road in the early 1990s, was nicknamed 'Little

Marbella' for the crowd of orange-tanned businessmen it attracted. There was Ted Ball, the bald, braying boss of Landhurst Leasing, to whom Schneider referred bigger borrowers in return for kickbacks; Harold Tillman, the lean and wheedling chairman of the Honorbilt menswear group, who did not borrow from Schneider but dropped in for gossip; and Scot Young, an aspiring property developer from Dundee who was later believed to have become mixed up with London's notorious Adams crime family. After the mid-1970s, Green had no need for Schneider's money, but he continued to call and visit. He liked to keep Uncle Tony onside. 'Philip was frightened of him,' said Schneider's former associate. 'Not frightened so much physically, but frightened of his mouth, 'cos Tony would belittle him.'

Green's odd relationship with Schneider came back to haunt him when he made his next move. In 1986, the year he left Lee Cooper, Margaret Thatcher's 'Big Bang' stock market revolution blew away the remnants of the Victorian-style City encountered by Sir Charles Clore. Over the coming years, American banks injected a macho Wall Street culture into London's financial centre – an epochal change described by the historian Philip Augar in *The Death of Gentlemanly Capitalism*. In 1987, as Thatcher won a landslide third election victory, turnover of share dealing rose by £100 billion to £283 billion. The atmosphere was captured by the Harry Enfield character Loadsamoney, an obnoxious plasterer who waved wads of banknotes around. The boom came to a dramatic end in October 1987, when a sudden rise in US interest rates knocked confidence on Wall Street. A burst of panic-selling in Hong Kong moved across to London, where the sense of chaos was exacerbated by the worst storm in decades. Between 'Black Monday' on 19 October 1987 and the following day, the stock market fell by 22 per cent. It was the first real City crash since 1974, and it traumatized a generation of investors.

Before the market turned sour, a consortium led by Irvine Sellar, founder of the Mates flared trousers chain, bought a 29 per cent stake in Amber Day, a lacklustre clothing manufacturer. A year later, in August 1988, Sellar engineered a fiddlier deal. He and his partners sold a menswear retailer called Review to Amber Day in return for shares, which they placed with Green and Blue Arrow, a recruitment company chaired by Tony Berry, one of the City's rising stars. Amber Day was a name that would come to have huge resonance for Green and his growing band of critics in the business mainstream over the next four years.

Green paid £3.1 million for a 16.4 per cent stake. Blue Arrow paid £1.8 million for 9.6 per cent. Berry was a grammar-school boy from Edmonton in north London who had steered Blue Arrow into the FTSE 100 through the takeover of Manpower, an American competitor more than twice its size. Berry had trialled for Tottenham Hotspur in his youth, and in 1987 Green had persuaded his friend Irving Scholar, Spurs' chairman, to make Berry a non-executive director of his beloved club. A year later, Berry returned the favour. Although Green boasted of investing more than £3 million of his own money in Amber Day, £300,000 came from Blue Arrow in the form of an undisclosed and unsecured loan. A letter to Green from Berry's deputy, David Atkins, said Blue Arrow had been 'disappointed to learn that you are unable to find the £3.1m'. It said the recruitment company had 'no alternative' but to lend him the money for a year. Green was installed as Amber Day's chief executive. Atkins joined the board as a non-executive director.

Green's arrival as the boss of a public company put him on the radar of the national press for the first time. Amber Day's stock market quote also gave him new financial clout. One of Green's first moves was to make a vengeful takeover approach for his old employer, Lee Cooper, by then renamed Vivat. Years later, Green told the BBC's Robert Peston that he did it 'just for a bit of sport' and 'it really pissed them off'. Through the abortive bid, he met Sir Laurie Magnus, an amiable investment banker who was advising Vivat. Green should have hated Magnus, a baronet who was educated at Eton and Oxford, but Magnus was impressed by Green's grasp of Vivat's trading numbers and the way he ran rings around its French directors. Green must have sensed the warmth, because after the deal died he rang Magnus and said, 'I'd like you to be on my side next time.' Samuel Montagu, Magnus's employer, had a record of working with risk-taking entrepreneurs such as Jimmy Gulliver, whose Argyll Group triggered a multibillion-pound bidding war for the Distillers Company in 1985 (although the merchant bank would later come spectacularly unstuck with its work for the Mirror Group pension plunderer Robert Maxwell). Magnus checked out Green with the bank's librarian, who kept an index of anyone who had appeared in *Private Eye*'s Slicker column. At that point, Green's name was fairly unblemished. Magnus became the first in a long line of City grandees to be lured in by the perceived glamour of the wisecracking trader. Green's irreverent sense of humour made him an attractive diversion from Magnus's more strait-laced clients, and for Green the presence of Magnus gave him a badge of respectability.

Amber Day's new boss had discovered Hong Kong in his time at Martin Geminder ('Very fast. Very quick. Nobody goes to sleep,' he told *The Guardian* in 2004). He set about cutting costs and moving production to Asia. In Green's first year, sales fell by 14.3 per cent to £8.6 million, but pre-tax profits more than tripled to £503,000. Ronald Metzger, the outgoing chairman, saluted his 'energetic' successor, who was to become executive chairman. In June 1989, Amber Day bought a second, more upmarket menswear chain, Woodhouse, and in September it made a flaky takeover approach for Moss Bros, the suit-hire business. Around the same time, Green tried to mount a takeover bid for Sears, the remains of Clore's retail empire, which still included Selfridges. Green persuaded an American investment bank, Citi, to fly over what one insider described as 'an army' of advisers. When Citi's bankers looked at Amber Day's tiny size in comparison to Sears, they laughed at Green and flew home. Nevertheless, in his second year, Green announced a near-doubling in sales to £15.7 million and a quadrupling of profits to £2.1 million.

Jeff Randall, City editor of the *Sunday Times*, stumbled across the whip-smart newcomer while looking for sources to tell him about a rumoured boardroom rift at Tottenham Hotspur. He found

Green beguiling and witty, and quickly realized that he was also deliciously indiscreet. Randall marvelled to colleagues about how Green managed to make himself the middleman in so many deals, so becoming a veritable 'supermarket' of stories. Green invited the ambitious young journalist to wine-fuelled dinners at his home on Avenue Road with eclectic guest lists, where the likes of Michael Knighton, a moustachioed property tycoon who tried to take over Manchester United, sat next to Jilly Johnson, a Page Three model. These were the days when business journalism – Sunday business journalism in particular – was about getting close to influential figures and trading favourable coverage for the inside track on big stories. Randall began to call Green every Friday. He talked up Amber Day's prospects, telling readers the company's 'hyperactive' boss was 'lining up support from several large merchant banks for a blockbusting move'.

Green's reputation was growing, but Tony Berry's career collapsed almost overnight in December 1988. To fund its takeover of Manpower in 1987, Blue Arrow had raised £837 million through what was then Britain's biggest-ever rights issue – the sale of new shares. The rights issue was a flop: just 38 per cent of Blue Arrow's investors participated. To disguise its failure, Blue Arrow's advisers, County NatWest and UBS Phillips & Drew, secretly bought some of the shares themselves after the deadline had passed. They then misled the stock market by saying that 50 per cent had been sold, and manipulated disclosure rules to avoid revealing their purchase of more than 13 per cent, which they planned to drip out into the market quietly. The arrangement was exposed by the Black Monday crash of October 1987, which forced County NatWest to announce heavy losses on its hidden Blue Arrow shareholding. In December 1988, the Department of Trade and Industry announced an inquiry into County NatWest's role.

In parallel, Blue Arrow was torn apart by a power struggle between Berry and the American boss of Manpower, Mitchell Fromstein. Berry forced Fromstein to resign, prompting a rebellion among Manpower's US franchisees. Pressure mounted on Berry after news of the DTI investigation broke, and Fromstein returned through a counter-coup in January 1989, taking the title of chief executive and relegating Berry to non-executive chairman. In April, Fromstein shocked Blue Arrow's shareholders by revealing a previously undisclosed £25 million loan – an amount representing a third of the previous year's profits. The recipient turned out to be Peter de Savary, a lively property developer whose America's Cup yachting challenge had been sponsored by Blue Arrow. It was curtains for Berry, who had made the loan without proper board approval. He resigned two days later. *The Times* reported, 'Tony Berry, the stock market star, finally came to earth last night. He left the City headquarters of the group he created, almost certainly for the last time, in pouring rain and drove off into the night.'

The DTI launched a new inquiry into the de Savary affair in May 1989. Blue Arrow disclosed its £300,000 loan to Green the same month. Although Blue Arrow sold its shares in Amber Day that June and Green repaid his debt in August, news of the relationship was damaging for two reasons. First, Green was rumoured to have lined up Berry as chairman, but to have been dissuaded by Amber Day's stockbroker, Hoare Govett, which pointed out Berry's obvious conflict of interests. Second, it hinted at Green's links to a web of businessmen – some of them distinctly unsavoury – centred around Tottenham Hotspur. *Private Eye* started to make the connection in June 1989. It described Green as a 'supporter pal of Berry'.

When the DTI published its report into the de Savary affair in 1991, it revealed more links between the two. Green had lent Berry £275,000 of Amber Day's money in December 1988 to help him buy 400,000 shares in Spurs. Berry had repaid the loan in January, but some of Amber Day's institutional shareholders were alarmed at the corporate governance breach and the amount of time Green seemed to be spending interfering with the football club. One of them thought that Green was 'hand in hand' with Terry Venables, Spurs' manager. In his autobiography, *Superfan*, a Spurs obsessive called Morris Keston described watching Green try and fail to help Venables buy the club from Irving Scholar during an evening meeting at Amber Day's Baker Street offices on the Friday before the 1991 FA Cup final. Keston said that Green tore up his £1 million cheque when Scholar insisted on closing the deal that night.

In May 1990, the *Sunday Times* broke news of an abrupt change in direction at Amber Day. It revealed that Green was planning to buy What Everyone Wants, a chain of forty discount shops based in Glasgow. What Everyone Wants had been set up in 1971 by the husband-and-wife team Gerald and Vera Weisfeld, who accepted their customers' £10 Provident Financial cheques and sold fashions at the lowest possible prices. The Weisfelds were tough, quirky operators who ran What Everyone Wants like a family. They encouraged their staff to sing and rewarded them with cars and cash bonuses for hitting sales targets. The Weisfelds had decided to step back from business and dedicate themselves to charity after a plane they were travelling in caught fire over Rio de Janeiro and was forced to make an emergency landing, but Vera was reluctant to sell their baby to Green. Tina won the day for her fiancé by calling Gerald and begging him, 'Philip really needs this deal.'

To amuse the Weisfelds, Green arranged for the Coldstream Guards' band to march in during the deal's closing dinner. At £47 million, What Everyone Wants was twice Amber Day's size, but the move initially pleased the City. Sales leapt to £31.2 million in 1990 and then £103 million in 1991. Pre-tax profits went from £3 million to £10.1 million. Having stood at 42.5p when Green arrived, Amber Day's shares shot up to a peak of 129p in November 1991, making it one of the best performers that year. Green's pay packet increased by 50 per cent to £450,000, including a bonus. The first cracks appeared when Gerald Weisfeld walked out after six months. Vera Weisfeld, who left at the time of the sale, said, 'It changed very quickly . . . The prices went up, and the Glasgow people are streetwise.' The *Sunday Times* continued its unwavering support for Green, but other papers began to question his leadership. John Jay, who was then City editor of the *Sunday Telegraph*, said Amber Day needed 'a more measured hand on the tiller' and mentioned that one of Green's heroes was Robert Maxwell, prompting Green to offer him 'a kick in the bollocks'. When David Hellier, an *Independent* journalist, wrote a short piece accusing him of comprehensively denying a story that turned out to be true, Amber Day's boss roared, 'I just thought you should know I tore your fucking article out and put it under the cat's arse where it fucking well belongs.' A dossier of unflattering details about the personal finances of another critic, Dominic Prince at the *Sunday Express*, was couriered to rival papers – followed by calls from Green to gauge the recipients' reactions. These were tastes of trouble to come.

In June 1991, Amber Day raised £24.4 million through a rights issue to pay down debt taken on to fund What Everyone Wants. As a condition of the fundraising, institutional investors such as Midland Montagu, John Govett & Co. and the Prudential insisted that Green hire a finance director and two non-executives to give the board a more sober feel. Graham Coles, the new finance director, and Leslie Warman, the first non-executive, joined in the late summer. Coles and Warman were amazed by the shambles they discovered. Amber Day's 'guv'nor', as he called himself, would typically arrive at Baker Street at 10 a.m. after a late night in the casino. There were no proper board meetings, board papers or monthly financial accounts. A cast of characters apparently unconnected with Amber Day's business traipsed in and out, including a property dealer known as 'Black Jack' Dellal and the rag trader Harold Tillman. According to a colleague, when Green was not flying to Glasgow or Asia, he would sit in his office 'showing off, doing several telephone calls at the same time, wheeling and dealing'. Hoare Govett and Laing & Cruickshank, Amber Day's first two brokers, had resigned – apparently because Green kept interfering with the trading of the company's shares. Green boasted to the new directors that he had a 'direct line' to the market maker at the replacement stockbroker, Smith New Court. His contact there was named Richard Osmond, although Green insisted on calling him 'Donny'. 'You would hear about him placing loose shares,' said a source who was close to the board. 'The business of the chief executive is to be shifting jeans and T-shirts, not placing lines of stock.'

In New Year 1992, Green went to Hong Kong and Sri Lanka on business. In mid-January, while he was away, Amber Day's shares suddenly fell off a cliff. The price dropped by more than a third to 66p in a fortnight. Jeff Randall at the *Sunday Times* thought the strange collapse bore the hallmark of a 'professional bear raider' – a speculator who sells a stock short, then wages 'an undercover campaign of lies and misinformation' to drive the price down. Attention focused on Simon Cawkwell, a comically fat trader who resembled a character from a P. G. Wodehouse novel, after a critical journalist received a letter thanking him 'on behalf of all public schoolboys bullying Philip Green', signed 'EK'. Cawkwell went by the name Evil Knievel. Cawkwell later denied being the shadowy spiv who spread rumours from a phone box. 'I haven't used telephone boxes since I was a teenager,' he said. However, he admitted that he had made 'several terms' school fees' betting against Amber Day: 'You could not, in my humble opinion, run that business from St John's Wood when it was operating in Glasgow.' Cawkwell sold the shares short on the basis that Green struck him as 'a joke character'.

The slide in Amber Day's share price brought simmering tensions between Green and his new colleagues to the boil. In late January, while Green was still in Asia, Graham Coles called an emergency board meeting. The most worrying item on the agenda was his discovery that Green had bought a wholesale parcel of videos on the grey market and sold it to a friend, Stephen Kay, the head of a company called Intervision. Kay still owed Green £2 million for the videos, but in the previous fortnight Kay had bought almost 400,000 Amber Day shares, slowing the steep fall in the share price. To Coles and the other directors this looked dangerously like an illegal share support operation, where a buyer is incentivized to prop up a company's stock. Kay had bought the shares through Bikuben-Whitefriars, a firm of stockbrokers that had already barred Green as a client after becoming uncomfortable about certain trades he had carried out. By phone, Green assured Sir Laurie Magnus there was nothing untoward, and when he returned to London he said the amount outstanding from Intervision was less than £1 million. Magnus channelled Franklin D. Roosevelt, telling Amber Day's directors the only thing they had to fear was 'fear itself' – meaning they should not worry about City gossip and should concentrate on the positives. The board accepted Green's answers, but the incident was terminal for Green and Coles, who was also concerned that Green seemed to have borrowed heavily from Barclays against his stake in Amber Day, leaving him facing personal financial ruin if the share price fell further.

Green had more problems. Some of Amber Day's shareholders picked up unsettling rumours of company staff being transferred to help his wife, Tina, with her struggling boutique in Knightsbridge. Harabels went bust in April 1992. Green, who had taken a debenture over the business three months earlier, controlled the process and installed as receiver his old Tollington grammar friend Panos Eliades, who had become an insolvency professional. Eliades had managed the demise of Tarbrook, the imports business set up by Green and his mother. He had also acted as receiver to two other Green companies, Buzzville and Cupcraft. Eliades said, 'We kept in touch, and when he was in trouble, obviously who would he go to? I suppose he went to his old school pal.' *Private Eye* noted that Eliades lived next door to Roger 'Ferret' Levitt, a bow tie-wearing, cigar-chomping insurance salesman. Eliades had stood bail for Levitt when he was arrested for theft after his Levitt Group collapsed with debts of £34 million in 1990. Green had introduced Levitt to Tony Berry, who had tried to put Blue Arrow into a joint venture with Levitt and also considered using him as his personal financial adviser. Tina soon opened a new boutique in Mayfair, named Alma – perhaps a tribute to Green's mother. It was on South Molton Street, in a shop previously occupied by Amber Day's Woodhouse brand. The lines between Green's family, friends and business interests appeared to be very blurred. He did not react well to questions about the overlap. When John Jay at the *Sunday Telegraph* mentioned Tina's problems with Harabels, Green told him, 'I don't mind you writing about me, but if you write about my wife things could get uncomfortable.' 'What does that mean?' Jay asked. 'I will leave you to be the judge of that,' Green replied.

In a June 1992 issue, *Private Eye* unpicked the relationship between Green and Tony Schneider. It said that Schneider, his wife Julie and their company, Eastcheap General Trading, had at various times owned 255,000 Amber Day shares worth more than £150,000. The Slicker column had already asked, 'Just why a man who has featured as a target criminal for Scotland Yard's organized crime squad – he was acquitted in the 1970s on charges concerning alleged pornography and extortion – should be investing in Green's company remains to be explained.' According to Schneider's old associate, Green encouraged him to buy shares in the company, promising they would continue to rise. The loan shark was none too pleased when the share price fell consistently for the next few months. Eventually, Green offered to buy Schneider out at the original price. Green then sold the shares for a profit. Schneider was outraged. 'Tony phoned Philip up and he's screaming and shouting, and Philip made a remark to him that he didn't like,' Schneider's friend recalled. 'He said, "Well, you're over twenty-one." '

The disputed investment in Amber Day led to one of the most notorious incidents of Green's career. A few years later, in November 1996, Green came across Schneider at Langan's Brasserie in Mayfair, one of the most fashionable restaurants of the time. Schneider was having lunch with friends. When Green bounded over to say hello, Schneider leapt up and punched him in the face twice, sending him sprawling. According to a bystander, the manager hurried to help Green to his feet. Schneider apparently said, 'Leave that prick where he is. He can crawl out.' There was a ripple of appreciative applause and several diners stood to raise their glasses in a toast. One onlooker told the *Mail on Sunday*, 'It quite put me off my spinach soufflé.'

(When he heard that I was looking into Tony Schneider for this book, Green told me, 'You really are a sick fucker.' He insisted that Schneider had 'no relevance to my business career whatsoever', and said he had 'no recollection' of the Langan's story. 'If I went into

Langan's twice in my life it would be a lot,' Green said. 'It's a load of rubbish.' He did not quite deny having borrowed from Schneider in the 1970s, although he said, 'You got evidence of that? Show me the cheques.')

Most of Green's friends were connected in some way. Through Schneider, Green was linked to Ted Ball, the hard-drinking boss of Landhurst Leasing. Ball had grown up on a council estate in south London and felt the need to prove himself by throwing money around. When Landhurst secured a £120 million credit line from a syndicate of banks led by Guinness Mahon in 1990, he gifted all his staff Dom Pérignon champagne and Montblanc fountain pens. Landhurst, which lent money to the likes of Frank Warren, the boxing promoter, was put into receivership in August 1992 when its bankers discovered a black hole in its accounts. Records soon showed that Schneider's company, Eastcheap General Trading, had leased an Aston Martin Zagato, a Bentley Turbo R and two Mercedes from Landhurst. Green had leased a £60,000 kitchen for his home in St John's Wood and a £160,000 Cougar Sportscat powerboat. Harabels had leased a Mercedes 300SL. Amber Day had leased a Bentley Turbo, a Jaguar Sovereign and a Saab Turbo. Tony Berry had borrowed £800,000 for antique furniture and cars. Terry Venables had borrowed £1 million to buy shares in Spurs. *Private Eye* described Green's circle as a 'clique . . . united by a love of Tottenham Hotspur as well as their wallets'.

The steady drip of allegations about Green's private life and the see-sawing of Amber Day's share price began to spook some of its biggest shareholders. A fund manager at one of the investment institutions felt that he was being compromised by Green, who would call him constantly with informal updates about Amber Day, in contravention of City practice. He said, 'I got hauled in by my management and told in no uncertain terms that if I didn't step back, I would be sacked. I was pretty appalled by the things I was learning and I couldn't get away from it fast enough.' The fund manager said that after he stopped answering Green's calls, Amber Day's boss leaked his name to the press, which he interpreted as a veiled threat 'not to shoot my mouth off'. He decided that Green was a 'nasty, vicious character'.

By May 1992, Green and Graham Coles were no longer speaking. Green was avoiding Leslie Warman altogether. On the last Sunday of that month, Coles and Warman visited Green at home in St John's Wood. They threatened to leave unless the boss agreed to separate the roles of chairman and chief executive, and bring in the second non-executive director he had promised. The next day, Warman gave Sir Laurie Magnus a handwritten note headed 'Secret memorandum', warning that he was close to walking out. It said, 'Since the January problems (which you know have not been resolved) trust on the board has not been what it should be . . . It goes without saying that I would have preferred it if matters had not reached this point.' A week later, there was what one source called a 'High Noon' stand-off at a rare board meeting. The motion to split the roles of chairman and chief executive was put to a vote by the board, which was packed with Green supporters such as Ian Grabiner and Elaine Gray, both of whom he had promoted from What Everyone Wants. They voted against Warman's suggestion. The following Sunday, Jeff Randall broke the news of Coles' and Warman's departures. He reported that Coles had been headhunted by First Leisure, a disco operator, and that Warman was leaving owing to 'a disagreement with Green over corporate strategy' – which was not strictly accurate, given that the dispute had been about Green's dominance. Randall went on to say that Green had been 'subjected to a campaign of personal abuse, including hate-mail at his north London home, and anonymous faxes at his office. Newspapers have probed his private life and have delved into the business problems of his wife, Tina, who recently had their second child.'

Randall believed there was a vein of anti-Semitism to some of the City criticism of Green. It was two years after the Guinness share-trading trial, when three Jewish defendants (and a fourth who had a Jewish father) had been convicted of market manipulation for helping to prop up the share price of Guinness while it tried to take over a rival, Distillers. Several Gentile bankers, including the City grandee David Mayhew of Cazenove, had walked free. Randall told friends that his support of Green had prompted anonymous letters calling him a 'Jew lover'. On one occasion he was even said to have received photocopies of cartoons printed by Julius Streicher, a publisher of grotesque Jewish caricatures in Nazi-era Germany. However, it is worth noting that both of Green's most vociferous critics, John Jay of the *Sunday Telegraph* and Leslie Warman on the board of Amber Day, were themselves Jewish. Jay in particular felt that Green's behaviour was offensive to the code of Jewish business ethics, which holds as a key principle that both sides of any transaction should benefit. According to Talmudic tradition, the first question asked of those who pass into the next world is, 'Were you honest in business?'

Green's victory over his City babysitters turned out to be pyrrhic. The departures of Coles and Warman stripped him of credibility. News of their departure was accompanied by a profit warning. A few months later, in September 1992, Amber Day delivered pre-tax profits of £7.5 million – far less than the £16 million Green had originally promised, and a decline on the previous year's £10 million. It was enough for Amber Day's three leading shareholders to demand his head. Sir Laurie Magnus delivered the news by phone to Green, who was eventually persuaded that it would be less embarrassing to stand down than to be forced out. He issued an angry statement blaming 'adverse and undeserved publicity'. 'Not a moment too soon,' was the verdict of the *Sunday Telegraph*. In the *Sunday Times*, Jeff Randall wrote that Green had 'walked on the wild side, and his enemies would not let him forget it'. But the farewell results also revealed a £6 million loss on the sale of Review and Woodhouse to their founder, who was working with Green's friend Harold Tillman. The bear raiders had been on to something.

Aged forty, with a wife and two young children, Green was back where he had started: unemployed, and smarting with an acute sense of failure. From Carmel College to Bond Street Bandit, Lee Cooper and now Amber Day, his career had been an uninterrupted series of calamities. Amber Day was a more public humiliation than the others. It gave Green a deep loathing of the City and its conventions. Inexplicably chippy, despite his education at one of the most expensive private schools in Britain, he 'felt very strongly the establishment was out to get him', according to a banker who tried to help him cling on at Amber Day.

In the years to come, Green would be contemptuous about 'all those tossers running public companies' and 'people [in the City] talking off-the-record in their posh accents'. For the time being, he had to console himself with a £1.1 million payoff, described as 'obscene' by *The Guardian*. His replacement, David Thompson, defended Green, who agreed to stay on as a consultant for three months. However, 1992's pre-tax profits of £7.5 million were later revised to a loss of £7.8 million, and Amber Day lost a further £2.1 million in 1993. There were further write-downs on the menswear business sold to Harold Tillman. Green's ignominious exit was capped by leaked news of a DTI investigation into Amber Day. DTI inspectors interviewed the main players but took no further steps. One individual who was interviewed thought the process 'amateurish' and said he was 'amazed and appalled nothing ever came out'.

Green's circle of friends seemed to be cursed. The DTI published its report into Blue Arrow's £25 million loan to Peter de Savary, which had been intended for a development at Canvey Island in Essex. It described Tony Berry as 'likeable and charming' but concluded that he had failed to show 'acceptable conduct for someone in a position of authority of a public company'. Peter Lilley, the trade secretary, sought Berry's disqualification as a director. The DTI pursued Berry for five years but finally gave up in 1994, by which point he had run up £1.1 million in legal costs and gone through 'untold pain and suffering'. He never held a major City job again, although he remained Tottenham Hotspur's deputy chairman. The Serious Fraud Office initially secured the conviction of four bankers involved in Blue Arrow's 1987 rights issue, but five months later an appeal judge ruled the trial unfair and overturned the verdicts.

★

Ted Ball's wild behaviour came to worry his friends. He kept a double-decker bus and a tank in the garden of his mansion in East Sussex, where he hosted extravagant parties. He drank Chablis in the office during the day and moved on to Bacardi and champagne at night. There was an infamous story about a charity auction at a banqueting hall below the Western Marble Arch synagogue, where Ball was said to have made the winning bid for a signed football, then drunkenly kicked it up into a chandelier, sending fragments of glass shattering. He apparently told the distraught maître d' he would cover the cost – about £10,000 – and continued to smash the chandelier to pieces, insisting that he now owned it.

When Landhurst Leasing collapsed, many of its loans turned out to be backed by worthless collateral. Ball and his finance director were charged with fraud for accepting bribes from the owners of the Brabham Formula One racing team in return for loose loans, including money advanced against racing cars with no engines. As the court heard stories about briefcases of cash being handed over on the M1, Ball pleaded guilty to eight charges and was sentenced to three years in jail in 1997. He died a few years after his release. The administrators appointed to Landhurst uncovered a morass of excess. They had to liquidate 'so many bloody Ferraris' they affected the market for supercars, according to a source who was involved in the administration. He explained that Landhurst's borrowers were divided into two camps. 'There was a group around Philip Green and his associates, but there was also a group of fairly unpleasant people,' he said. 'There were drug dealers and someone that had a conviction for murder.'

Landhurst's demise would prove catastrophic for Terry Venables, the Tottenham Hotspur boss (and later England manager). In 1991, Venables had bought Spurs with Alan Sugar, the Amstrad tycoon. The pair fell out viciously over money and the way Venables was running the club. In 1993 and 1994, the BBC's *Panorama* programme revealed that £2 million of Venables' initial investment in Spurs had come from Norfina, a finance company. A further £1 million to take up the issue of new shares had come from

Landhurst. Venables had pledged the assets of four pubs owned by a company called Transatlantic Inns as security for the Landhurst loan. There were two problems: he had ceased to be a director of Transatlantic two months beforehand, and one of the pubs – The Miners in Cardiff – did not exist. After a lengthy DTI investigation, Venables decided not to contest nineteen different charges. He was banned from acting as a director for seven years in 1997, although he was still allowed to work as a coach.

Roger Levitt, the financial adviser who lived next to Green's schoolfriend Panos Eliades, left 18,000 clients facing destitution when his Levitt Group fell apart – including the thriller writer Frederick Forsyth, who lost £2.2 million. Levitt declared himself bankrupt. Desperate to secure his conviction, the SFO agreed to whittle down sixty-two charges to one of fraudulently trading in return for a guilty plea. There was outrage when Levitt walked free from court with a 180-hour community service sentence in 1993, proclaiming his innocence despite having been branded 'thoroughly and markedly dishonest' by the judge. But he became the first person in Britain to be banned for life from working in financial services, and he was struck off as a director for seven years. Levitt fled to New York to work as a boxing promoter just before the DTI issued a warrant for his arrest for breaking the terms of his director's ban in 1996. The DTI failed to extradite him and he stayed in America with his family.

Sir Laurie Magnus's association with Philip Green dented his reputation. Beyond Amber Day, however, Samuel Montagu had a bigger problem in the form of Robert Maxwell, the belligerent tycoon who was found to have looted £425 million from the Mirror Group's pension funds after his dead body was found floating by his yacht off the Canary Islands in November 1991. The DTI eventually censured the merchant bank over its role in the stock-market listing of the Mirror Group, but in any case Samuel Montagu was subsumed into HSBC in 1992 as part of HSBC's takeover of its parent company, the Midland Bank. Magnus, who left three years later, said of Green, 'I and my colleagues knew there was some reputational risk in working for him. Looking back, I don't regret it . . . He felt there was some sort of establishment vendetta against him. I sympathized with him. He faced real prejudice at times.'

Tony Schneider died of a heart attack in May 2003, aged seventy-nine. According to his former associate, he was on holiday at the time with his wife, Julie, in the flat he had bought her near Athens. His last words when he woke up at 4 a.m. with heart pains were said to have been, 'Make me a cup of tea.' Schneider left Julie an estate worth £273,180. She fell out with Schneider's closest friends over money, sold their house near Regent's Park and moved to a suburban road in Wood Green, north-east London, where she installed bars over the doors and windows. Schneider's funeral at Edgwarebury cemetery in north London was attended by several hundred people. Green was not there, but Harold Tillman was among the mourners. Tillman, meanwhile, defied the DTI's attempts to ban him from acting as a director after Honorbilt went into administration in 1990, but was banned for three years in 2001 over the collapse of a company called Launchexception, which ran the O Bar in Soho.

There was a sinister postscript to the Amber Day saga. In the late summer of 1992, David Hellier, the *Independent* journalist who had been critical of Green, went into the *Sunday Times* for a contract shift. He received a call from Leslie Warman, the non-executive director who had just stood down. Warman had been angered by the way Green had leaked the news of his departure, which was followed by a smattering of other articles mentioning Warman in a disparaging light. He wanted to explain the background properly and help Hellier piece together the Amber Day 'jigsaw puzzle'. John Cassidy, the *Sunday Times'* business editor, was keen to investigate the story, but Jeff Randall opposed it. That afternoon, Warman received a hysterical call from Green. Amber Day's boss shouted so loud down the line that Warman's wife, Linda, a GP, could hear him from the other side of the room. Green allegedly threatened him, 'If you don't shut your fucking mouth, I'll get my friends south of the river to come for you and your family.' Randall always denied having given Warman's name to Green, but he accepted that he might have mentioned the prospect of a negative article to Green, leaving him to guess the likely source. The story died. For the next few days, Warman's wife felt uneasy whenever she took their children to the park or the shops near their home in Golders Green, imagining that Green's friends were among the crowds, watching them from behind newspapers.

(Green denied having threatened Warman or having mentioned any 'friends south of the river' when I asked him about the incident for this book. 'That's all bollocks,' he said. 'I don't talk like that. That's not my style.')

Revenge was Green's first instinct after leaving Amber Day, as it had been after Lee Cooper. He still had an 8 per cent stake, and for a while he was in danger of losing his house as the share price languished below the level of his borrowings. In April 1993, Amber Day bounced on an unexpectedly good set of results and Green sold his shares for £7.5 million, more than clearing the debt against them. The following month he went into direct competition with his old employer, buying fifty-four discount stores out of receivership. Green paid £3.3 million for Parker & Franks, which was sold by one of his closest insolvency contacts, Philip Monjack at Leonard Curtis. David Thompson, Amber Day's new leader, had to explain why Green was able to buy a rival business less than eight months after receiving a £1.1 million golden goodbye. 'Mr Green did have an exclusion clause in his contract but this deal does not breach it,' he said. Green rebranded the chain Xception and opened the first refurbished store in Manchester.

Next, Green took over Owen Owen, a group of loss-making department stores. He threw a 1995 Valentine's Day party at the famous Lewis's department store in Manchester, part of Owen Owen's portfolio. There was pink champagne and a Glenn Miller-style band in 1940s GI uniforms. Green told a *Sunday Times* reporter that Owen Owen had been cleaned up and 'prepared for us, who as retailers can really take it forward'. But the reality did not match the rhetoric. A year later, Green sold eight of its thirteen stores to a rival, Allders, for £23.6 million. A further four were closed or sold.

In 2004, Green offloaded the remaining Liverpool shop to David Thompson, his successor at Amber Day, who had tried to follow him into dealmaking. What was left of Owen Owen went bust less than three years later.

He also tried his hand at jewellery. Owen & Robinson – no relation to Owen Owen – had sixty loss-making shops trading as The Gold Centre and thirteen more-promising trainer stores branded as Foothold. Green gained control by buying its £6 million outstanding bank debt for a discounted £3 million and taking an equity stake. It was clear to Owen & Robinson's boss, a jovial Irishman called Alan Gaynor, that Green still needed to scratch the Amber Day itch. The company was listed on the stock market, and Green demanded to meet its biggest shareholders. Gaynor corralled twenty reluctant fund managers into a room. Green turned up late after what one observer guessed had been 'a big lunch'. He proceeded to walk up and down, lecturing them. 'You suits don't have a fucking clue,' he said. 'You've never run a fucking company.' One of the investors mouthed to Gaynor, 'I told you so.' Green's City comeback proved short lived. He and Gaynor were forced to put the jewellery business into administration.

But these were scrappy little deals. Looming over Green like a mountain to be climbed was Sears, Sir Charles Clore's once-mighty empire. Green had longed to take it over since the late 1980s, when the bankers from Citi had scoffed at him. There was an element of emotion – a break-up bid for the company Clore built would be rich in symbolism – but it was also logical. In its glory days, British Shoe Corporation, owned by Sears, had sold one in four pairs of footwear. Sears had begun to lose momentum even before Clore stepped down as chairman in 1976. He was succeeded by his lawyer, Leonard Sainer, whom Clore's biographer Charles Gordon described as 'seemingly tired and weary, with layers of skin draped around his eyes'. Sainer lacked Clore's vision – as did Sainer's successor, Geoffrey Maitland Smith, a tax adviser who was once Paul McCartney's accountant. Maitland Smith sold some of the peripheral businesses, like Mappin & Webb and William Hill, but Sears' processes remained antiquated. John Lovering, who went on to become one of the most powerful figures in private equity, remembered arriving as finance director in 1988 and asking to see the group's cash balance. 'Some little lad held out a Woolworths notebook,' he said. 'Sears worked out its cash balance by calling up every subsidiary and asking how much cash they had.'

In 1995, Maitland Smith was replaced by Sir Bob Reid, the former chairman of British Rail. Reid's chief executive was Liam Strong, an urbane but overpromoted former British Airways marketing director who quickly alienated his senior team by refusing to take advice. The combination gave off a smell of weakness. Sears had effectively become a property portfolio with a collection of badly managed retail businesses on the side. One of the unloved parts was Olympus, a loss-making chain of 200 sports-equipment stores.

Olympus caught the eye of Tom Hunter, a softly spoken greengrocer's son from New Cumnock in East Ayrshire. Hunter's family had closed their shop in a local downturn caused by a miners' strike in 1984 and gone into shoe wholesaling. With £5,000 from his father, Campbell, and £5,000 from Royal Bank of Scotland, Hunter had started out supplying Nike and Adidas trainers to retailers from the back of a van. He had gradually developed the business into Sports Division, a chain of forty-five stores. Eager to expand, Hunter approached Liam Strong about a bid for Olympus. Strong dismissed the thirty-four-year-old as inexperienced. Hunter knew Green through a contact at What Everyone Wants, Ian Grabiner, who had introduced them over an Italian meal on one of Green's trips to Glasgow. Hunter called the arch dealmaker and explained his predicament. 'Leave it to me, Thomas,' Green said.

Green had hardly any money, but he happened to know the boss of Olympus, Derek Lovelock, from his days bustling around Great Portland Street. When Lovelock finally called to confirm the potential for a deal, Green was in hospital. Already overweight and wheezy – his father's genetic inheritance – he had suffered his first heart attack. Doctors discovered that two of Green's coronary arteries were partially blocked and fitted him with two stents. 'It's a bit difficult today,' Green croaked to Lovelock. 'Can it wait until next week?' When he emerged from hospital, Green called Hunter. 'The good news is we've got a lock-out period,' he said. 'The bad news is *I've* got the lock-out period, and you've got to deal with me.' Hunter asked how much money Green intended to put in. Green was astonished. 'I want to take money *out*,' he said. He demanded £1 million cash upfront for his services, plus a 13 per cent stake in the enlarged Sports Division. After a fierce bout of haggling, during which Hunter's lawyer warned Green that his client was 'not the kind of guy you can shout at', they agreed on a stake of 12 per cent.

In need of cash, Hunter turned to Bank of Scotland and its head of corporate lending, who would become crucial to his and Green's careers: Peter Cummings. Hunter put up his home and shares in Sports Division as security for a £20 million loan. Green agreed a price of £20 million for Olympus with Lovelock, keeping the identity of the buyer secret. At the final meeting in the offices of Sears' law firm, Titmuss Sainer Dechert, Green welcomed Hunter with a theatrical flourish. 'You'd better let him in,' he told the Sears side, ''cos he's got the fucking cheque.'

From their office on an industrial estate near Kilmarnock, Hunter and his father now oversaw a business with almost 250 stores and £250 million of sales. Green visited only once, when he declared there were 'too many fucking sheep' in Scotland and went back to London. Hunter confidently rebranded the Olympus stores to Sports Division. In 1997, two years after the Sears deal, Green pushed Hunter to float the group on the stock market, which would crystallize their combined fortune of several hundred million pounds. One of the analysts appointed to prepare the listing was NatWest Securities' John Richards, who had sometimes clashed with Green at Amber Day. Richards thought Green was 'a demon in terms of doing a deal' but joked that 'if you shook hands with him, you had to check whether you still had all your fingers afterwards'. They embarked on what Richards could 'only describe as one of the most embarrassing series of store visits in my life. Every store we went into was a mess in one way or another. One store manager got a complete bollocking in front of me – "the way you've organized your stock room is totally wrong" – to which he said, "Well, your fucking system doesn't work." '

The merger of Olympus and Sports Division had clearly been a mess. But Green and Hunter were determined to press ahead with the float, so Richards and his colleagues began writing detailed research notes. 'And then we started getting the numbers,' he said. 'And the like-for-like sales were down literally 15 per cent, 20 per cent, at which point I had to say to Philip and Tom, "This just isn't going to happen." ' There was a crisis meeting in March 1998, at which Green and Hunter discussed the prospect of an emergency sale to one of Sports Division's rivals, Blacks Leisure. Then, out of the blue, Hunter took a call from Dave Whelan, the owner of Wigan Athletic and the boss of JJB Sports – another rival. Whelan was eager to buy Sports Division and willing to pay a big price. 'One condition,' he told Hunter. 'Don't tell Philip Green. This needs to be private and he can't keep a secret.' Hunter negotiated a price of £290 million, which Richards said was 'even more than we were going to float at – it was a total get-out-of-jail-free card'.

When the finalized deal was presented to Green, his first reaction was, 'I could have got more.' Hunter retorted, 'No you couldn't, and if you fuck about, I won't do it, I'll go back to my sheep and you can fuck off.' Green relented, and JJB Sports announced the acquisition in July 1998. Like Lee Cooper with Bonanza Jeans and Jean Jeanie a decade earlier, JJB soon realized that it had horribly overpaid. Hunter resigned from his new job as JJB's deputy chairman before Christmas, and Whelan had to issue two profit warnings as he grappled with Sports Division's trading problems. Green walked away with almost £36 million. It was the lucky windfall that put him on the road to the big time.

Over the years, the Greens would give a variety of reasons for their move to Monaco. In her 2005 *Daily Mail* interview, Tina said they decided to leave London after Green was mugged outside their home by 'three guys, one of them with a great big sword, which he held to Philip's throat'. In his 2016 parliamentary evidence, Green said he had 'wanted to put my children in school somewhere, and I had two or three choices'. According to someone who knew them at the time of the Sports Division sale, it was simpler: Green ordered his wife to whisk the children off to the tax-free principality a few days before the start of the tax year in which his big Sports Division payday arrived. From that moment on, all Green's business interests were held offshore in his wife's name. Tina was said to have been 'in tears' about leaving their home in St John's Wood. She rented a flat in Le Formentor, a building on Monaco's sought-after Avenue Princesse Grace, and her husband started commuting weekly to London.

Green had become the retail industry's shark. He could taste Sears' blood in the water. He continued to build his private empire, paying £7.5 million for the discount chain Mark One from the insolvency practice Leonard Curtis in February 1996 after a bidding battle with the Mancunian rag trader Shami Ahmed, which he likened to fighting 'ten rounds with Mike Tyson'. Some journalists compared him to Stephen Hinchliffe, a dealmaker from Sheffield whose Facia Group was buying up ailing brands such as Red or Dead and Sock Shop – until Facia went bust in 1996 (Hinchliffe was later jailed twice for fraud).

But Green remained focused on Sears. In April 1997, less than a month before Tony Blair swept into Downing Street, Sears finally sacked its hapless boss, Liam Strong. At the same time, its chairman, Sir Bob Reid, announced plans to demerge Selfridges, effectively signalling a break-up of the group. First, Green moved in on Shoe Express, one of its footwear chains. His negotiating team, which included his stepson, Brett Palos, outmanoeuvred Sears mercilessly. At an early stage of the talks, the Sears side left a sheet of paper in a meeting room listing all the rival bids. Green urged Palos to stuff it down his trousers and they ran outside to read it in the car. Green then wore down the Sears team. The night before the deal was due to be announced in December 1997, the two sides were still arguing over a sum of £40,000. Green looked across the table with a glint in his eye. 'We either stay here all night discussing this, or we toss a coin for it,' he said. Sears tossed – and lost. The next morning, Green bought Shoe Express for £8.3 million. He humiliated Sears by converting some of the shops to Mark One and selling the rest for £20 million within months, making a huge profit.

Green was not the only predator circling. Richard Caring, a clothing supplier who had lived in Hong Kong, was also planning a takeover of his own. Caring was a sleek, slight figure with a glossy mane of hair and dazzling white teeth. His Italian-American father, Louis Caringi, had been a GI who was stationed in Britain during the war. In 1945, Louis tumbled down the steps of Warren Street Tube station and broke his leg. The nurse in the ambulance taking him to hospital was Sylvia Parnes, who came from a family of successful clothing retailers (and also happened to be a cousin of Larry Parnes, manager of the pop star Billy Fury). Louis and Sylvia fell in love and married. Louis, who anglicized his surname, pretended to be Jewish to blend in with Sylvia's family. Lou Caring, as he became known, set up one of the biggest dress manufacturing companies in London. His son, a talented golfer, went to Millfield public school in Somerset on a sporting scholarship, until his father's company went bust and he had to leave at fifteen – an experience that 'hurt him desperately', according to a family friend. Lou and his son then relaunched the business. Richard had first met Green on the rag-trade scene of the early 1970s – although Caring, who was four years older and infinitely smoother, initially saw Green as an irritating little boy. They became closer on regular trips to Hong Kong in the years when they both felt like pioneers exploring a new land of cheap sourcing.

In early 1998, Green picked up a rumour of Caring's plan. Caring was particularly interested in Sears' catalogue business, Freemans. He believed that he had a buyer lined up already in the shape of a German mail-order company, Otto Versand, which had bought a catalogue called Together from Caring in the late 1980s. Green bombarded Caring with voicemails telling him that he was 'doing it all wrong', but Caring was silent. In a fit of frustration one evening, Green sent his chauffeur to Caring's house in Highgate, north London. The driver knocked on the door and handed Caring an envelope containing a pound coin and a note. It said, 'I know what you're up to and I know you're mean. Now you can afford to call me.'

A few weeks before Christmas 1998, speculation over a mystery bid for Sears reached fever pitch. Despite the company's denials, an analyst called Richard Ratner told the *Daily Express*, 'My belief is that people are out there ready to move on Sears.' Ratner, nicknamed 'Ratty', was speaking from knowledge. Ratty was a public-school eccentric who once welcomed the boss of Railtrack for lunch by dressing as a stationmaster, but his clownish sense of humour masked a sharp mind. He called Green 'Monsieur Vert', and he was one of the few people Green trusted in the City. Ratner had already put Green in touch with a merchant bank called Rea Brothers, which had been impressed by Green's analysis of Sears and agreed to work with him.

A few days before Christmas, Green struck. He and Tom Hunter announced a £460 million takeover approach for the wounded giant, with Richard Caring's involvement kept quietly in the background. They offered to pay Sears' shareholders in cash – which was bold, because they didn't yet have any money. The stock market laughed at Green's flimsy raiding party. Sir Bob Reid, Sears' chairman, rejected him out of hand. A few days later, Green tabled a new offer. Reid rejected him again. The explosion of action confused the City, which hesitated between its scepticism of Green and its usual desire to see a sluggish company ripped apart.

Green now needed increased firepower. He got very lucky. Out of the blue, he received a call from Frederick Barclay, a reclusive tycoon who lived with his twin brother David in a mock-gothic castle on Brecqhou, one of the Channel Islands. The Barclay brothers were familiar with corporate raids, having made their first fortune buying a shipping and brewing company called Ellerman on the cheap and breaking it up for a profit. Green and Hunter flew to Monaco to meet them in the Hôtel de Paris, Monte Carlo's answer to the Ritz. The Barclays were waiting at their usual table at the back of the hotel's famous Bar Américain. The ageing brothers had a reputation for strangeness – it was said you could only tell them apart because David parted his hair on the right, Frederick on the left – and on the way in, Green muttered to Hunter, 'I'll handle this.' He confidently sketched out the Sears bid to the Barclays, explaining how they would make their money back by selling the retail brands, effectively getting the property portfolio for free. As they chatted, Fred Barclay leaned across the table. 'Young Tom, do you want to know the best business advice of your life?' he asked. Hunter nodded eagerly. 'Never do business with arseholes,' Fred said. The Barclays looked at each other and burst out laughing. Bemused, Green and Hunter shook their hands and left. On the steps outside, Hunter breathed in the grandeur of Monte Carlo's Place du Casino in the cold December air. Green turned to him, shaking his head. 'Fucking weirdos,' he said.

Despite the bizarre meeting, the Barclays agreed to put £100 million into a new bidding company, January Investments. Green, Caring and Hunter chipped in £25 million. BankBoston and Bank of Scotland provided loans of £415 million. As with the Olympus deal, Peter Cummings, the Bank of Scotland financier whom Green and Hunter had befriended, played a crucial role. It was testament to Green's growing clout that he was able to put together a fighting fund of almost £550 million in such a short space of time.

Sears cowered in anticipation of a second strike. Green returned from his traditional winter break in the Caribbean and established a war room at his suite at the Dorchester, the Park Lane hotel favoured by Sir Charles Clore's business partner, Jack Cotton. David Barclay seconded his sons, Aidan and Howard, to help with the preparations. Aidan was the more serious of the two. Howard liked to lean back expansively in his red braces, puffing on cigars. Green chain-smoked cigarettes, frantically juggling phone calls. From time to time he would stop, jab a butt in Howard's direction and say, 'In my next life, I want to fucking come back as *you*!'

In mid-January 1999, Green raised his offer to £519 million. Sir Bob Reid rejected him again, but this time the presence of the Barclay brothers and their hard cash persuaded Sears' biggest shareholder, Phillips & Drew, to fold its hand. The defence was crumbling. A week later, Green and the Sears team faced off in an evening meeting at the Dorchester. Green said he would make a final bid of £548 million if the board surrendered. As Sir Bob Reid prevaricated, Green's bankers published a humiliating analysis describing Sears as the 'incredible shrinking company'. Emasculated and exhausted, Reid accepted the deal. As a condition of their backing, the Barclay twins had asked Green to use the blue-blooded bank Robert Fleming alongside the smaller Rea Brothers. In the early hours of the morning, observing Green become twitchy, one of his advisers popped out to buy him cigarettes. He came back to find Green chasing a tearful Flemings banker around the meeting table, shouting, 'I'll rip your fucking throat out!' At the end of a tense night, the Flemings man had made the mistake of handing Green the bill.

Sears was the ultimate back-of-a-fag-packet deal. But the gamble paid off. Green took over in January 1999 and asset-stripped the company with cold precision. The old board had already agreed a £141 million sale of its store-card business to Groupe Cofinoga, a French conglomerate. In April, Green sold the Freemans catalogue to Otto Versand for £150 million. Arcadia Group, the owner of Topshop, paid £151 million for Sears' fashion brands, including Miss Selfridge and Warehouse. The Adams childrenswear chain went to its management team for £87 million. By the end of July, the 108-year-old empire was gone. Green's consortium had recouped almost the entire £548 million purchase price – and it still had Sears' valuable property portfolio, which turned out to be worth about £300 million. Having put in little more than £120 million of their own money, Green and his friends made profits of more than £280 million. His wife also had a piece of the action. Tina had bought 1.8 million Sears shares in late 1998, before her husband's interest became public knowledge. She was sitting on a paper profit of £3.6 million.

Eight years after the disgrace of Amber Day, Green had suddenly caught the attention of every banker in London. He had ruthlessly dismantled Sears into its component parts and shown the City he possessed the one quality it prizes above all others: the ability to make money.

5

High Times

The 220 guests who arrived at Luton airport on the morning of 14 March 2002 had been told only to pack for hot days and cold nights, and to bring a piece of flesh-coloured underwear. They were greeted by a check-in sign: 'PG50 Airways. Getting a great party off the ground.'

In the departure lounge, a muzak-style band played Frank Sinatra's 'Fly Me to the Moon'. Philip and Tina Green mingled, embracing newcomers and serving glasses of Buck's Fizz. As well as Green's business contacts – including Richard Caring, Tom Hunter and Stuart Rose, the new boss of Arcadia Group – there were B-list celebrities such as the TV prankster Jeremy Beadle, the former Page Three girl Jilly Johnson and the racing driver Sir Stirling Moss, who was married to Tina's sister, Susie. Caring's wife, Jackie, who thought Tina's tastes vulgar, was notably absent.

Green's fiftieth birthday, organized by Tina at an estimated cost of £5 million, loudly announced his arrival to the big time. A year earlier, Hunter's wife had hired an events company called Banana Split to put on his fortieth birthday party in Cap Ferrat, with entertainment from Kool and the Gang and Stevie Wonder. It had cost £750,000. Everything about Green's party was designed to be bigger and better. Tina had booked a new luxury hotel in Cyprus, the Anassa, and hired Banana Split to plan a weekend of ridiculous extravagance. The preparations required fifty-six people and took three weeks. Thirty articulated trucks delivered materials ranging from 18,000 flower stems to four drum kits. A fleet of mobile generators pulled up with enough power for the whole of Cyprus. Tina ordered 1,000 bottles of wine, 400 bottles of champagne, 400 oysters and 40 kilograms of caviar.

Even the flight safety video was personalized. 'It is vital at this stage that all your hand luggage is labelled correctly,' a polite voice told guests as they boarded the plane. 'The appropriate labels should read Louis Vuitton, Christian Lacroix or Chanel. For this flight only, British Home Stores is also acceptable.' There was a heavy-handed joke about cocaine. 'At this point, I would like to introduce you to the captain,' the voice said. An image of a boggle-eyed pilot appeared on the screen. 'His name is Charles . . . Some of you may have been this high with Charlie before, but for others it's a new experience.' There was applause and laughter.

A candle-lit champagne reception on the first night oiled the crowd for a performance by the jazz guitarist George Benson. The party carried on until 2 a.m., with Hunter leading a raucous round of Scottish country dancing. The next day, in the Anassa's sunny garden, Tina presented her husband with a series of gifts. The first was a solid gold Monopoly set from the jeweller Asprey, complete with real money. Every square referenced one of his deals. Then a scantily clad model revved up on a Harley-Davidson with the licence plate PG50, and Richard Caring gave his business partner a red Ferrari Spider. As the crowd tucked into a buffet lunch of lobster and scallops, a grey-haired figure in a jacket and tie trotted down the steps to the terrace with a microphone. Michael Aspel, the host of *This Is Your Life*, asked Green, 'Are you game?'

In the hotel's ballroom, Aspel invited the most important people in Green's life to the stage. Tina came first – then Alma took the microphone and opined that her son had done 'not bad, for somebody with no O levels'. There were several pre-recorded video appearances. Green's old headmaster from Carmel College, David Stamler, wished him 'a very warm mazel tov'. Looking like loony pensioners, Sir David and Sir Frederick Barclay – who had been knighted two years earlier – fired a six-gun salute from their castle. Puff Daddy, Sylvester Stallone, Britney Spears and Bruce Willis sent separate messages. Stallone promised, 'Men don't really become sexy until they're fifty, so I can imagine you've got nothing but green lights and blue skies ahead.' Morris Keston, the Tottenham Hotspur superfan, Jeff Randall, who had become the BBC's business editor, and Ian Grabiner, Green's lieutenant, came on stage wearing Spurs shirts with Green's name on the back and the number 50. Terry Venables toasted him via video link. He cracked a joke about his nightmare with the Department of Trade and Industry, saying, 'If you do take over Tottenham at some stage, remember – leave me out, will you?'

A black-tie dinner followed in a huge marquee. Randall stepped to the microphone. 'Ladies and gentlemen, I don't have to tell you what a star Philip is,' he said. 'We all know that. That's why we're here tonight.' Green took to the stage and sang, to cheers, 'Where do I begin, to tell the story of how strange my life has been?' He quipped, 'That's the cabaret tonight.' Then he launched into a speech, welcoming Prince Albert of Monaco, who had joined the party that day. Green raised a glass of red wine to Tina, saying, 'She has the will to win, and boy oh boy, can she deliver.' Tina clasped her hands to her face as her husband led three cheers for his wife. After dinner, waiters brought out an enormous five-tiered cake with miniature models of Green and his family enjoying the event. He turned to the crowd and announced 'our present to every-body' – Tom Jones. The music legend revived some of his classics like 'Help Yourself', but he was only the warm-up. Green returned to the stage to introduce 'thirty-five guys, one of the best live acts in the world – Earth, Wind and Fire'. The band went down a storm, and the set ended with Green and his entourage dancing wildly on stage. On the way out of the marquee at the end of the night, he was mobbed by drunken friends singing Stevie Wonder's 'Happy Birthday'. 'How are you going to deal with tomorrow?' Green asked Chris Gorman, the future millionaire owner of the Gadget Shop, who was singing lustily in a top hat, clutching a bottle of champagne. 'Philip, I always deal with it,' Gorman giggled.

The best was yet to come. The next morning, guests awoke to find togas hanging on their bedroom door handles – hence the need for flesh-coloured underwear. 'They look completely see-through, but they're not,' Tina reassured the crowd at breakfast. 'Anyway, we like to see bums – men's bums, women's bums.' That evening, Green dressed and behaved like Emperor Nero. Wearing a gold-trimmed toga and a laurel wreath, he led a procession down an avenue of flaming torches to the marquee, which had been opulently redecorated as an amphitheatre. Holding his eleven-year-old daughter by the hand, Green barked in a photographer's direction, 'No pictures when I come with Chloe, or I'll break his camera.' After dinner, Green again praised a tearful Tina. He said, 'Tonight, you've made everybody sparkle, so I thought it's only fair I do my bit.' Chloe and her eight-year-old brother, Brandon, gave their mother a pair of diamond earrings in champagne flutes. 'I love this man,' Tina declared. Rod Stewart bounded onstage and sang hits such as 'Maggie May', then there was a final round of speeches. Tom Hunter said, 'Philip Green has taught me to believe in the impossible, and I think this weekend the impossible has been achieved.'

Green's scramble to the top of the business food chain was all the more remarkable for its speed. In three years, he had gone from pariah to emperor. The starting point was Sears. In January 1999, the burly corporate raider swung into the retail group's dilapidated headquarters behind Selfridges in the West End like a human wrecking ball. He delighted in undermining the senior staff who had presided over its decline, such as Roger Groom, the property director. 'Roger, go and make us some tea,' Green would snap as he arrived in the morning. Groom left at the end of January with a £318,000 pay-off. One of the few people to stand up to the new owner was Paul Coackley, an analyst in the finance department. Coackley told Green, 'You own the business. You can have whatever information you want, but not if you speak to me like that.' Green immediately made him Sears' finance director.

The Sears takeover electrified the retail industry and set the newspaper market columns fizzing with rumours of bids for House of Fraser and Storehouse, the parent company of BHS, Habitat and Mothercare. Having burned their fingers on retail deals in the late

1980s, private equity firms started prowling the high street again. John Richards, the analyst who had worked on the abortive float of Olympus, said, 'People saw Philip Green making loads of money and everyone said, "I want some of this, this is a gravy train." Which it was, until 2007.'

In July 1999, before Green's break-up of Sears was even complete, the *Mail on Sunday* linked him to possible bids for Marks & Spencer and J. Sainsbury. As a strong, self-willed character, he was beginning to see himself as the natural heir to M&S's two towering patriarchs, Simon Marks and Israel Sieff. Green became obsessed with taking over their business.

M&S, founded in 1884 as a penny bazaar at Kirkgate market in Leeds, represented the crown jewels of British retail. But it was not the invulnerable fortress it had once been. While Green had been concentrating on Sears, M&S was in the throes of a bloody succession battle. Sir Rick Greenbury, its autocratic bully of an executive chairman, had pushed the company to make record pre-tax profits of £1.1 billion in 1997, topped by £1.2 billion in 1998. Stretching the business that far proved unsustainable, and in 1999 profits collapsed to £634.6 million. At the same time, Greenbury's relationship with his successor turned poisonous. Greenbury resigned in June. Peter Salsbury, an oddball who had until then concealed his contempt for Greenbury behind a mild veneer, rampaged around sacking staff and severing decades-old contracts with suppliers. M&S's share price tumbled as it slipped from success story to crisis.

Green quietly began putting together a takeover plan code-named Project Mushroom. To run M&S if he won, he lined up Allan Leighton, the charismatic boss of Asda, Richard North, the finance director of the Bass leisure conglomerate, and Terry Green, the boorish yet high-profile chief executive of Debenhams (who was no relation). He sounded out Rupert Hambro, a silky-smooth old Etonian, to be chairman. Hambro was struck by Green's greediness in terms of the shareholding he expected to take, and he also noticed the only thing Green talked about was realizing value from M&S's properties. But he agreed to think about it.

Green approached the investment bank Merrill Lynch to see if it would act as their lead adviser, which prompted a discussion among the bank's senior ranks. Paul Roy, head of equity markets, had come across Green when he worked at Smith New Court, Amber Day's broker. He dissuaded his colleagues with a simple message, 'No way.' Simon Mackenzie-Smith, a Merrill Lynch managing director, was friendly with a member of Green's bidding team. He gave his contact some off-the-record advice. 'The only way I can see this working is if you keep Philip in a box where he's just doing the finance,' he said. 'You'll have to do all the City-facing stuff and talk to the press.' Green's team member asked the banker if he could sketch out the structure on a piece of paper. Puzzled, Mackenzie-Smith obliged. The individual then took the idea to Green. 'Box?' Green exploded. 'You're not putting me in a fucking *box*!' The paper in his acolyte's hand began to tremble. Green snatched it from him. 'You didn't write this!' Green said. 'Who did?' The disintegrating executive stammered, 'M-M-Mackenzie-Smith from M-M-Merrill Lynch.' Green growled, 'That double-barrelled cunt. What the fuck does he know?'

With Merrill Lynch out of the picture, Green turned to his old friend Sir Laurie Magnus, who had moved from Samuel Montagu to an American investment bank, Donaldson, Lufkin & Jenrette. Magnus persuaded his new bosses in New York to give Green a chance.

Green was amazingly fortunate that his emergence as a serious player coincided with a brief period when a handful of banks were prepared to lend large amounts of money to lone-wolf dealmakers. The previous summer in St-Tropez, he had been introduced to Robin Saunders, a young American woman who was head of something known as 'securitization' at the London office of WestLB, a German state-owned bank. Securitization is a way of raising money by issuing bonds backed by a company's future income stream, and in the late 1990s it was still seen as a fairly exotic tool in Europe. Saunders, who was born in North Carolina and raised in Florida, was ambitious and cool. After pulling off pioneering securitizations in Italy and Portugal, she became famous overnight for helping the Formula One tycoon Bernie Ecclestone refinance the sport in 1999 through a $1.4 billion bond backed by its future broadcasting revenues. The *Daily Telegraph* called the American banker 'Formula One's fairy godmother' and *The Sun* dubbed her 'the City's answer to Claudia Schiffer'. When they met on the French Riviera, Green was still basking in the glory of his Sears break-up. Saunders saw him as a talented underdog. She agreed to provide almost £6 billion of debt from WestLB to support his move on M&S.

M&S's shares sank to an eight-year low of 228p in November 1999. They rallied to more than 300p before Christmas as newspapers floated rumours of a takeover bid from Tesco. At that price, M&S was valued at £9 billion. As with Sears, the hidden gem was the property portfolio. M&S owned almost all the freeholds to its 300 stores. The properties were valued at less than £3 billion in its books, but they were probably worth a lot more. Like Sears, M&S had been sloppily run, with high costs at its Baker Street headquarters and poor performance from its fashion division. It was still without a chairman after Greenbury's departure. Through Sir David Sieff, the last remaining family board member, Green tried to contact Greenbury's temporary replacement, Brian Baldock, but the tough former Guinness director refused to meet him.

On 13 December, Green broke cover. After a weekend of intense press speculation, he confirmed that he had hired DLJ to look at a possible offer for M&S. The prospect of being taken over by the Bond Street Bandit was the nightmare scenario for M&S – worse even than a bid from Tesco and its aggressive Liverpudlian boss, Terry Leahy. Baldock's war cabinet comprised Brunswick, the PR firm famous for its hardball defence of Imperial Chemical Industries against Hanson Plc in 1991, the stockbroker Cazenove and the investment bank Morgan Stanley. First blood went to Green when M&S reported a fall of more than 11 per cent in like-for-like Christmas clothing sales. In late January, M&S hired a replacement for Greenbury, a dapper but unconvincing Belgian called Luc Vandevelde. The real fightback came when its advisers served Green's team with Section 212 notices under the Companies Act, demanding disclosure of any shares they owned. Green had none, but Tina's reply revealed that she had bought 9.5 million shares in M&S in early December, before news of Project Mushroom broke – similar to the trades she had made on Sears. Tina had used fifteen nominee accounts in the Channel Islands to keep her identity secret. She was sitting on a theoretical profit of about £2.5 million.

The M&S team was jubilant. In fact, the Greens had sought legal advice and cleared the purchases with the City's Takeover Panel in advance. The share trades had been approved because Tina was deemed to be in a 'concert party' with her husband and had promised to hand the shares over to the bidding entity at cost price when the time came. But M&S's advisers leaked her Section 212 reply to two Sunday newspapers, ensuring a splash of lurid headlines about secret share buying. The *Sunday Times* pushed the story too far. John Jay, the managing editor of business news, filed an article about a 'share dealing row', which was transformed by an overenthusiastic news editor into an 'insider dealing row' – effectively an allegation of criminality. It was accompanied by a longer piece headlined, 'Wife of Raider Makes Killing on M&S Deal'. The paper soon apologized, but Green was not satisfied. He launched a libel action. The two sides eventually reached a £100,000 out-of-court settlement.

Jay's story also contained an interesting nugget that might have been more troublesome for Green on a marital level. Aida Dellal Hersham, attractive, dark-haired and Iranian born, had bought shares in M&S nine days after Green announced his possible bid in December 1999. She had bought several more tranches over the next couple of months, at one point holding a stake worth £200,000. The unexplained connection between Green and a stunning divorcee became the talk of London. Tina was rumoured to have been highly displeased – by the gossip, if nothing else. When the matter was raised again a few years later, in 2004, Green irritably told the *Mail on Sunday*, 'I said I had a friendship . . . My wife is standing here. She knew about it. What's the issue?'

Green put out a furious statement saying that his family had 'behaved entirely properly' over the M&S share trades. He denounced 'an unjustifiable campaign' to discredit him, but the damage had been done. Even before the weekend's stories, DLJ's New York office had grown sufficiently concerned by Sir Laurie Magnus's buccaneering client to commission a report from the investigations agency Kroll into Green's background. A few days after the revelations of Tina's stake building, the chairman of DLJ in London, Martin Smith, visited the Dorchester and told him it was over. Green pleaded, cajoled and lost his temper, but it was too late. He announced that he would withdraw his interest in M&S. He told *The Independent*, 'It's my prerogative to play or pass, and I don't need to stress myself with all this.'

Green retreated to Sears' headquarters behind Oxford Street to lick his wounds. He fielded calls from contacts, complaining bitterly about the City's smears. But he rebounded quickly. Storehouse, the high-street conglomerate put together by the designer Sir Terence Conran in the mid-1980s, had effectively put itself up for sale the previous year by planning to spin off Mothercare and keep its other business, BHS. The department-store chain, founded in 1928 by a group of Americans who wanted to emulate the success of Woolworths, was struggling with the introduction of cheap clothing by supermarkets like Asda and Tesco. In the six months to October 1999, BHS's like-for-like sales fell by 9.2 per cent and it made an operating loss of £8.3 million. It had a valuable property portfolio, however, with more than 150 stores. BHS was the acquisition that would change everything and transform Green's finances.

Storehouse held sale talks with two suitors – Brown & Jackson, the owner of Poundstretcher, run by a South African tycoon called Christo Wiese, and Iceland, the supermarket group. In March 2000, both sets of talks fell apart. With backing from Barclays and Robin Saunders from the German bank WestLB, Green pounced. He called Storehouse's dour chairman, Alan Smith, and made him a take-it-or-leave-it offer: £200 million for BHS, and four days to think about it. Richard Caring hovered in the background during the operation, which was codenamed Project Boris, although he 'never appeared in the front-line negotiations', according to an adviser who was involved. Green's purchase of BHS was announced on 27 March 2000. Touchy about his growing reputation as an asset-stripper, he emphasized his intention to run it as a going concern.

The following month, Terry Green, the Debenhams chief executive who had worked with Green on the M&S project, denied that he was taking a job at BHS. Terry Green was a beefy bruiser with a big ego and an appetite for money. He had just bought a ten-bedroom mansion near Tunbridge Wells, and he told an interviewer from *Management Today* that he had realized his boyhood dreams of 'having a flash car, a sexy girlfriend and a house in the country'. It was later said that he boasted of having paid for his girlfriend's breast implants. Terry Green saw the opportunity to take his earnings to the next level. In September 2000, despite his earlier denial, he left Debenhams to become Green's chief executive at BHS. Two months later he was joined by Allan Leighton, the former Asda boss, who became chairman. Green offered Terry Green and Leighton respective stakes of 5 and 10 per cent in his deal.

Hiring the successful boss of Debenhams should have been a coup, yet Green enjoyed demeaning Terry Green. 'He treated him like dirt,' said a Green adviser who watched them together. Richard Hyman, founder of the retail analysis firm Verdict, was invited for a buffet lunch with BHS's new owner in his office at its headquarters on Marylebone Road. Hyman observed that Terry Green, usually boastful and ebullient, sat in meek silence throughout the meal. At one point, Hyman made the mistake of suggesting that Green hadn't been serious about his tilt at M&S and had been 'in it for the ride' – an unfortunate phrase, given the furore over Tina's share buying. 'In it for the fucking ride?' Green roared. He got up, rummaged through the papers on his desk and produced a cheque for £6 billion from WestLB. 'If I was in it for the ride, what the fucking hell is this?' he demanded, waving it in Hyman's face. Terry Green, himself a hard man who had grown up with poor parents in a terraced house in Stoke-on-Trent, seemed to be overawed by his new employer's alpha-male swagger.

Green and his team hit BHS like a storm, working eighteen-hour days. Terry Green derided BHS's womenswear department for buying '10,000 little dresses – the sort of thing Pocahontas would wear'. Green liquidated £60 million of unsold stock at '20 per cent, 30 per cent or 50 per cent off'. When their gruelling shifts ended on time, they decamped to Les Ambassadeurs casino on Park Lane, where Green would smoke slim-line cigarettes and hold court. Under his ownership, BHS's profitability began to improve miraculously. In the first year, the chain's sales fell by 1.1 per cent to £815.2 million, but it swung from a loss of £58.8 million to a pre-tax profit of £18.5 million. In the second year, sales came in at £875.1 million, but profits multiplied to £94.9 million. It was one of the most remarkable recoveries the retail industry had ever seen, and it turned Green into a hero. He gave reporters stories illustrating his attention to detail, claiming he had saved £40,000 a year by changing coat-hanger suppliers. In January 2002, Rory Godson of the *Sunday Times* announced that Green had 'made the fastest billion pounds in British history', on the basis that retail companies were valued at roughly ten times their pre-tax profits. On that measure, BHS had gone from being worth £200 million to £1 billion in less than two years.

Green pretended not to care – 'I don't pay any attention to all that crap,' he told *The Independent* – but he obviously lapped it up. When he and Tina flew their friends to Cyprus for PG50 three months after Godson's story, he basked in adulation. During his mock *This Is Your Life* presentation, Michael Aspel mentioned that Green had won personality of the year at the *Retail Week* awards a few weeks earlier. For the first time in his life, Green felt he was receiving the recognition he deserved. It was intoxicating. A former colleague said, 'It wasn't just that he was running BHS – he felt he was running the rest of the high street as well. He would go into places, buy a garment with the worst mark-down on the rail and hand it to a member of staff. He'd say, "Send it to your boss with my compliments." It was like a Sicilian message.'

Sir Alan Sugar, who had been knighted two years earlier, had been on 'chinwag' terms with Green since the Tottenham Hotspur days. He remarked on the change wrought on Green's personality by the BHS phenomenon. 'Recently when I bumped into him at the Dorchester, I got a very regal down-your-nose look and was then ignored,' Sugar wrote in the *Evening Standard* in June 2002. 'This must be because he is worth £1.3 billion and feels he does not have to talk to anyone unless they are in the top thirty of the Sunday Times Rich List.'

Beneath the grander exterior, the insecurities stoked by his ousting from Amber Day still burned. Green harboured a particular jealousy towards Gerald Ronson, one of the 'Guinness four' convicted for their roles in the 1980s share-support scandal. Ronson, who insisted that he had not known his actions were illegal, emerged from prison with his head held high and rebuilt his billion-pound property business while earning respect in the Jewish community for giving generously to charity. Ronson wore double-breasted suits and disliked 'champagne bullshit', but every year he hosted a big lunch for his contacts, filling the Savoy hotel's vast River Room. In 2002, the guest list included Robin Saunders. Green called Saunders on the morning of the lunch and pleaded with her not to go – presumably prompted by ego or spite. Saunders reluctantly agreed to cancel, and sent one of her managing directors in her place. She was mortified when she found out she had been seated next to Ronson himself.

The two Greens inevitably fell out. Terry Green urged his boss to move BHS upmarket and introduce designer collaborations, as he had done at Debenhams with the likes of Ozwald Boateng and Jasper Conran. Green rejected most of Terry Green's ideas as a matter of course, especially if they involved spending money. Their relationship culminated in an infamous shouting match in Green's office, where the two men ratcheted up the volume against each other until Green's secretary and the whole floor could hear. In the end, Terry Green decided that his boss simply had a louder voice and gave in. He left BHS in April 2002, eighteen months after joining. Green cancelled his underling's right to a 5 per cent stake. Terry Green realized that his contract had been drafted with a loophole in it, and decided to go without a fight.

*

Green had bought BHS at a time of uncertainty on the high street. The rise of discount fashion stores like New Look and Primark was putting pressure on the established middle-market retailers. A month after Green sealed his deal with Storehouse in May 2000, C&A, the second biggest player after M&S, announced that it would close all 109 of its British shops, with the loss of 4,800 jobs. Sentiment was further dampened by the bursting of the dot-com bubble, which coincided with the £571 million stock-market float of Lastminute.com. That was followed by the 9/11 terrorist attacks on New York. By the time of PG50 in March 2002, confidence had begun to stabilize. New Labour had won a decisive second election victory, and the economy was entering a long upswing that would run until the financial crisis of 2007. In November 2003, the former Sears finance director John Lovering and his business partner, Rob Templeman, took over Debenhams for £1.6 billion – a swoop that became highly controversial as they extracted £2 billion for their private equity backers while selling off the chain's properties and squeezing its suppliers. Money was in the air and deals were there for the taking.

By late 2000, the County NatWest analyst John Richards had moved to Deutsche Bank. A few days before Christmas, he returned to his desk from a meeting and found a Post-it note on his phone asking him to call a Mr Bergs. He dialled the number for Helgi Bergs, deputy head of investment banking at Kaupthing, a small Icelandic financial firm. Bergs told Richards that one of his clients wanted to bid for Arcadia Group, the clothing retailer that had bought Sears' womenswear brands from Green. At first, Richards thought he was joking. Arcadia was struggling, and its market value had fallen to about £90 million by November, but its American boss, John Hoerner, had been ousted in favour of Stuart Rose, a smooth-talking fashion veteran, and its share price had started to recover. Bergs' client, Baugur, was a tiny company run by a thirty-three-year-old Icelandic entrepreneur called Jón Ásgeir Jóhannesson. Intelligent but shy, with long blond hair, blue eyes and a penchant for black leather jackets, Jóhannesson seemed an unlikely buyer for one of the most significant groups on the high street.

Out of curiosity, Richards flew to Iceland to check out Baugur. He realized it held the local franchises for Arcadia brands including Topshop. He decided Jóhannesson was not the ingénue he looked. Between Christmas 2000 and May 2001, Deutsche Bank lent Baugur enough money to build a 20 per cent stake in Arcadia, whose share price continued to rise. In October 2001, Arcadia's advisers accidentally sent a confidential fax to a fish-and-chip shop in Devon, and Arcadia was forced to confirm that it had received a takeover bid from Baugur worth £568 million. The plan foundered in early 2002 as Baugur failed to raise the financing, but it sounded an alert to other potential buyers. Green was one. On the surface, he and Stuart Rose had little in common – whereas Green liked to gamble and swear, Rose enjoyed fine wine and gardening – but both were driven men who had lost a parent early (Rose's mother had committed suicide when he was twenty-seven). They were friends and sometimes rivals.

Green had first contacted Rose during his bid for M&S, when Rose was running Booker, a food-and-drink wholesaler. Green offered Rose a role managing M&S's distribution network, which Rose thought was 'about the least good fit of a job as he could have offered me'. Nonetheless, they met for what Green liked to call 'chitty chatty bollocks' and stayed in touch. Green's way of congratulating Rose over his appointment at Arcadia was to call and say, 'Have you found it?' 'Found what?' Rose asked. 'It,' Green said. 'The black hole. There's a big black hole in there, son. Go and look harder.' The accounting nasties Green predicted never materialized. As Baugur popped up on the share register and Arcadia's stock price climbed, Green's bantering calls became more serious. He would ask about Arcadia's debt levels and trading, although he made sure never to compliment Rose on the unfolding turnaround.

In the summer of 2002, John Richards put Jón Ásgeir Jóhannesson in touch with Green. They quickly drew up a deal whereby Jóhannesson would throw Baugur's 20 per cent stake behind a Green takeover bid for Arcadia, in exchange for the right to buy its young-fashion brands, including Topshop and Miss Selfridge.

Green would keep the middle-market chains, such as Burton and Dorothy Perkins. They dubbed the move Project Anaconda, after the snake that squeezes its prey to death. Having missed the chance to buy Arcadia when the share price was far lower, Green engaged in a round of haggling with Rose. He was relaxed enough to direct most of the action from his yacht in the Mediterranean. Arcadia's former boss remembered, 'Basically, the negotiation was done by me and Philip, and it was about, "OK son, how's the business looking? Any problems, tax liabilities, lease liabilities?" He gave me a handwritten list of things he wanted to know about. I gave him a verbal reply. He didn't really do any proper due diligence. He trusted that what he was getting was what he was getting.'

Merrill Lynch had refused to work for Green three years earlier. Suddenly, his arrival as the coming man in retail made him irresistible. The investment bank signed up as his adviser. To help with the press Green also hired Finsbury, one of the top financial PR firms. In mid-August, Green and Jóhannesson made a £690 million approach, which Arcadia's board rejected. The news appeared almost immediately in two Sunday newspapers. At the end of August, the bidders returned with a higher offer worth £770 million, or £850 million including share options. The night before it was made public, Green called Rose and teased him by singing 'If I Were a Rich Man' – a reference to the £25 million bonus Rose stood to collect if he accepted the bid.

Green's mirth evaporated the next day. At 2 p.m., Reuters flashed news that Baugur's headquarters in Reykjavik had been raided by the Icelandic police's fraud unit over allegations made by a disgruntled former business partner (the case would rumble on for years before it collapsed). There had already been tension in Green's relationship with Jóhannesson. A well-placed source said that Green had made 'a very determined effort to elbow Jón Ásgeir out of the deal' so he could control it. The raid would obviously make it impossible for Jóhannesson to buy any of the Arcadia brands. Green screamed that he could not get hold of 'that fucking Viking cunt', who happened to be away on a fishing trip. At 8 p.m., there was an emergency meeting at BHS's building on Marylebone Road. Green sat fuming in the half-lit canteen, chairs stacked on the tables, his most senior bankers gathered around him. Jóhannesson's colleagues came to the glass entrance door and sheepishly met his unblinking stare. Eventually, Green motioned to his bodyguard to let them in. As they entered, Green shouted at one of the Icelanders, 'You have left me standing on a ladder that is getting kicked over. I wish I had never met you . . . So far as I know there are not that many people in Iceland. How unlucky can I be that of the four that I meet, three are under a fraud investigation?'

Peter Cummings at Halifax Bank of Scotland saved the day. He had already agreed to lend Green £700 million. Based on a single phone call, Cummings raised that to £800 million so he could cut out the Icelanders. As angry as Green was that night, Jóhannesson's arrest turned out to be the freak event that made his career. The fraud raid was the act of God that handed him Topshop. Had the original deal gone ahead, Jóhannesson would have owned it. The following week, Green negotiated the purchase of Baugur's 20 per cent stake in a fractious late-night meeting. At 3 a.m., he grabbed one of the Icelanders' advisers from Deutsche Bank by the lapels and shouted, 'If you're going to play poker, make sure you have some fucking cards.' He had the banker thrown out of the BHS building by his security guards. After a final 'willy waving' argument with Stuart Rose outside the George club in Mayfair, where Rose demanded that Arcadia's shareholders get to keep a 4p dividend they were due, Green bought Arcadia.

Jóhannesson was left with a sour taste in his mouth. He believed that Green had promised to sell him Topshop at a later date as part of their final agreement over Baugur's stake. In Jóhannesson's version of events, he went to see Green with his wife and lawyer, and Green shook his wife's hand, saying, 'I'd never lie to a woman.' For the next five years, as Green held onto the booming Topshop business, Jóhannesson sent him a text message on every anniversary of the conversation, asking, 'When are we going to close the deal?'

Added to BHS, the takeover of Arcadia put Green in charge of

2,000 shops and £3 billion of sales. By the end of the summer, he really was the Emperor Nero character he had played at PG50 a few months earlier. Green told the *Financial Times*, 'People talk about those like Hanson as great empire builders. But that was all done through the stock market money. I have done this as a solo artist.' With hindsight, one of his closest advisers thought Arcadia was 'probably one deal too far' because 'it got too big for one man to know everything'. A friend believed the acquisition of Topshop in particular began to change him. 'Philip went from being a seriously underrated businessman with some interesting contacts to someone who was now mixing in the world of celebrities and wanted to be part of that world,' he said.

Green had left his old life behind, but characters from his murky past occasionally surfaced like monsters in a bad dream. Amid all the glory, the loan shark Tony Schneider said to the *Daily Mail*, 'I lent him money and he let me down. If he had asked me to his party, I wouldn't have gone. There are many others who feel the same.' Green told the *Mail* he was 'astounded that anyone can ring you up just because they want their name in the papers'.

Green announced that he would take a break from dealmaking – 'I cannot afford Arcadia and a divorce at the same time,' he joked to the *FT* – but his hunger for the next deal soon returned. He watched as Baugur went on a spree with the £70 million profit from its stake in Arcadia, buying shares in Big Food Group – the parent company of Booker and Iceland – House of Fraser, Somerfield, Selfridges and Hamleys. Having already looked at merging BHS with Woolworths, Green flirted with takeover approaches for Safeway and Sainsbury's. But M&S remained the ultimate prize. And it now looked tantalizingly within his reach.

In 2003, the former *Sunday Times* business editor Rory Godson brokered a crucial introduction. Godson had left journalism for a PR job at the investment bank Goldman Sachs. Keen to impress both his new bosses and Green, he organized a dinner at Pied à Terre, a discreet French restaurant with a Michelin star in London's Fitzrovia. As well as Green, he invited Charles Dunstone, the co-founder of

Carphone Warehouse, and Mike Sherwood, one of Goldman's most senior bankers in Europe. There are generally two types of investment banker. M&A advisers, who deal with corporate clients, tend to be public school-educated and Savile Row-suited. Bond traders – brasher, rougher characters – wager millions (and sometimes billions) of the bank's money on market movements. Woody, as he was known, was the consummate bond trader. He struck up an immediate rapport with Green. Like Arcadia's new owner, Sherwood was a middle-class Londoner who presented himself as an outsider. By coincidence, his family had also lived on Bancroft Avenue in Hampstead Garden Suburb, although they did not move in until 1967, when Sherwood was two and Green would have been at Tollington grammar. After attending the fee-paying Westminster School and Manchester University, Sherwood joined Goldman and shot up the ranks, becoming a partner in 1994 before he was even thirty. Woody was entranced by Green's market-trader patter and his billionaire status. As they became friendly, Sherwood piled on weight and began to brush his greying hair back. He even eventually hired Banana Split, the events company that had put on PG50, to organize a 'joint 100th' birthday party with his wife at the luxurious Hotel Cala Di Volpe in Sardinia. For Green, Sherwood provided an entrée to the most powerful investment bank in the City – one that had hitherto turned up its nose at him.

In September 2002, Roger Holmes was named M&S's new chief executive. Holmes was a boyish former management consultant in his early forties. For a few months, Holmes and his chairman, Luc Vandevelde, enjoyed a City honeymoon. But Vandevelde showed several lapses of judgement as he launched a private equity firm on the side and took non-executive roles at Vodafone and Carrefour, the French supermarket. As the more experienced Vandevelde grew distracted, Holmes lost his way. M&S's sapling chief executive had the misfortune to run into Green at an industry dinner at the Grosvenor House hotel on Park Lane in October 2003. A few months earlier, the compilers of the Sunday Times Rich List had estimated Green's wealth at £1.9 billion. Holmes was walking down the stairs to the seating area when the king of the high street, who was in a boisterous mood, called out to him, 'I was in your Oxford Street store yesterday.' Holmes made the mistake of asking what he had thought. 'I've never seen a bigger pile of shit in my life,' Green pronounced, at a volume that ensured anyone who mattered in retail heard. According to another chief executive, Holmes 'was so taken aback he went white and ran away to his table'. From that moment on, his authority was critically damaged.

Holmes bled further credibility in January 2004, when M&S delivered far worse Christmas trading numbers than analysts had expected. The contrast between his and Green's fortunes was widening dramatically. Green had been the star attraction at the *Sunday Times'* Christmas party that December, when journalists and bankers had queued up to congratulate him. Even David Mayhew, the aloof Cazenove stockbroker who had helped thwart his first bid for M&S in 2000, had laughed at Green's jokes and whispered confidences into his ear with an easy, Old Etonian charm. At the end of January 2004, Green had lunch with Mike Sherwood and Goldman's European chief, Peter Weinberg. The bankers bought his pitch. M&S was struggling, as it had been in 2000. This time, Green's retailing prowess, apparently established through BHS and Arcadia, would make him a more believable takeover candidate. Project Mogul took shape quickly. Green's first tilt at M&S had resembled a highwayman trying to hold up a stagecoach with a water pistol. Four years on, he armed himself with the heaviest artillery the City could provide – Goldman Sachs and Merrill Lynch, who agreed to act as his advisers. Green offered to put in up to £1 billion of his family's money as equity. Goldman, Barclays Capital and HBOS also said that they would commit equity. A club of five banks signed up to provide billions of pounds of debt. The pieces came together within weeks.

At the end of the final advisers' meeting before they pulled the trigger, Bob Wigley, Merrill Lynch's European chairman, had a quiet word with Green. He said, 'You're fifty-two, you're heavily overweight, you've had a heart bypass operation, you smoke like a chimney and you must have an income of about £190 million a year. You don't need any stress and you certainly don't need a job.' Wigley questioned the wisdom of pursuing the blockbuster deal. A smile broke across Green's face. 'Bob, I like your thinking,' he replied. 'No one's ever said that to me before. But with respect, that's why you're chairman of an investment bank and I'm worth two billion quid.'

In April, M&S put out another dire set of results. Having fallen from a high of 420p in May 2002 to about 245p, the shares fluttered up slightly in the following weeks amid rumours of a takeover bid and a replacement chairman for the unpopular Vandevelde. On a Friday in early May, Green called Stuart Rose, who had been taking a career break since selling Arcadia. 'You've got fuck all to do,' he said. 'Why don't you come over for a cup of tea?' Rose went to BHS's headquarters on Marylebone Road five days later. Green asked him to sign a non-disclosure agreement. When that was done, he revealed that he was planning to bid for M&S, and offered Rose a job as head of food. Rose promised to think about it, but he remembered how the domineering billionaire had reduced former high-fliers like Terry Green to gofers. A week later he called Green and said, 'I don't want to play.'

Unknown to Green, Rose already had good reason to believe he was in the running for one of the top jobs at M&S. Working from an office near Fitzroy Square with a few friends, he had picked up the rumour of Vandevelde's imminent departure and started lobbying persistently for the chairmanship with the help of a PR firm, Tulchan. Little more than a week after his meeting with Green, a headhunter rang Rose to arrange a coffee with one of M&S's non-executive directors, Kevin Lomax. They met on the morning of 27 May. Rose gave Lomax 'both barrels' about the company's shortcomings. Lomax listened with interest.

That afternoon, Green telephoned Roger Holmes. He sounded strangely calm, as if he was reading from a script. 'We've got something we want to put to the board,' the tycoon said. Minutes later, Revival Acquisitions, his new company, announced its intention to bid for M&S. The share price shot up by almost 20 per cent. Rose's phone turned red hot as Green tried to call him repeatedly, perhaps sensing that his frenemy was manoeuvring. Green knew that Rose was the one person who could plausibly defend M&S. Rose told his secretary, 'Give him any fucking excuse – just get him off my back.' The next morning, Rose had breakfast with more M&S board members, including Paul Myners, a corporate silverback who saw himself as the next chairman. Myners knew that Holmes was far too weak to defend a hostile takeover bid. He needed a new frontman.

On Friday lunchtime, Rose finally saw Green again. He dodged questions about M&S, but Green warned him that he would see any Rose involvement with M&S as a betrayal. 'If I come bumper to bumper with you on Monday morning I'll punch your headlights out,' he threatened. In the evening, Rose drove to his country house in Suffolk. Myners called and told him the board was about to fire Holmes. Myners dispatched an investment banker with a briefcase of papers to Rose's home so he could spend the bank holiday weekend thinking about becoming M&S's chief executive. Simon Robey, Morgan Stanley's star dealmaker, wandered around in the garden while Rose and two former Arcadia colleagues, Steven Sharp and Charles Wilson, looked through the business plan. Rose had dreamed of the M&S job ever since he started his career there at twenty-three, having blown his modest £3,000 inheritance in fashionable restaurants. He told Myners that he would accept. On the bank holiday Monday, he drove to M&S's headquarters on Baker Street. Rose entered by the back to avoid the press pack gathering at the front. 'We didn't know you were coming,' said the security guard, scanning his list of names. Rose raised a patrician eyebrow. 'No, you didn't,' he said.

Roger Holmes and Luc Vandevelde were carrying their possessions out through the front door as Stuart Rose and his team arrived at the back. The announcement of the palace coup went out at 5 p.m. Over the course of a long weekend, M&S had given itself a fighting chance. Green was enraged. 'You fucking dicked me over,' he shouted at Rose down the phone.

M&S scored a second early point by raising a tripwire it had originally laid in case of a takeover bid from Tesco. A few years earlier, M&S had changed legal advisers from Freshfields to Slaughter & May, but it had kept Freshfields employed on a small strip of work involving its Per Una range because it was Tesco's law firm. Freshfields would be ruled offside due to a conflict of interests if Tesco were to make a bid. Green happened to be using Freshfields. M&S managed to secure an injunction by raising the Per Una point, forcing Green to drop the Magic Circle firm before the war had even begun. At the same time, Green set out his opening offer of £7.5 billion for M&S, comprising cash and shares in Revival Acquisitions, which he planned to list on the stock market. Green was deploying a device known as a 'virtual bid'. Rather than make a formal approach, which would set the clock ticking on a takeover deadline and expose him to expensive banking fees, he tabled a highly conditional and non-binding offer. In any case, Rose immediately rejected it. It was a fiery start.

The next morning, Rose was getting out of his car by the side entrance of M&S's headquarters when he was confronted by an agitated Green, who seemed to have been waiting in a chauffeur-driven Mercedes. 'Oi!' Green shouted. 'I want a fucking word with you.' As staff crowded at the windows to watch, Green grabbed Rose by the lapels and berated him for taking the M&S job. He dialled Tina and handed the phone to Rose. Green's wife, who had invited Rose to PG50 two years earlier, told M&S's new boss he was a 'cunt'. Shaken, Rose went inside and relayed what had happened to his advisers. Someone pointed out that the incident must have been captured on CCTV. It took several days to retrieve the tapes from an offsite facility. When they arrived, the twenty-minute period covering the confrontation was missing.

Green subjected M&S to a relentless shelling through the Sunday papers. In mid-June, he raised his offer to £8.4 billion. Rose rejected him again. The fight turned nastier on the weekend of 20 June. The *Mail on Sunday* reported that Rose had bought a block of M&S shares. It turned out that Rose had bought 100,000 a few hours after Green called to invite him for a cup of tea on 7 May. Rose insisted he had not known what Green wanted to talk about when he made the trade. It also emerged that some of Green's friends, including Tom Hunter and the brothers David and Simon Reuben, had bought shares in April. Michael Spencer, head of the stockbroker Icap, had bought 2 million shares worth £5.5 million after having lunch with Rose in May. The City's regulator, the Financial Services Authority, launched an investigation.

The FCA cleared all the parties involved in less than a fortnight, but the story poisoned the atmosphere. It worsened still when Rose's mobile-phone company, O2, said that his call records seemed to have been accessed by a third party. Rose spoke to a few contacts and found that every number he had dialled since January had received a mysterious call from someone who quickly hung up. He also believed he had been followed on several occasions, and there were signs that his wife's mail had been intercepted. As a precaution, the entire M&S team was equipped with pay-as-you-go mobiles. Green denied having hired private investigators. 'We know where George and Harry's Bar are without Kroll,' he quipped, referring to two of Rose's favourite playboy hangouts. But when M&S approached the two biggest agencies, they both cited conflicts of interest, suggesting they were already engaged on the deal. Paranoia spread. The M&S office was swept repeatedly for bugs, without any being found.

Rose issued Green and his advisers with data protection notices asking for disclosure of any information they held on him. The notices were accompanied by £10 notes to cover the cost of sending back the material. Green's reply to Rose contained two prostitutes' calling cards and a message, 'Here's a picture of the two girls that had dinner with you at Harry's Bar a few weeks ago. I enclose the £10 which they told me to return to you.' When he heard about the prank, Lord Stevenson, the Cambridge-educated chairman of HBOS, was incensed. His bank was helping to fund Green's bid. He had also agreed to sit on the board of Revival Acquisitions as its senior non-executive. Stevenson had tangentially crossed paths with Green years earlier: he was the Blue Arrow board director who had blown the whistle on Tony Berry's undisclosed £25 million loan to Peter de Savary. He had warmed to Green in the intervening period, telling acquaintances the tycoon could 'read figures like music'. But now, without counting to ten, he stopped in the middle of Eaton Square and called Green. 'Frankly, I can't speak for my colleagues, but I couldn't blame them if they pulled the financing,' he said. Green apologized and said he wouldn't do it again, but he couldn't help adding, 'Dennis, remind me to buy you a sense of humour.'

The farce signalled the beginning of the end game. Green raised his offer again – this time to 400p. It valued M&S at £9.1 billion, or £11 billion including debt. Green was now putting in £1.6 billion of equity. Goldman was committing £850 million and Barclays Capital and HBOS were contributing £550 million. Five banks were providing £8.1 billion of loans. Operation Socrates, as the project had been portentously renamed, had swollen to a mammoth size. M&S's biggest shareholder was an American fund called Brandes. Its manager, Amelia Morris, was kingmaker. She gave Green's enlarged offer her backing – a development many thought would force Rose to open M&S's books to Green for scrutiny. Green rang favoured journalists and sang, 'We're on our way to Wembley, we're on our way to Wembley.' But the M&S board still insisted that 400p undervalued the company, and the pension trustees refused to meet Green. He accused their chairman, David Norgrove, of spouting 'pious nonsense' and treating him like 'an ignoramus'. Norgrove, a mild-mannered former civil servant who looked like a vertical caterpillar, hit back by warning that M&S's pension contributions might have to rise significantly if Green took over because of the amount of debt he planned to pile onto the business.

The evening before the drama reached its climax, tempers frayed spectacularly in a bizarre incident at the Dorchester. Jeff Randall, the BBC's business editor, and Will Lewis, business editor of the *Sunday Times*, were waiting to have dinner with the tycoon in the hotel's restaurant. As Green walked in, unclasping his mobile from his ear and promising to tell them about a 'late twist', a voice cried out from another table, 'So now we know! Philip Green and Jeff Randall – ah ha!' Green muttered to Randall, 'It's that fat cunt Lord Soames.' And indeed it was: Nicholas Soames, the Tory trencherman and then shadow defence secretary, was chuckling away with two dinner companions, his face full and red. 'So that's why the BBC coverage is like it is – nice cosy chats,' Soames guffawed. 'Ho ho ho! We'll all be able to see your coverage now, won't we? Their kind keep it all together, as ever.'

Green took this last remark to be an anti-Semitic slur, although neither Randall nor Lewis was Jewish. Soames afterwards strongly denied there had been any such colouring to his comments, and insisted that 'nobody said anything remotely offensive'. But Randall was already highly sensitive about his friendship with Green. A year earlier, *Private Eye* had described it as 'one of the cosiest relationships between a BBC journalist and a businessman ever seen'. Randall called Lord Maurice Saatchi, joint chairman of the Conservative Party, and complained that Soames had 'impugned the integrity of the BBC in a very public place'. Soames reportedly contacted Randall the next morning to apologize.

Despite all the heat, Green had not actually tabled a proper bid for M&S. He had merely stated his intention to bid. He was trying to carry out what is known in the City as a 'bear hug', where a predator dangles a price in front of a company's shareholders, hoping they will put pressure on the management and squeeze them into consenting. Claiming the backing of a third of M&S's share register, which had become crowded with sharp-toothed American hedge funds hungry for a deal, Green ordered the board to open the company's books so he could formalize an offer. The siege came to a head on 14 July, the day of M&S's annual shareholder meeting at the Royal Festival Hall on the South Bank. Rose put on a confident performance, promising to give investors a £2.3 billion windfall if they kept the company independent. As evening fell, Green and his bankers anxiously strafed the M&S camp with calls, hoping for a change in the board's position. Perhaps because of his strange obsession with the City, Green placed disproportionate confidence in the views of David Mayhew, M&S's impeccably upper-crust broker at Cazenove. In fact, Mayhew had been sidelined for most of the takeover, and he was fishing in Scotland when Green called. Mayhew gave a cryptic and unhelpful response.

Green had no idea how close he came to winning. Andrew Grant, the boss of Tulchan, M&S's PR firm, was horrified to arrive halfway through a crunch board meeting at 6 p.m. to find two different press releases waiting – one of them announcing M&S's surrender. Some members of the board, including Rose's right-hand man, Charles Wilson, felt it was impossible to keep holding out at 400p. At that moment, Grant received a call from Kate Rankine, the *Daily Telegraph*'s deputy City editor. Rose instructed Grant to fob her off by saying there was no change in the board's stance. Rankine, who was close to both Green and Rose, called Green and relayed the update. The M&S board continued to debate the position fiercely. At 8.30 p.m., Robert Swannell, one of M&S's bankers, looked at his BlackBerry and announced in a surprised baritone, 'It's all academic now.' Green had withdrawn. The message from Rankine seemed to have been the final ingredient that made him lose his nerve. Like that, Green's dream of assuming Simon Marks and Israel Sieff's great mantle slipped through his fingers.

The king of the high street was anything but magnanimous in defeat. 'I expected to be treated with an element of respect,' he ranted to the *Sunday Times*. 'It was very, very shabby. I was treated like someone waiting for a taxi.' He blasted the M&S board for 'continually mucking me about' and branded Paul Myners, M&S's chairman, an 'anti-Semitic left-winger'. Myners pleaded guilty to the left-wing charge but threatened to sue for defamation on the first point, prompting an unreserved apology from Green. A few months later at a cocktail party, Green cornered David Norgrove, the M&S pension trustees' chairman who had helped scupper the bid. Green arrived on bullish and defiant form. He took Norgrove by the lapel with one hand and jabbed a finger into his chest with the other, bellowing, 'Your behaviour was disgraceful!' At the same party, he was introduced to Maurice Helfgott, M&S's outgoing director of clothing. By that point, he had loosened up and slipped into a jokier mood. 'I'm going to take you lot to the cleaners,' Green promised. Then he mischievously recited the opening words of the Kaddish, the Jewish prayer for the dead, to amusement from Helfgott and the crowd around him.

Green's scattergun apportionment of blame was met with scepticism from some of his closest advisers. 'He simply bottled it,' said one. The tycoon had come under pressure from Tina and their teenage daughter, Chloe, who had both called Rose during the siege to accuse him of making Green ill by refusing to sell him M&S. Chloe had rung her father, sobbing, 'Dad, you promised you wouldn't buy anything else. You said you were busy enough. Why do you want another business?' There was a funereal post-deal dinner at the Dorchester. Green served Château Cos d'Estournel claret. Bankers from Goldman Sachs and Merrill Lynch took it in turns to say through gritted teeth what a privilege it had been to work with him. Richard Sharp, Goldman's head of private equity, introduced a dose of reality. 'We lost,' he said, despondently. 'We didn't fucking lose,' Green snapped. The embarrassment of Green's behaviour during the M&S battle caused deep recriminations inside Goldman. It contributed to the departure of one of its most senior bankers, Simon Robertson, who felt that Goldman's brand was being tarnished by Mike Sherwood and his unbiddable client.

Stuart Rose sent a case of Château Cheval Blanc to BHS's headquarters as an olive branch. Green gave Rose a clock from the jeweller Asprey – a pointed joke about the amount of time he would have to spend in the office turning M&S around. Rose liked to quip that Green had planted a bug inside. During board meetings he would order colleagues, 'Speak up – PG can't hear you.' Green told Rose the dirty tricks of the preceding months had been nothing more than 'the normal bing bang bosh' of a takeover battle. The two retailers kept up a playful rivalry. Green would call Rose and complain about M&S's products ('I've been eating your chicken breasts every lunchtime for the last ten years and they've gone dry'). Rose would sometimes admit that he had a point.

A year after the M&S affair, Green had a cake made for Rose's birthday, which coincided with the *Retail Week* industry awards. It was topped with an edible Rose figurine wearing a brown T-shirt mocking the various initiatives he had implemented since settling in as chief executive. It said, 'Green/Ethical/Fairtrade/Won't leave a bitter taste/There's nothing woolly about us/Got you hook, line and sinker/Don't get caught.' The front read, 'Happy birthday Stuart. £3.50 or two for £5.' When he was sure that plenty of people were watching, Green made a point of plunging the serving knife deep into the Rose figurine's back.

On the second anniversary of Green's withdrawal, the M&S defence team held a reunion dinner at Harry's Bar in Mayfair. The Citigroup banker Robert Swannell gave out M&S wallets containing four £1 notes as a memento of Green's 400p-a-share offer. After the main course, Rose announced another present. Green entered in a spirit of bonhomie, the hostilities of the campaign gone. As they sipped coffee, Nigel Boardman, the Slaughter & May lawyer who had tripped up Freshfields, asked Green why he had given in. Green, who must have been in an unusually candid mood, said he had not wanted to risk so much of his family's money.

In the immediate aftermath of M&S, Green turned to Arcadia for consolation. He had repeated the BHS formula, attacking the cost base, moving to cheaper suppliers and mortgaging the Oxford Street flagship store to pay down the acquisition debt as quickly as possible. It was a frenetic period. Someone who worked with him closely said, 'You could get your first call from Philip just before 6 a.m. and your last call just before 1 a.m. His attention to detail was formidable. It was as tough as I've ever worked.' At BHS, Green had repaid his loans to Barclays and WestLB within two years. In October 2004, three months after his failure to buy M&S, he announced that the entire £808 million provided by HBOS for Arcadia had been settled. With 'Ain't No Mountain High Enough' pounding from the speakers, Green told his senior staff that Arcadia's operating profits had more than doubled in two years, despite barely any movement in its £1.7 billion of sales. Tina, standing at the front of the crowd, dabbed away a tear. Next to her was HBOS's Peter Cummings, Green's favourite banker. As with BHS, Green was lauded as a genius who had changed the paradigm of retailing.

Green's estimated wealth soared from £1.9 billion in 2003 to £3.6 billion in 2004 and £4.9 billion in 2005 as the perceived values of BHS and Arcadia ballooned. In 2005, Arcadia's owner reloaded the balance sheet with debt and paid his wife a £1.2 billion tax-free dividend in Monaco. A further £100 million of dividends were sent to minority investors, such as HBOS, which owned 7 per cent. It was the biggest payday in British history, and it was the superlative answer to the grey suits he believed had denied him M&S. An old friend thought it was also his way of flicking the middle finger at his loathed rival, the property developer Gerald Ronson, who was a mere multimillionaire. Green had risked just £9.2 million of his own equity in the original Arcadia deal. The dividend represented 130 times his investment, and it propelled the Greens into the top tier of the global super-rich. In May 2005, they flew 300 guests to the south of France for the bar mitzvah of their son, Brandon. The party at the Grand-Hôtel du Cap-Ferrat cost £4 million. The tenor Andrea Bocelli performed on the first night. Beyoncé played on the second evening. At the end of the ceremony in a pop-up synagogue, Brandon sang in uninterrupted Hebrew for fifteen minutes. A business contact whispered to Green that he must be very proud. 'Why, what's he ever done?' the tycoon retorted. 'I paid for all this.'

With his increasing prominence, Green exercised unrivalled power over the media. A partygoer who attended Brandon's bar mitzvah tried to sell a DVD of the event to the *News of the World*, the now-defunct Sunday tabloid. Instead of running it as an exclusive, as it would have done with most other celebrities, the paper couriered the disc straight to Green's office so he could have it destroyed. The source never received the £5,000 he was promised because the contract had been carefully worded to stipulate payment only after publication. A little while later, the *Daily Telegraph*, which had recently been bought by Green's friends Sir David and Sir Frederick Barclay, squashed a readers' poll that voted BHS the most unpopular chain on the high street. The unprecedented deference shown to Green only encouraged his innate control freakery.

The Greens took delivery of *Lionheart*, a new 210ft superyacht with six bedrooms, a gym and a hammam, at the end of 2005. At around the same time, they moved from Le Formentor to a penthouse flat in Le Roccabella, a tower near the infamous nightclub Jimmy'z on Monaco's eastern fringe.

It was a time of uncontrolled bloating for Green's ego and spending. One of his oldest friends, who stopped attending Green's parties after his fiftieth in Cyprus, thought the £1.2 billion dividend 'destroyed him in more ways than have ever been analysed'. He said, 'It destroyed his judgement, his humanity and in some respects his soul. It did something to him.' There was the obvious external effect. The sheer amount of cash now at his disposal made people treat him differently. The Greens' deposits in Barclays and HSBC put them among the banks' top customers in the world, and they were lavished with attention. 'He became a very big money tree,' his friend observed. 'Under all money trees there are lots of people sitting there hoping to catch a few things, and he surrounded himself with those kinds of people.'

Then there was the internal effect, which was less immediately obvious but possibly more damaging. Green had grown up without a father. In the past he had taken advice from male friends such as Morris Keston, the Tottenham Hotspur superfan, and Kenny Tibber, the job buyer. After his big payday, he gradually stopped listening. 'Subconsciously, he started to go down the route of being someone who said, "I've got a billion pounds, what have you got?"' his old friend said. 'It pushed him beyond the point where he felt he had to take the views of dissenters seriously.' With Green's mother playing less of a role, Tina 'fanned the flames' of his greed. The friend added, 'No one I've ever met has worshipped at the temple of Mammon so assiduously. It was about conspicuous consumption, about spending the money and making sure everyone knew you were spending it in excessive and vulgar ways.'

In 2007, Tina asked the events company Banana Split to top the

PG50 party. PG55 cost an estimated £20 million and took place on a private island in the Maldives. So many private jets parked at Malé airport that latecomers were told there was only enough landing space to drop off passengers. Tina ordered 3,000 bottles of champagne and had a giant granite Buddha built for a Balinese-themed party, which was said to have upset some of the Muslim labourers. There was live music from Gladys Knight & the Pips, George Michael, Jennifer Lopez and Ricky Martin. Green and his friends sprayed champagne around on the beach. The inflation in his birthday celebrations could be measured easily. Guests at PG50 had been given a single souvenir DVD of the event. Guests at PG55 went home with a four-disc box set. The opening segment of the first DVD was modestly titled, 'In The Beginning'.

6.

Dreams Come True

Project Centipede was at an embryonic stage when an unhelpful story appeared in *The Times*. 'Bugger!' Paul McGowan typed to a colleague. 'We need to move fast . . . Get some rest.'

McGowan was an insolvency expert with an impish face and a sharp glint to his eye. He had been tracking one of the retail industry's wounded beasts through the early Christmas trading season (for some reason, he chose Project Centipede as the vaguely comical codename for his hunting expedition). It was December 2004, and Allders was on its last legs. After his unhappy departure from BHS, Terry Green had gone across to run the careworn department store. Allders resembled Grace Brothers from the sitcom *Are You Being Served?* Terry Green's original plan had been to merge Allders with House of Fraser. When that failed, he had attempted to take the group upmarket by bringing in Debenhams-inspired designer collaborations. That had flopped, and Lehman Brothers, the company's main lender, had warned of its intention to call in its loans. Allders had until the New Year to find a saviour or face going bust. One of McGowan's colleagues, Robert Schneiderman, remarked in an email, 'It is very much the talk of the town.'

On 8 December, its owner announced an emergency auction. The statement irritated McGowan. The Northern Irishman and his business partner, Paul Taylor, ran Hilco, a small fund set up to take over struggling retail businesses – and to liquidate them if that turned out to be the most profitable route. The advent of Hilco pointed to an emerging trend. Having survived for years despite offering unremarkable products and service, older high-street chains were beginning to feel the internet nibbling at their sales.

McGowan had been planning to gain control of Allders by buying its debt from Lehman. He worried that the news might alert other predators. It did – although it actually worked in McGowan's favour. One billionaire in particular took a liking to the deal but chose to hide his involvement by using Hilco as a front.

Philip Green negotiated the purchase of Lehman's £90 million debt for less than £30 million from Jeremy Isaacs, the American bank's European chief executive. Project Centipede came to fruition on 19 January 2005. Minerva, the property company that owned Allders, announced to the stock market that Lehman's loans had been sold to Epsilon Investments, a mysterious company based on the island of Nevis in the West Indies. Epsilon was said to be working with Hilco. Green liked to refer to the people who fronted his financial interests as his 'jockeys'. McGowan was the jockey who would ride Allders towards its highly profitable collapse.

Andrew Rosenfeld, Minerva's cigar-chewing boss, felt betrayed by Lehman. He made sure the statement included a pointed reference to the Monaco domicile of Epsilon's directors. Rosenfeld also authorized his PR man to brief journalists off the record that Green was the force behind Epsilon. Green denied any involvement. Someone who dealt with him on Allders watched him repeatedly take calls from the press, lie and hang up, chuckling, 'They'll write whatever I tell them to.' When Green found out who was behind the briefings, he called Rosenfeld's PR man and warned him, 'You've landed the first punch, but believe me, when I punch you back, you'll feel it a lot more. I'll have my lawyers onto you.'

The speculation died away. Green and Hilco spent a further £45 million buying loans Barclays had made to Allders, then pushed the business into administration. Hilco appointed the insolvency division of Kroll, the investigations agency, which in turn employed Hilco as a paid adviser. Someone who worked with them described the way Green controlled the administration and brutalized McGowan, who was himself hardly a soft character. Green would shout, 'Paul, you're not fucking listening, otherwise you wouldn't have asked that fucking stupid question!' Allders was a classic smash-and-grab. Through BHS, Green bought the ten best sites from Allders' portfolio of forty-five stores. A further fourteen were sold to rivals including Debenhams and Primark. Most of the others were shut, with the loss of at least 2,000 jobs. The flagship Allders in Croydon was sold to Green's friend Harold Tillman, with Hilco and Terry Green also taking stakes. The disposals were overseen by Malcolm Dalgleish, one of Green's closest allies in the property industry. Dalgleish, a wily, self-made agent from Wandsworth Common in south London, had first worked with Green on the dismantling of Sears, helping to sell off its £300 million property portfolio.

The proceeds of the administration went tax free to Nevis, then on to Green and Hilco. Within a few months, the 143-year-old company had all but disappeared. Having put £75 million at risk, the raiders roughly doubled their money. Allders' pensioners fared less well. There were 3,000 members of its scheme, which had a shortfall of £68 million. It had to be bailed out by the Pension Protection Fund, a recently created insurance programme, resulting in benefits cuts for 2,400 people. The Pensions Regulator tried to pursue Minerva, Allders' former owner, but abandoned the case fourteen months later. Perhaps the incident stuck in Green's memory.

When I asked the tycoon about Allders in 2016, he continued to deny his involvement. 'I had nothing to do with Allders, at all, ever,' he said. With an almost audible smirk, Green added, 'I don't even know the name of the company. Epsilon what?' McGowan's response was similarly unhelpful. 'Fuck you,' he said. 'You're trying to build this big bloody conspiracy and you are *so* barking up the wrong fucking tree.' However, one of the many well-placed sources who confirmed the details of the deal gave me a copy of the draft contract for Epsilon's purchase of Lehman's £90 million debt. The signatory was one Philip Green.

Six years earlier, Green had been happy to boast about his lucrative demolition of Sears. His strange coyness over Allders might have reflected a growing desire to protect his celebrity status. It might also have reflected a growing desire for a knighthood. Green had first shown an interest in politics in October 2003, when he attended a Breast Cancer Care charity auction and bid £18,000 for a game of tennis with Tony Blair at Chequers, the prime minister's country retreat. Richard Caring, his business partner, was reported to have tagged along for the match. With his bouffant hair, high-wattage grin and £15 million house in Hampstead nicknamed the Palace of Versailles, Caring was far from the typical Labour sympathizer. Yet he came to play a significant and controversial role in the party's financing three years later.

In June 2004, Green donated £4.25 million to Jewish Care, a health and social services charity. He topped that in 2007 with a gift of £5 million, to be given in five annual tranches of £1 million. Jewish Care's president was Lord Levy, the master fundraiser known to his more cynical colleagues as Lord Cashpoint. Levy, who was among the guests at Brandon Green's extravagant bar mitzvah weekend in 2005, was a tough accountant-turned-music-industry entrepreneur. He had made £10 million in 1988 from the sale of Magnet Records, the label he co-founded. After helping to raise £15 million for New Labour's first election campaign, he had been installed in the House of Lords by Blair in 1997. Levy was known to be the most direct route to the prime minister's heart for the wealthy. Visitors to his home in Totteridge, which had its own tennis court and swimming pool, would mingle with key figures from Blair's inner circle, such as Tessa Jowell and Jonathan Powell. They would rarely leave without opening their chequebooks. Levy would make clear that generous donors to his charities could occasionally expect letters of recommendation for honours – although, of course, there was never any guarantee of a knighthood or peerage.

Labour had overhauled the political funding system in 2001, requiring parties to name donors giving more than £5,000 following a row over a £1 million payment from the Formula One tycoon Bernie Ecclestone. In September 2004, under pressure from Gordon Brown, Blair announced that he would serve only one more term. The prospect of Blair's political mortality, combined with the longer-running issue of transparency, slowed Labour's donations to a drip. Lord Levy calmly suggested a solution. He said that Labour could deploy its own version of a trick used by the Tories: solicit loans rather than gifts to get around the disclosure rules. Blair approved the idea, and Labour secretly raised almost £14 million from twelve businessmen to fight the 2005 election. The prime minister came a cropper when he proposed four of the lenders for peerages. One was Sir David Garrard, the former chairman of Minerva, who had lent Labour £2.3 million. The peerages committee raised concerns over the collapse of Allders and the fate of its pensioners under his stewardship. Another was Chai Patel, a care-homes owner, who had lent £1.5 million. The Liberal Democrat frontbencher Vince Cable wrote to the panel questioning Patel's suitability (there had been allegations of poor standards in one of his homes in south-west London, although he was cleared of wrongdoing in a judicial review of the case).

When he was turned down for a seat in the House of Lords, a furious Patel spoke to the *Sunday Times*, which exposed the scandal. Richard Caring was revealed to be among the twelve businessmen who had provided loans. He had lent Labour £2 million. Caring was known to be close to Levy, and was sometimes described as his tennis partner. In 2005, Caring had raised £10 million at a lavish ball in St Petersburg for the NSPCC, one of Levy's charities. The guests included Bill Clinton and Liz Hurley. Elton John performed. Blair filmed a message of support for the event. Barry Townsley, a stockbroker who was on the board of several Caring companies, had also lent Labour £1 million, and was one of the four businessmen put forward for peerages.

Lord Levy was arrested twice in the ensuing police investigation into cash for honours. Blair was questioned three times. Almost eighteen months after the story broke, the Crown Prosecution Service decided that it had insufficient evidence to bring charges and dropped the case. Labour repaid all the loans, and none of the four proposed by Blair entered the Lords.

That was the backdrop to the government's surprising decision to knight Philip Green. It was a time when money and politics mingled giddily. After Lord Levy, the next most direct route to Blair's heart was to build a city academy. In 2006, Des Smith, a council member of the trust that recruited sponsors for academies, told an undercover *Sunday Times* reporter that funding the prime minister's favourite type of school made an honour 'a certainty'. In September 2004, three months after his first Jewish Care donation, Green unveiled plans to build a vocational college for the retail industry. The Fashion Retail Academy opened near Tottenham Court Road in October 2006, offering one- or two-year diplomas for sixteen- to eighteen-year-olds. Green's Arcadia Group invested £5 million. Other retailers, including Marks & Spencer and Tesco, put in £6 million. The government provided £10 million. At the ceremony to celebrate the arrival of the first 220 students, Blair awkwardly picked out a pair of women's shoes to go with grey shorts and a woollen jumper. Green joked, 'You could have missed your vocation in life.' Blair replied, 'You would have to start me right at the bottom.' As usual with Green, there was a kink that ensured his family had a stake. The academy's building on Gresse Street was owned not by the college but by Tina through Taveta Investments, Arcadia's holding company. In the decade after 2006, the property soared in value from £12.5 million to £41.5 million, helped by a refurbishment in 2015 that was partially funded by a one-off grant of £544,000 from the Greater London Authority. The property's appreciation accrued to Green's family, not the academy.

Philip Green was knighted for services to retail on 17 June 2006, less than eighteen months after his break-up of Allders. Next to him on the front page of the *Financial Times* was another Monaco-based tycoon, the easyJet founder Stelios Haji-Ioannou. Jack Dromey, Labour's treasurer, later said the party had been keen to present itself as pro-enterprise as well as pro-worker, which was 'legitimate'. But he added of Green, 'Were we quite as discriminating as we should have been? In the zeal to become the party of business, it was too embracing."*

By the time the Fashion Retail Academy opened its doors, the economy was hurtling upwards on a steep trajectory. Prices of assets were booming, from property and shares to fine wine. Green was among a crowd of dealmakers who clustered around the honey pot of Halifax Bank of Scotland. HBOS's head of corporate lending, Peter Cummings, was a mild-mannered banker from Dumbarton who had started his career as a tea boy, but he was willing to risk huge amounts of debt and equity on high-profile deals sourced by entrepreneurs who put in little money of their own. Like Green, Cummings was particularly drawn to companies whose value appeared to be underpinned by property. The banker went on a spree after his stunning early experience with Arcadia, where he received a £96 million dividend for investing £800,000 of the bank's equity alongside £808 million of debt, which was repaid in a flash.

Cummings backed Tom Hunter's failed takeover bid for Selfridges in 2003, followed by his successful moves on Wyevale Garden Centres, House of Fraser, the retirement homes group McCarthy & Stone and the housebuilder Crest Nicholson between 2006 and 2007. Cummings also financed the Icelandic fund Baugur, which partnered with Hunter on House of Fraser, and Robert Tchenguiz, an Iranian-born playboy with pink-tinted glasses. He liked to reassure HBOS's investors, 'I just make sure I don't lend to idiots.' In 2007, Cummings earned a total of £2.6 million – more than his youthful chief executive, Andy Hornby. Green was one of Cummings' top clients. An internal HBOS briefing note drawn up by two of his managers in October 2006 said, 'The Sir Philip Green connection has been highly remunerative for the bank in recent years with

* Before this book went to print, Green's lawyers wrote to reiterate that he was awarded his honour for services to the retail industry, not for his charitable work, that he had never 'desired' an honour of any kind, and that the decision to knight him was made independently by the honours and appointments secretariat at the Cabinet Office. In fairness, many of his retail achievements had long pre-dated the cash-for-honours scandal of 2006 and 2007, and Green was not implicated in it.

significant dividends paid to us . . . Our relationship with the executive team is strong and further banking opportunities are likely to arise for the bank from this source.' The following summer, Green had dinner with Paul Myners, M&S's chairman, at Scott's in Mayfair. The evening was supposed to have been a peace summit between Green and Paul Dacre, editor of the *Daily Mail*, brokered by Myners after both he and Green bid for an audience with the newspaper boss at a charity auction. But it had gone badly, and Dacre had left early. As they smoked cigars outside the restaurant, Green boasted to Myners, 'I could call Peter Cummings now and have a term sheet for £1 billion tomorrow morning.'

Yet Green was less reckless than his public image suggested. 'There is a difference between risk and calculated risk,' he liked to say. After his second attempt to buy M&S, he pulled back from big acquisitions and kept debt levels at BHS and Arcadia low. The swashbuckling days were coming to an end, but he was still plugged into every deal on the high street through his network of contacts. An adviser who worked with him said, 'It was a moment when it was just things happening all the time. It was really quite exciting. Everything that came into play, he was involved with in some way or another, or people came to him for advice.' Green's access to information and willingness to leak stories about his friends made him the perfect contact for a generation of journalists, who competed for his favour.

By the summer of 2007, the economy was overheating dangerously. Hubris was in evidence. Baugur installed a ten-foot-tall statue of a Viking with a rock guitar strapped to his back in the lobby of its office on Bond Street. In May, Jón Ásgeir Jóhannesson flew 300 contacts to Monaco for an event called 'Baugur Day'. After a series of financial presentations, there was a black-tie dinner. Jonathan Ross, the compère, welcomed the crowd to 'the glittering heart of Europe's tax-evasion district'. Green appeared on stage as a judge in a live production of *The X Factor* alongside Louis Walsh, Sharon Osborne and Simon Cowell. Baugur screened a bespoke episode of *Little Britain* where Matt Lucas's character hypnotized Jóhannesson. The evening culminated in a live performance from Tina Turner, who was backed by a full orchestra. Two months later, Sir Tom Hunter, who had been knighted in 2005 for services to philanthropy, gave an interview to the BBC's Robert Peston in the garden of his mansion in the south of France. He pledged to give away £1 billion to charity.

It was a remarkable promise for a remarkable time, but it didn't last. The seven-year boom had been driven by a fantasy combination of cheap debt and rising asset prices. A fortnight after Hunter's BBC interview, the first thunder cracks of reality broke across the Atlantic. Two hedge funds run by the investment bank Bear Stearns collapsed. They had invested heavily in American mortgage-backed securities. It was the first sign of trouble emerging from the sub-prime market, where banks extended money to homebuyers with poor credit ratings, then sliced and diced the loans into complicated financial instruments and traded them on Wall Street. The storm moved across to Britain in September 2007, when a request to the Bank of England for emergency funding sparked a run on Northern Rock. By the end of 2008, the landscape was unrecognizable. HBOS had merged with Lloyds Bank and the enlarged group had been partially nationalized – as had Royal Bank of Scotland. Iceland had become the first European country to receive an International Monetary Fund bailout since 1976. Britain was in the deepest recession since the Second World War. The party was over.

Hunter and Robbie Tchenguiz both saw their £1 billion fortunes wiped out as their investments plunged in value. Hunter said, with gallows humour, 'I did want to give my money away – I just didn't expect it to be in quite this way.' Peter Cummings was fired from HBOS and turned into one of the villains of the crisis, along with Sir Fred 'The Shred' Goodwin, the boss of RBS, who was stripped of his knighthood four years later. Green, who had resisted the headiest temptations of the debt-fuelled years, weathered the hurricane in a position to play godfather to his broken associates. In October 2008, a month after Lehman Brothers collapsed, Green flew to Iceland to negotiate the purchase of Baugur's bank loans. He humiliated the Icelandic lenders by offering as little as 10 per cent of their face value, and the talks broke down. When Baugur was put into administration the following February, Jón Ásgeir Jóhannesson predicted that Green would be 'dancing a war dance in his living room'. But the tycoon did not scoop up any of Baugur's retail collection, which ranged from the fashion chains Coast, Karen Millen, Oasis and Warehouse to the Hamleys toy emporium.

When Peter Cummings became the only HBOS employee to be subjected to an investigation by the Financial Services Authority, Green put him in touch with a PR man, Neil Bennett, former City editor of the *Sunday Telegraph*. Cummings was given a lifetime ban by the regulator. He denounced 'an extraordinary Orwellian process by an organization that acts as lawmaker, judge, jury, appeal court and executioner'. Lord Stevenson, Cummings' former chairman, sent Green a case of first-growth Bordeaux wines from 1961 and 1982 as a thankyou for helping the banker find PR support. He never heard anything in reply.

The king of the high street was increasingly preoccupied with other interests. Green was jabbing his fingers into as many pies as possible, and retail was just the start of it. He had dabbled in football since 1987, when he persuaded the Tottenham Hotspur chairman Irving Scholar to put his friend Tony Berry on the board. In 1991, he helped Terry Venables raise the money for his ill-fated purchase of a stake in Spurs, and in 1999 he underwrote the West End theatre producer Bill Kenwright's takeover of Everton. Green later told *The Observer* he had written 'a £30 million letter' to help Kenwright secure debt from Bank of Scotland because 'I liked him'. In 2002, he brokered the transfer of the Leeds United defender Rio Ferdinand to Manchester United. (Terry Venables was the manager of Leeds at the time. Allan Leighton, BHS's chairman, was deputy chairman, and Richard North, who knew Green from his first M&S approach, was also a non-executive.) In 2004, Green intervened in talks between Fulham's owner, Mohamed Al-Fayed, and Manchester United's chief executive, David Gill, clearing the way for the striker Louis Saha's transfer to Old Trafford. Football's dealmaking appealed to his trader's instincts, and he loved the reflected glamour and power.

A financier who attended an intimate charity dinner hosted by Sir Alex Ferguson, then manager of Manchester United, and Harry Redknapp, then manager of Spurs, at Searcys private dining rooms in Knightsbridge in January 2012 described how Green dominated the conversation. He had been invited by the Goldman Sachs banker Mike Sherwood, who had paid for the evening alongside Manjit Dale, co-founder of the private equity firm TDR Capital. 'Everything Ferguson said, Philip was like, "Oh, I did that deal, I financed that deal,"' the guest said. 'He gave the impression he had been the cashpoint. He made it clear he was at least partly the power behind Tottenham. Harry was very scared of him. There were times when I expected Ferguson to give him a slap, but he didn't. He seemed slightly nervous as well.'

In December 2016, Chris Matheson, the Labour MP for Chester – and an Everton season-ticket holder – used a select committee interview with the chairman of the Football Association, Greg Clarke, to raise the question of Green's influence over the sport. Matheson suggested that Green had played 'something of a role as a shadow director at Everton'. In 2004, Green had organized a £15 million credit line when Everton's finances came under strain, and in 2006 he arranged the sale of a 23 per cent stake in the club to his friend Robert Earl, the founder of Planet Hollywood, who invested through a company in the British Virgin Islands called BCR Sports. When Earl sold the shareholding in 2016 to Farhad Moshiri, a Monaco-based businessman, bankers wondered whether Green was in fact the true owner of BCR Sports.

Simon Cowell, the sharp-tongued creator of *The X Factor*, provided another distraction. Green had first met Cowell at the Monaco Grand Prix in 1999, and the boyishly vain pop promoter had been among the guests at PG55. As he acquired a taste for celebrity through Topshop, Green appointed himself Cowell's superagent, flying around the world for free to negotiate deals on his behalf, including the formation of a joint venture with Sony for the rights to *The X Factor* and *Britain's Got Talent*. In October 2009, Tina paid Banana Split £3 million to stage Cowell's fiftieth birthday party at

Wrotham Park, an eighteenth-century mansion in Hertfordshire. Cowell's face was projected onto the outside of the building. The 450 guests were greeted by waiters wearing Cowell masks and top hats. The dining marquee was decorated as a boudoir, with blue satin curtains on the walls and gold and silver on the curved tables. On the ceiling was a replica of Michelangelo's *Creation of Adam* from the Sistine Chapel, with the image of God replaced by Cowell. There was a live performance from Earth, Wind & Fire, the Greens' favourite band, and a burlesque show from The Box in New York featuring dancers dressed as giant vaginas. Green, who was in his element as he swaggered around greeting guests, leered to one, 'Dreams really do come true, don't they?'

Four months earlier, Green and Cowell had announced plans to build a multibillion-pound showbiz and merchandising company to rival Disney. Through poor business planning, Cowell had allowed the rights to the shows he produced so obsessively – *The X Factor* and *Britain's Got Talent* – to be owned by third parties including Sony. Green wanted to take them back, launch new formats and sell clothes based on the acts they discovered. The venture was hyped as the ultimate collaboration between the creator of One Direction and the billionaire boss of Topshop. Kate Moss was lined up as style director. However, Green's rambunctious approach irritated Cowell's negotiating partners in Hollywood, and when Syco Entertainment finally emerged, it was in the form of a 50:50 joint venture between Cowell and Sony. Green was relegated to the role of adviser. His vision of a showbiz empire quietly faded.

By 2010, Green was one of the few people who could claim to straddle the worlds of business, entertainment, sport and politics. He even boasted of having helped London win its bid to host the 2012 Olympic Games, dialling the ambassador Lord Coe and putting him on speakerphone to convince incredulous journalists. Having ridden the New Labour wave, he switched his allegiances to David Cameron, the forty-three-year-old Conservative leader, a fortnight before the general election in May. Cameron unconvincingly ousted Gordon Brown in coalition with the Liberal Democrats.

Three months later, he appointed Green to review public sector efficiency – to the rumoured chagrin of senior colleagues such as Francis Maude, the cabinet office minister.

There was an immediate backlash as Labour pointed out that Green's wife lived in Monaco, and stories resurfaced about his extravagant birthday parties. Green angrily told BBC Radio 4's *Today* programme, 'My wife is not a tax exile. My family do not live in the United Kingdom – it's somewhat different.' David Crow, a reporter at the free business daily *City AM*, was among those who challenged the Arcadia boss on his tax affairs. Green called him a 'fucking tosser'. Vince Cable, the Lib Dem business secretary, told *City AM*, 'There's a lot I could say on this, but I'd better miss this one out.' Green responded, 'What difference does it make if I live on the moon? The real question is whether I'm qualified to do the job.'

Green refused to produce a proper report. In October 2010, he delivered a thirty-three-page PowerPoint presentation to the Cabinet Office suggesting the government centralize procurement of basic materials like paper and printing cartridges and use more videoconferencing to cut down on hotel bills. Green told the BBC's Robert Peston that 'the lights would be out' if he ran his retail businesses with the level of data the government had. Green's review went nowhere, and it was tacitly shelved. Meanwhile, UK Uncut, a campaign group set up to protest against the Tories' austerity programme, targeted Green's stores, staging a sit-in at the flagship Topshop on Oxford Street and glueing themselves to the windows in Brighton. Green later complained that he had tried to contribute to the public debate but had 'got my windows broken'.

The powerful image Arcadia's owner presented to the outside world through his catholic range of interests belied a dysfunctional family life. Sir Philip Green and his sister, Elizabeth, had continued their childhood feud into adulthood. While he pursued material wealth, she trained as a teacher, then ran off to live in an ashram in India. She eventually settled in north London and married a graphic designer, David Neville, with whom she had three children – Simon, Jacob and Georgia. Green's antipathy towards his sister extended to her offspring. Simon, his eldest nephew, became a journalist who happened to cover retail for the *Evening Standard*. In November 2013, Green hosted his annual Arcadia results breakfast at the Langham hotel. I sat next to him and watched with grim fascination as he cut a huge slab of blue cheese, pinned it to a hunk of French bread and shovelled it into his mouth, washing the combination down with gulps of black coffee. A few weeks earlier, a rumour had gone around the assembled press pack that Green had helped Neville buy a house in Brixton. With his sixth sense for weakness, Green must have known. As his nephew rushed out of the room to meet the *Standard*'s early print deadline, Green called out in a loud voice, 'If you don't write something nice, I'll take the fucking house back.'

But in October 2007, Green and his sister put on a rare display of solidarity. The tycoon threw a ninetieth birthday party for their mother at the Four Seasons hotel on Park Lane (although he belatedly realized it was actually her eighty-ninth). Alma still exercised a powerful hold over her son. She was one of the few people who could criticize him. She would also mock Tina, sometimes remarking of her garish choice of clothes, 'Ooh, Tina – I remember when that was in fashion!'

A long queue of shiny cars disgorged guests including Richard Caring and his then wife Jackie, the former *Sunday Times* business editor Will Lewis and the Goldman Sachs banker Mike Sherwood. Some of the Greens' relatives had flown over from Canada. Tina, wearing a black dress and dripping with sparkling diamonds, led Alma into the champagne reception to a chorus of 'Happy Birthday'. After the crowd had taken their seats in the candle-lit dining room, Green gave a speech to the woman who had dominated his life. Alma looked on impassively, her blonde hair in a neat bob. 'I was very, very lucky . . . that my mother was an entrepreneurial businesswoman,' Green began. 'That was a good start for me, and I'm pleased to say, Mum, I put it to good use.' There was a round of applause. He went on to say that Alma had 'even phoned me yesterday to discuss one of the properties – "I think maybe we should do this sort of deal, but I don't think we should do it because I don't really like the tax situation" . . . She's still energetic, enthusiastic, she travels the world with her friends, she still looks after the same properties she's had for fifty years, she still phones the solicitors, writes to the accountants – and bravo, well done to you, Mum.'

Chloe and Brandon awkwardly performed a specially prepared song. 'Hello, Grandma,' they sang. 'It's you we should be thankin', for what Dad's been bankin'. It's 'cos of you that we don't have to work.' Simon and Georgia Neville, two of Elizabeth's children, gave a speech. They reminisced about Sunday lunches at Alma's flat in Maida Vale, where she served home-made chicken soup with matzah balls, and about trips to see *Beauty and the Beast* and *Starlight Express* in the West End. They joked about her love of gambling. 'If anyone in this room thinks that Alma's lost any zest for life, you only need to turn up at Les Ambassadeurs on a Saturday night to see that she's lost none of it,' Georgia said. Simon mentioned Alma's right-wing politics and 'her favourite topic of asylum seekers'. 'You can ask her later on her views on that, but be prepared,' Georgia warned the crowd.

Green introduced the main entertainment, 'a special surprise from us' – the 'Diana' crooner Paul Anka, who had flown in from Los Angeles. Anka danced with a delirious Tina during a rendition of 'Put Your Head on My Shoulder'. She tried to lean into the microphone. 'I'll do the singing, lady,' Anka quipped. 'You've got as much chutzpah as he does,' he added, looking at Green. Anka tried to sing 'Puppy Love' with Robert Tchenguiz, the overfed property tycoon, who bellowed the lyrics like a drunken walrus. 'Don't quit the day job,' Anka advised him. The evening ended with a bespoke version of 'My Way' for Alma, who joined Anka on stage. 'You are it, my darling,' Anka told her, gazing into her eyes. 'Your voice is it,' she replied. Then Anka sang, 'We wish you love, and mazel tov, for living your way.' Tina's cheeks glistened as Alma cut a giant cake decorated with ninety candles. On their way out at the end of the night, guests were given copies of a newspaper from the day Alma was born in 1918. Goldman's Mike Sherwood remarked, 'We were all in tears and Alma was completely unfazed.' Green's mother said, 'I had a very good night . . . It was not like being in London, it was like being in Las Vegas.'

While the attention of the Green family's matriarch shone on Philip, Elizabeth was left in the shade. Alma's flat in Maida Vale was like a shrine to her son. The walls were covered with newspaper cuttings reporting his success, and the mantelpiece was crammed with photographs of him and Tina. There was also a huge collection of dolls and trinkets she had picked up at Church Street market near the Edgware Road. On one occasion, when Elizabeth was featured in the *Jewish Chronicle*, she framed the article and asked Alma if she would put it up on the wall. 'Yes, when you actually achieve something,' her mother snapped.

Alma died of a heart attack at the Wellington hospital in St John's Wood on 15 January 2015, aged ninety-six. Her will contained a final bitter pill for her daughter. As executors, she had nominated Philip and his best man, Edward Landau. She left £100,000 to Elizabeth, £20,000 to her helper Anicia Wass and £25,000 each to her five grandchildren, Chloe, Brandon, Simon, Jacob and Georgia. The rest – about £2.3 million – was to be put into a trust for Sir Philip and Lady Cristina Green, who were already billionaires several times over. Alma said she wanted them to 'provide for the wellbeing, comfort and needs of my daughter Elizabeth in the future'. But she was careful to make the request 'without creating any legal obligation'.

7.

Steak and Chips

To begin with, Topshop was the one part of Arcadia Group that resisted Green's cost-cutting. Jane Shepherdson, its brittle but brilliant brand director, guarded the fast-fashion business like her baby, denying Green access to key meetings and carefully protecting its network of quality suppliers. Shepherdson was about as different from her boss as it was possible to be. A lithe, elven fortysomething with a blonde bob and a head-girl's accent, she enjoyed dropping into the Almeida, her local theatre in Islington, and making weekend trips to the Tate Modern art gallery with her husband, a criminal defence barrister. She had joined the Arcadia brand Burton after graduating from North London Polytechnic and worked her way up, drawing attention when she moved to Topshop and ordered a tank top that sold half a million units. Surrounded by an inner circle of about sixty fiercely loyal, mostly female staff, she had an intimate understanding of the business. Shepherdson liked to say that 'Topshop is run by people who are also its customers, and that is really important'.

By the time Green took over in 2002, Shepherdson's team had already gone a long way towards turning Topshop into the hottest young-fashion destination in Britain. The year Arcadia left the stock market, Topshop sold 750,000 pairs of its £35 Ria skinny jeans. Celebrities like Cher and Madonna could be spotted among the 180,000 weekly shoppers entering its Oxford Street flagship store, a giant sweet shop full of gumball-shaped earrings and peppermint-striped bangles. Fashion editors cooed over its cheap catwalk designs, rifling through the rails for big-buttoned coats resembling much more expensive versions from Marc Jacobs and floral tops similar to the ones produced by Marni. The flagship received two deliveries a day, 300 new lines a week and 7,000 new lines a season. Shepherdson was clear on her demographic. 'We target 18-to-30-year-old, opinionated, cutting-edge fashion cognoscenti,' she said. 'However, our market stretches from 12 to 45 years old.'

Green realized he had accidentally acquired a swan among Arcadia's ducklings. However, Shepherdson's relationship with her new paymaster was never going to be easy. She told an interviewer that he had promised 'no decisions would be made without consulting me' and that he 'doesn't really understand our customer base'. But Topshop's ra-ra skirts were infinitely more glamorous than BHS's squeaky puppy toys, and Green could not resist trying to interfere. His relationship with Shepherdson turned into a struggle for control. In November 2003, the industry magazine *Drapers* ranked her first in its list of the hundred most influential people in high-street fashion – one place above Green. He rang Eric Musgrave, the magazine's editor. 'You've caused me a lot of fucking problems,' Green complained. 'Her head'll be even fucking bigger than it is already.' The sting was sharpened by an anecdote in the accompanying interview, which named Shepherdson 'Fashion's First Lady'. *Drapers* said the marketing department at Burton had been forced to use a single member of the boyband Blue for its autumn campaign because 'Arcadia's top brass' had been unwilling to pay for all four. It added that a 'top-ranking Arcadia boss' had shouted at Shepherdson, 'Do you fucking realize that we spend more on fucking photography than fucking *Vogue*? Can't you do it fucking cheaper?' She was said to have given a curt 'no' and turned on her heel.

By 2005, Topshop's Oxford Street store alone was turning over close to £100 million, but the tensions between Shepherdson and Green were surfacing. She pointedly said that her business was 'driven by ideas and creativity, and that's something money can't buy'. The following year, as Green's £1.2 billion tax-free dividend inflated his ego, he began to plan for international expansion. He wanted to follow in the footsteps of European retailers like H&M and Zara, which had travelled from their respective homes in

Sweden and Spain to become globally renowned high-street chains. At the time, Topshop was buzzing on Camden rock chic inspired by Amy Winehouse and the Libertines. Shepherdson openly contradicted her boss's ambitions. 'I am generally nervous about Topshop abroad,' she told *The Guardian* in June 2006. 'I don't think for one minute it's an easy or obvious thing to do . . . I don't see Topshop as an H&M, for example, which is everywhere.' Shepherdson said that British people were 'more interested in fashion for the sake of it, as opposed to fashion to make you look sexy or pretty'. The implication was that Americans wouldn't understand its quirky styles.

Three months later, Kate Moss materialized on the front row of Topshop's London Fashion Week show for the first time. The supermodel had long been a fan: in 2002, when Topshop's buyers ordered a colourful range of £6 tank tops based on her look, Moss had bought three. Green had sent a helicopter to her garden in Gloucestershire at 1.30 p.m. that day to fly her to London in time for the show's 3.30 p.m. start. As Moss sat giggling between Green and her hairdresser, wearing flares rather than her trademark skinny jeans, speculation swirled that she was about to be unveiled as the face of Topshop's spring 2007 campaign. A year earlier, Moss had been dropped by luxury brands including Burberry and Chanel after the *Daily Mirror* obtained a video apparently showing her snorting cocaine with her then-boyfriend, the former Libertines frontman Pete Doherty. Three days after her appearance at Topshop's show, a far wider-ranging collaboration was announced to the world: Moss would design her own range of clothes, shoes and accessories, on a three-year contract said to be worth an initial £3 million. That evening, Green and Moss retreated to China Tang in the Dorchester to celebrate their deal. Accompanied by Shepherdson, Shepherdson's marketing director Jo Farrelly and Moss's agent Sarah Doukas, they ate oysters, dim-sum and rare duck. Green reportedly toasted his new muse with Cristal champagne and the words, 'It's not every day you sign up Kate Moss.'

A fortnight later, Jane Shepherdson quit.

Many of Shepherdson's staff were said to have burst into tears at the news. Green insisted the plan to hire Moss had been under discussion for three months, and dismissed suggestions of a row over the supermodel's role as 'absolute rubbish'. A week later, Shepherdson told the *Daily Telegraph*, 'It is absolutely not true . . . It is a shame that people think I am that trivial.' But many of Shepherdson's colleagues were convinced that Green had forced through the deal with little or no input from his brand director. 'It might have been the straw that broke the camel's back,' said one, who worked for another Arcadia brand. 'As strong as she was in pushing back on his influence, I guess over time it wears you down. It was probably the cumulative effect.' A month after the Moss announcement, Arcadia reported a 20 per cent slump in pre-tax profits to £202.3 million. It was only a year after the ebullient results breakfast at which Green had taken his £1.2 billion dividend, but the mood was very different. 'I don't want today to be about Jane,' he said in a pre-speech briefing at his office, dragging on a super-slim cigarette. When Green handed her a farewell jeroboam of champagne on stage later, the *Financial Times* reported that Shepherdson 'could barely look him in the eye'.

The Arcadia tycoon gave his former queen bee a green Nissan Figaro as a leaving present, which she drove for years. He tried to play down her significance, telling *The Independent*, 'Look – are Arsenal still going to play football without Thierry Henry? Or will they take the goalposts down?' Shepherdson moved to Whistles, which had passed from Green and Richard Caring into Icelandic ownership. When her appointment was announced in January 2008, her former boss was reported to have growled, 'Why would you end up in a tiny 30-shop chain if you're that good?' Green badmouthed Shepherdson to journalists, describing her as egotistical, and she spoke of him with distinct froideur. When I met her in 2013, she said coolly, 'Our paths cross occasionally. We don't tend to go to the same clubs.'

Shepherdson was followed through the door by two of her closest lieutenants, Jo Farrelly and Karyn Fenn. Green tried to come across as unperturbed. When Chris Blackhurst, City editor of the *Evening*

Standard, asked him if Topshop was in crisis, the billionaire demanded to know where the journalist was. 'London,' Blackhurst told him. 'I'm in 40-degree heat, on my yacht off Turkey, sipping Cristal champagne,' Green replied. 'Now, which one of us is in crisis?'

For many years, Shepherdson had managed to keep Green out of the business. 'After she left, he started to force his way in,' said the same former colleague who thought Kate Moss was the final straw. 'It became the Philip Green show rather than the Topshop show.' The newly empowered owner gave a self-indulgent interview to *The Guardian* in February 2007, presenting himself as the master tastemaker. 'I think I've got a good feel,' he said. 'I mean, I went shopping with Beyoncé the other day. I said, "Let me pick the things for you." And eight out of ten, I got right.' Green dropped in a mention of Moss's thirty-second birthday party, which he and Tina had attended. 'You saw the pictures of Kate in the papers this morning?' he asked. 'Awesome. Right? Awesome. I mean, we were having fun at . . . whatever time it was.'

The first Kate Moss collection was the subject of wild anticipation and hype. The few journalists marshalled in to see it at London Fashion Week were made to sign non-disclosure agreements. *Vogue* was given exclusive rights to cover the fifty-piece range, and its editor, Alexandra Shulman, received a rare audience with Moss herself, who said that she had 'kind of got bits from my closet' for inspiration. The fashion designer Jeff Banks questioned whether the supermodel could 'sharpen a pencil or draw a matchstick man', speculating that Moss had simply 'turned up at Topshop's head office in Oxford Street for a quick hour's briefing with the in-house designers'. But hundreds of young women queued outside the flagship store for an evening launch event on 30 April while Green chaperoned Moss around a small area dedicated to her collection. Moss appeared in the shop window wearing a £195 red dress, to cheers from the crowd. She was heard to whisper nervously, 'He's fucking well getting his money's worth.' *Vogue Italia* photographed the collection – an honour the recherché publication almost never bestowed on a high-street retailer – and the fashion press generally approved of the micro hotpants and vintage rock T-shirts. Ten days later, Topshop repeated the successful launch at Barneys department store in New York – despite hostile reviews from the influential *New York* magazine, which summarized the collection with the word 'snore', and the *New York Post*, which described the styles as 'oddly familiar' under the headline, 'Duplikate'. Barneys had ordered just ten copies each of the two most popular items, a barbed wire-print dress and a long black gown. *Women's Wear Daily* described how American fashionistas descended like locusts. 'Shoppers ripped clothes off the mannequins, grabbed items from racks and out of the hands of sales associates,' it said. Green was vindicated. He had poured petrol on the fire Shepherdson had built, and it had worked. Twenty-five years after the flop of Joan Collins Jeans, he had created a proper celebrity fashion hit.

Green was clear that he saw an American store-opening programme for Topshop as the corollary of the Kate Moss deal. The US had long been known as the graveyard for overambitious British retailers. Marks & Spencer lost its shirt on the acquisition of Brooks Brothers in the late 1980s, and Tesco was soon to be humbled by the failure of its Fresh & Easy chain on the West Coast. Undeterred, the weekend after the Moss announcement, the emperor told the *Sunday Times* that 'America has to be the ultimate retail challenge because it is the biggest market. For me, utopia would be Topshop, Kate and New York all tied up with a big bow round them.' In May 2007, surfing the wave of excitement caused by her launch, he told the *Sunday Times* that he wanted to open three stores in New York. 'We are definitely going ahead with the American expansion – we have just pressed the button,' he said.

Gilbert Harrison, founder of an independent US investment bank called Financo, helped Green find the first site. Harrison, a restaurateur's son from New Haven in Connecticut, had known the Topshop billionaire since he was under fire at Amber Day in the early 1990s. Harrison had followed him to Sears and then BHS, where he was impressed by Green's office on Marylebone Road, which was 'filled with racks and racks of clothing'. 'He was the type of hands-on entrepreneur that basically looked at every piece of clothing that was sold – a true garment genius,' Harrison said. Green picked a building on West Broadway in Manhattan's SoHo district, close to Bloomingdale's department store. On April Fool's Day 2009, the TV presenter June Sarpong led a countdown. 'Even *I'm* nervous,' Green confided to Moss as they walked hand-in-hand through the store to the front, where a crowd was waiting. 'You're good nervous,' she replied. 'I'm not, I'm shit.' Amid a shower of red, white and blue confetti, a curtain lifted to reveal them arm-in-arm on a podium like a newlywed couple. The store, modelled on Topshop's Oxford Street flagship, was stocked with $40 jeans and two-for-$20 T-shirts. When *The Guardian* asked how he felt about opening it in the teeth of a global recession, Green retorted, 'Where are the people walking around nude? People are still wearing clothes. They want to be inspired. They still want to shop. Get real.'

The worldwide attention generated by Topshop's push into America fed Green's lifelong addiction to press coverage. Amid the endless interviews, an old friend worried that he was beginning to 'suck up his own exhaust'. As ordinary people came to terms with the shattering effects of the financial crisis and attitudes towards ostentatious consumption slowly hardened, Green was gleefully barging his way into the top fraction of a per cent, throwing cocktail parties where David Walliams of *Little Britain* cracked jokes and the supermodel Naomi Campbell grooved with Tina. He seemed blissfully unaware of how he must have come across to the average BHS customer. In February 2010, he allowed a *Times* journalist to shadow him for several weeks. He put on a hubristic display as he led her around stores and took her to dinner at Scott's in Mayfair. Green boasted about how *Vogue*'s US editor Anna Wintour would always call him back within six minutes, showed off a text message from Sir Howard Stringer of Sony and insulted the new chief executive of Marks & Spencer, Marc Bolland ('Does he know anything about fashion?'). Green was like an overgrown child who had woken up one morning to find himself the ringmaster of a giant circus. The media loved it, and he loved the media. He was caught in a feedback loop.

The first Topshop in New York was followed by openings in Chicago, Las Vegas, Los Angeles, Washington, San Diego, Atlanta, Houston and Miami. Green added a second store in New York, on Fifth Avenue, and struck a deal to sell the brand in Nordstrom's department stores in America. A banker who was involved at an early stage of the expansion doubted whether Green and Arcadia's chief executive, Ian Grabiner, had done enough market research before diving in. 'I don't think they did anywhere near what they should have done,' he said. 'I don't think the US customer understood the fashion as well as the UK customer.'

Beneath all the headlines and hype, it was difficult to tell whether Kate Moss and America really improved Topshop's finances. Green chose not to disclose the performance of Arcadia's individual brands, possibly because the likes of Evans and Wallis were beginning to struggle badly. Between 2006 and 2009, the group's overall sales rose slightly from £1.8 billion to £2 billion, although pre-tax profits actually fell from £202.4 million to £200.3 million. In 2010, Arcadia and BHS merged, raising the total sales to £2.8 billion. In the following two years, sales fell to £2.7 billion and profits dropped from £213.2 million to £103.7 million – or £166.9 million once BHS's losses were stripped out. It was not quite the stellar stuff readers of Green's interviews might have imagined.

The consensus among fashion insiders was that Jane Shepherdson had left Topshop with enough fuel in the tank to keep it motoring ahead for several years. The Kate Moss collaboration turbo-charged it for a short time, but by 2012 the business had reached a plateau and was about to start rolling downhill at pace. That was very bad news for Green's next business partners – although they would not realize until it was far too late.

Leonard Green & Partners was one of the most powerful private equity firms on the west coast of America. Its eponymous founder (again, no relation), a donor to animal rights causes and the Los Angeles opera, had been known as the 'nice guy' of the takeover industry. Leonard Green had helped to pioneer the 'friendly' buyout, where an investment firm works with a company's management to purchase it from the stock market consensually. His business was on the opposite end of the spectrum from the likes of Kohlberg Kravis Roberts, whose hostile takeover of the Oreo biscuit maker RJR Nabisco was immortalized in Bryan Burrough and John Helyar's book *Barbarians at the Gate*. Despite its herbivorous approach, LGP had often made juicy returns for its investors and partners. In the early 1990s, managers of the Thrifty Drug retail chain made more than ten times their money when LGP took over, merged it with a rival and floated the combined group on the stock market. In more recent times, LGP had profited handsomely by taking a 17 per cent stake in the upmarket grocery store Whole Foods during the financial crisis.

Its founder died of a heart attack in 2002, having spent the last two years of his life mired in a messy divorce battle with his third wife and a boardroom dispute with his partners. Since then, LGP had been run by three of Leonard Green's protégés, including Jon Sokoloff (one of the trio stepped down in 2014, leaving Sokoloff and another in charge). A serious, white-haired man known as 'Sok', Sokoloff was introduced to Sir Philip Green in late 2009, while Moss-mania was still raging. In the words of an associate from the Owen Owen era, Green in dealmaking mode could be 'the world's nicest person and also the world's most obnoxious person'. He threw every ounce of charm he had at Sokoloff, who became besotted with Topshop and its canny owner. By early 2010, they were discussing a joint venture in America, jokily describing it as 'the marriage of the Greens'. Private equity firms tend to like taking risks, and LGP was not averse to working with rough-hewn entrepreneurs. In November 2010, LGP and another firm announced a $3 billion plan to buy the preppy fashion brand J Crew, which was run by Mickey Drexler, a rag trader from the Bronx who liked to make spontaneous staff announcements over loudspeaker (and who happened to be friendly with Sir Philip). Green was at pains to point out that he didn't need LGP's money. Instead, he said, he wanted a partner to be his eyes and ears in the US. Green flew Sokoloff around Britain on his private jet to see its best shops and entertained him on his yacht in the south of France. He reassured the American that LGP was the only party in the frame and urged him to keep their talks secret. The private equity boss went back to his colleagues in Los Angeles brimming with excitement, telling them that Topshop was 'one helluva company' and encouraging them to consider a deal.

As 2011 rolled on and the conversation evolved, Green proposed that LGP buy half of Topshop for anywhere up to £1 billion. Even for a heavyweight fund like LGP, that was a big cheque – and Topshop's financial performance was dipping after seven strong years. Green had started to jack up prices to compensate for the slowdown. Topshop's scope for international expansion was also severely limited by the fact that it had sold off the rights to many of its most important overseas markets to franchise operators. As Sokoloff hesitated, Green insisted the poor trading was a blip and painted a tantalizing picture of new growth in America, China and Germany, as well as online. He told Sokoloff that he planned to shed all his other brands in the next few years and float Topshop on the stock market. Perhaps a deadline to repay Arcadia's bank debt by the end of 2012 was also lurking somewhere in the tycoon's consciousness. He planned to use £250 million of his LGP windfall to pay down the debt, £200 million to buy out minority shareholders in Arcadia (such as Lloyds bank) and £450 million to fund a new offshore dividend to Tina. Even though Green intended to set aside £100 million for Arcadia's pension funds, PwC, Arcadia's auditor, warned that they would be mildly damaged by the transaction because of the value flowing out of the company and back to Monaco.

In August 2012, Sokoloff told his colleagues that Green had spoken to Tina and his closest advisers, and had decided it was 'all systems go'. Green and Sokoloff codenamed the burgeoning deal Project Steak and Chips – Steak being Arcadia, and Chips being Topshop. At LGP's request, the size of the investment was reduced to a 25 per cent share of Topshop for a sum of £350 million. There was to be no dividend for the Greens: the money would purely be used to pay down Arcadia's debt to Lloyds bank. The whirlwind romance alarmed some of Sokoloff's colleagues in California, including John Danhakl, his joint managing partner. The doubters at LGP were uncomfortable with the limited data Green was willing to share on Topshop's prospects and the way Sokoloff's new friend seemed to be hurrying the deal along. Danhakl emailed a group of colleagues to say that he was 'particularly struck and troubled' by the consistency of Topshop's profit margins relative to those at close competitors such as H&M and Inditex. He thought Green might have been flattering Topshop's financial results by allocating some of its costs to less glamorous Arcadia sister brands like Dorothy Perkins and Wallis. Danhakl raised the spectre of Bernie Madoff, the investment guru who was jailed in 2009 for running the biggest Ponzi scheme in history. 'Madoff kept the fiction alive and was a revered financial figure for decades NOT because of absolute returns, but because of consistency,' he wrote. 'I'm not suggesting by any means that we've the [same] situation here, but incredible consistency is [a big] red flag, as is great variation or sudden improvement in results . . . Also a concern that stepping back, it's hard to figure out why this makes a great deal of sense for SPG to do based on the numbers – why bother with this for £350 million if he owns all of a £300 million-a-year earner?'

Danhakl ran through Green's possible reasons for wanting to sell a stake. He said, 'If he's looking for a partner/friend, maybe, although we have to ask ourselves the question as to whether we can satisfy the promises here. If he's losing confidence in the business – an entirely different story. If he's looking for validation to the world that "retail" experts approve – troubling. We'll leave misdirection out of the equation completely.'

But Sokoloff was committed, and his enthusiasm won the day. The final details were hammered out in early December 2012. By then, LGP was falling over itself to make the purchase, and the shareholders' agreement gave the private equity firm very few rights. LGP had the ability to elect two of the five or more board directors, and to call for a stock-market listing after five years. It also secured indemnities against Arcadia's huge pension deficit and the liabilities of its non-Topshop brands. In all other respects, Green remained the majority shareholder and kept control – which was just the way he liked it. From his point of view, the courtship of Sokoloff had been a resounding success. Adding a touch of stardust, the American fashion tycoon Tommy Hilfiger came in to take a $3 million slice of Topshop shares alongside LGP.

Green announced the stake sale with unusual solemnity. 'Under my family's ownership, we have continued to invest in and grow the Topshop and Topman brands,' he said. 'Having had extensive dialogue over several months, the board felt that Leonard Green & Partners becoming our partner would be extremely beneficial.' It turned out to be far less beneficial for LGP, although it would be several years before Sokoloff and his colleagues realized the extent of their mistake. They had bought into Topshop after its peak. It never again recaptured the momentum it had enjoyed at the point of Jane Shepherdson's handover to Kate Moss.

Green had first met Moss at a charity auction at Annabel's night-club in May 2006, when he paid £60,000 for a kiss just before midnight and donated it to the next highest bidder, the socialite Jemima Khan. Two weeks later, Green and Moss bumped into each other outside China Tang. 'That was a bit of fun,' Moss reportedly said of her smooch with Khan. 'I suppose,' Green replied. 'It all depends on your idea of fun.' Then Moss put it to him, 'I'm a girl from Croydon, you're a boy from Croydon. Why don't we do something together?'

Green assumed the role of indulgent uncle. He banned journalists from asking about her alleged cocaine use. When an interviewer from *The Independent* dared to raise it over sushi and salad at Arcadia's headquarters, Green's fork stopped mid-air. 'You don't want to be thrown out before lunch, do you?' he asked. 'We're not even going there, OK? You've already got a yellow card and you've only been here for five minutes.' His protectiveness was said to have extended to intervening in her break-up with Pete Doherty, the drug-addled former Libertines singer. When Doherty left two beaten-up Jaguars on the road outside Moss's flat in St John's Wood, maintaining a tenuous link after their separation, Green was reported to have dispatched tow trucks to remove them. And even before she became engaged to Jamie Hince of The Kills, there were suggestions that Green had helped Moss's husband-to-be choose a ring for her (although he dismissed that as 'more press bullshit').

Partying with Moss in Mayfair and Manhattan drew Green deep into the celebrity world. After the LGP coup he embraced it wholeheartedly. There were still days when he worked until 1 a.m. to prove the establishment wrong, but they were fewer and further between. Paparazzi increasingly photographed him with the likes of Geri Halliwell, the former Spice Girl, and the soul singer Lionel Richie. There was also his special relationship with Simon Cowell. Green and Cowell would sometimes speak on the phone into the early hours, until Green fell asleep with Cowell still rambling on. He liked to describe the feline reality-TV judge as his 'only outside interest'. He seemed to view Cowell as some kind of hobby.

Over time, many of Green's older business acquaintances thought he became untethered from reality. The same friend who criticized Tina for feeding her husband's greed thought the 'monster' of his swelling ego gradually 'strangled the funny, interesting person that once existed'. In March 2012, Tina booked the Rosewood Mayakoba resort in Mexico for her husband's sixtieth birthday party. There were performances by Robbie Williams, Stevie Wonder and the Beach Boys. The guests, including Naomi Campbell, Leonardo DiCaprio and Kate Hudson, were asked to wear PG60-branded clothing as they played beach volleyball and ate £50 Japanese Kobe beef burgers. Ian Grabiner, Arcadia's chief executive, privately told colleagues that he estimated only 20 per cent of the crowd had been at PG50 a decade earlier.

A few months after the party, Green's sister, Elizabeth, went to a bikram yoga class in Primrose Hill, north London. By chance she spotted Kate Hudson across the room doing stretches. Keen to speak to a Hollywood actress, Elizabeth went over and introduced herself. 'Oh my God, I *love* Philip and Tina!' Hudson exclaimed, clasping her hands together. She rhapsodized about the long week-end in Mexico, recounting how the Rolling Stones guitarist Ronnie Wood had got on stage and spontaneously jammed with Carlos Santana on the first night. Elizabeth felt a stabbing sensation in her chest. She hadn't been invited.

8.

The Great BHS Plunder

BHS was the base upon which Sir Philip Green's fortune was built. As the years passed and Topshop prospered, the unglamorous foundation of his empire slowly rotted.

Senior staff at the department store's headquarters on Marylebone Road experienced a rude awakening when the tycoon first swept in with his entourage in May 2000. BHS had been neglected by its former owner, Storehouse. It was an old-fashioned company, in both good and bad ways. There were charming examples of its paternalistic approach to employees, such as the story of a buyer who left to set up his own business, fell on hard times and was welcomed back with the promise that his two sons' private school fees would be covered. But in the judgement of someone who joined shortly before Green's takeover, the existing management was 'neither up for it, nor up to it'. 'Paternalistic' was not a word commonly attached to Green. He showed little patience. He had a simple philosophy towards the people he inherited: a third would like him, a third would learn to put up with him and a third would hate him. It was better to be brutal, he reasoned, and push the final third to the door.

Tales of Green roastings became legendary. There was the logistics director who was still on the first page of a presentation for a £1.5 million investment when his new boss slapped a £20 note on the table. 'What's that?' Green asked. 'Twenty pounds,' replied the quavering director. 'No it's not, it's *my* £20,' Green corrected him, 'and if you expect me to put another 74,999 of those into your project you'll have to do better than that.' There was the womenswear buyer caught paying three times the lowest price for a range of products. 'You're absolutely fucking useless,' Green told her. 'I should throw you out of the window but you're so fat you'd probably bounce back in again.' A senior member of staff said he would often duck out of meetings to take calls and return to find several junior people in tears. He would ask Green what he had done. 'Nothing, nothing,' the owner would apparently insist, sidling away.

One of Green's first acts was to squeeze BHS's suppliers by demanding discounts on outstanding invoices and lengthening payment terms. Richard Paice, a footwear supplier whose company, International Shoe Agencies, had a £10 million-a-year contract with BHS, was among those to feel the pain. 'We suddenly found ourselves being screwed on price for deliveries we had already agreed,' he said. 'Our chap who was looking after the account actually had a mental breakdown trying to deal with them. We got out within six months of delivering everything and called it a day, so a multimillion-pound contract we'd developed over many years was out of the window and we were on our bike, doing new things.'

The supplier crackdown was followed by a rigorous programme of cross-costing, where every department was forced to check how much it was paying for products versus the price Green could obtain. Some of the rationalization was long overdue: twelve different jeans suppliers were whittled down to one, which provided sharper prices. Yet the way the process was managed caused much unhappiness. BHS staff discovered a breed of people they called FOPs – Friends of Philip – who would pop up offering better terms. Brian Hill, who was head of menswear when Green arrived, said, 'That's fair enough, providing you're looking at like-for-like quality. That's where things in my view went somewhat awry. The things we were looking at were not in most cases of a similar quality. They were cheaper and from some questionable sources. The people that seemed to be arriving were people that I'd never heard of.'

At first, Hill was in the group who were prepared to live with Green. He hoped the energetic new leader would be a catalyst for change. 'There was a lot wrong with BHS,' he said. 'It was very top-heavy with management, and one of the things Philip did was start to address all that. But shortly into his tenure I guess he began to show his true colours. Although I didn't necessarily disagree with what he was doing, I disagreed with the way it was being done.'

Hill's objections went beyond the way clothing quality was being sacrificed. He thought BHS's new boss was a 'vulgar bully'. 'You don't want to sit in meetings with young buyers, some of whom are inexperienced, and see them demolished and sworn at,' he said. 'You would see young women, particularly, reduced to tears. Philip would often have a meeting before he flew off in his jet to Monaco and he would pick on one person and just batter them. The horrible thing about it was sometimes you would sit there and think, "Thank God it's not me." '

A bad-tempered meeting about the next season's pyjama range brought Hill's tenure as head of menswear to an abrupt end. In a moment of frustration, he banged a lever-arch file down on the meeting table and announced that he was leaving. According to Hill, Green followed him across the open-plan office, 'effing and blinding and saying, "Nobody walks out on me." I didn't actually say anything. I just got my stuff and walked out.' A colleague persuaded him to come back, but a few months later he left for good. Hill had lasted almost exactly a year under the new regime. He decided that Green was 'a thoroughly disgusting human being'.

BHS's pre-tax profits rose from £18.5 million in 2001 to £94.9 million in 2002, £100.1 million in 2003 and £101.9 million in 2004. Green exhausted himself in hauling the chain towards ever-greater profitability. In January 2002, after the *Sunday Times* first dubbed him a billionaire, he told the *Sunday Telegraph* the turnaround had been 'like an assault course'. 'And for everyone who said I couldn't run a business, I've come here to a business that was in the doldrums and I've proved to people I can do it,' Green said. 'The secret is that I'm an all-rounder.'

As much as he liked to feed the press stories about coat hangers and dress designs, the true secret behind BHS's incredible surge in profitability was Richard Caring. Between 1979 and 1988, Green's suave business partner had lived in Hong Kong, where he built up International Clothing Designs, a sourcing operation that supplied clothes to high-street retailers such as Marks & Spencer and Next. Based in a shopping centre in the Kowloon district, overlooking the impressive scenery of Victoria Harbour, ICD was one of the biggest suppliers to BHS and Arcadia. Caring was known to be a particularly clever user of Hong Kong's quota system. The territory's garment industry was broken down into different categories. There was an overall limit on the number of women's dresses, men's jackets and other items that could be imported to Britain from Hong Kong every year. Within those categories, each manufacturer had its own allowance. Quota was a tradable commodity, and those who bought and sold at the right times had a pricing edge. Quota was a key component of the total cost of making a garment – and the lower the price of a garment, the less duty an exporter had to pay. Caring's nickname, according to traders who knew him then, was 'The Quota King'.

After Green acquired BHS, Caring took an office at its Marylebone building. He was the foremost FOP, sitting in on buying meetings and range reviews. He and Green were constantly on the phone to each other. 'They were working eighteen hours a day and they were joined at the hip,' said a friend. 'If you were with Caring, Green would be calling him every five minutes.'

Caring was not just a supplier to BHS. Although Green strenuously denied it for years, he was also a shareholder. Green's family owned 73 per cent of BHS through Global Textiles Investments, a company domiciled in Jersey, which was in turn owned by GH One and GH Two, trusts based in the British Virgin Islands. Green's friend Tom Hunter owned 5 per cent through his private equity firm, West Coast Capital. Caring had a secret 22 per cent stake through two BVI companies, Dar Jenna and Lineman Holdings. Caring's shareholding was not disclosed to any of BHS's board members, including Terry Green, the chief executive, or Allan Leighton, the chairman. As a result, none of Green's lieutenants could understand quite why he was so heavily involved in BHS's operations. 'Richard was always a bit mysterious,' said one. 'He'd just say, "I'm partners with Philip", and that would be it. And I thought, well, I'm not going to ask.'

With Caring's help, BHS's operating-profit margin shot up from 2.5 per cent in 2001 to more than 10 per cent in 2002, 2003, 2004 and 2005. His hidden role as the second biggest shareholder put him in a different position from other suppliers. In 2005, an institution considering doing business with Green and Caring commissioned a private investigator's report into their relationship. The report said, 'PG discusses almost every major commercial decision he makes with RC before proceeding.' It also noted that, in 2004, Caring rearranged his ownership of ICD so that it was held by Global Investments Trust, a company with a strikingly similar name to the Greens' Global Textiles Investments. Both were registered on Don Street in St Helier, Jersey.

The report floated the idea that Caring was selling clothes to BHS at unrealistically low prices to flatter BHS's profit margins and help Green beat down other suppliers. It included several spreadsheets that superficially appeared to back up the claim. One showed figures from a Caring business, Tapestry Design Company, which sold goods to BHS at a margin of 4.8 per cent. The same company supplied Debenhams at a margin of 12.6 per cent and Tesco at 17.3 per cent. However, the spreadsheet gave only a snapshot of a particular product range over a tiny period of time in 2005. When I asked Caring about the figures, his lawyers at Carter-Ruck replied,

> Our client does not recognize the margins to which you refer, and can only assume that these represent certain individual orders or styles . . . In 2005, as in any trading year, goods were sold by Tapestry in hundreds of different styles and at a variety of margins . . . Management records for 2005 show that Tapestry's average margin for goods supplied to BHS was 13%. This is entirely consistent with its average margin to other major retailers for the same period, including Tesco (14%), Next (16%), Debenhams (9%) and Asda (8%).

In 2016, Caring told Parliament that his stake was kept secret because he was a supplier to some of BHS's rivals on the high street, and also because other suppliers might have been concerned about his ability to see their product lines and wholesale price points.

With BHS's profits ostensibly motoring, Green stripped value out of the business on a scale that made his break-up of Sears look like childish tinkering. To investigate the Green family's transactions with BHS is to pass through a looking glass into a parallel reality where greed is king and almost anything is possible. As the majority shareholder of a private company, Green was free to do whatever he liked within the bounds of the law. It was a freedom he pushed to the limit. Despite the show he made of improving BHS's retailing, behind the scenes he seemed to be more focused on extracting huge lumps of cash, which were sent offshore.

'I invest my own money,' Green told the *Daily Telegraph* two years after he bought BHS. 'I stand or fall on my own decisions. I take on the risk.' In fact, Green put no personal equity into BHS at all. He later referred to an equity investment of £20 million, but that almost certainly came from his sale of stakes to Richard Caring and Tom Hunter, who paid £10 million each. Green borrowed more than the entire £200 million purchase price from Barclays and the London office of WestLB, the German bank that had been supercharged into a racy lending machine by Robin Saunders, the starry young financier from Florida. Barclays and WestLB made facilities of £264 million available to Green – the excess presumably being to cover the deal costs and to provide BHS with working capital. An adviser who was involved said the banks were prepared to lend so much money because the stock market had seriously undervalued BHS's property portfolio, which Green reckoned was worth £350 million on its own. Saunders was sold a 0.5 per cent stake in BHS from the Greens' family shareholding as a reward for her efforts.

The financing was expensive. Between 2000 and 2005, BHS paid £69 million of interest to cover the cost of Green's acquisition, including £9.5 million to his wife, Tina, who subscribed to £29 million of BHS bonds through a Jersey-based company called Tacomer (BHS repaid Tacomer's bonds in 2005). Green had to race to pay off the first slice of bank lending within five days.

Despite its trading problems, BHS owned some of the best real estate on the high street. Green's masterstroke was to transfer ownership of the nine stores in the best locations – plus BHS's Marylebone headquarters – to his family. Because he planned to own the properties through an offshore company, the arrangement would allow him to collect rent directly from BHS as a tax-free income stream. Green set up a Jersey-based company called Carmen, which would buy the BHS properties. Tina owned 75 per cent of Carmen through a Jersey-based trust called Nautilus. Hunter owned the other 25 per cent. Green was helped by Malcolm Dalgleish, the trusted property adviser who had worked with him since the Sears days. Dalgleish made sure that Carmen's properties commanded the highest possible rents.

As with the main BHS takeover, Green put no money into this deal. Carmen borrowed £106 million from a syndicate led by Bayerische Hypo- und Vereinsbank, an obscure German bank. (The German loan was later refinanced by HBOS.) Green used the German cash to pay BHS £106 million for the properties. BHS then put the proceeds of the property sale towards a dividend of £167 million that it paid to Green, Caring, Hunter and Saunders in 2002. In other words, Green used bank debt to buy the ten best-located properties from BHS and immediately refunded himself a figure in excess of the purchase price. One of Green's advisers pointed out the sale-and-leaseback device could have been carried out by Storehouse, but that the public company 'failed to do what is fundamentally a simple transaction that Philip saw the opportunity to do'. Assets and cash gushed from BHS and its lenders into the new owners' bank accounts. The dividends pushed BHS into a loss of £51.6 million for 2002.

As Richard Caring worked his magic and BHS's profits ballooned, Green took further paydays. BHS paid £57 million of dividends in 2003 and £200 million in 2004 – the latter funded by new borrowings from Barclays Capital based on its improving performance. The total came to £423 million. With their 73 per cent stake, Green's family received payouts of £308 million. Caring took

£93 million, and Hunter and Saunders shared the remaining £22 million. Green's family and Hunter also received £136 million of tax-free rental income via Carmen, having cranked up the rent BHS paid for the ten properties by 20 per cent. The £9.5 million Tacomer bond interest, £308 million of dividends and £102 million share of the Carmen rent took the Green family's haul from BHS to almost £420 million. Considering he had risked no money of his own, it wasn't bad – and there was a lot more to come.

During this period, journalists who admired Green's turnaround of BHS were rewarded with expansive interviews and tours of its flagship store on Oxford Street. The few who tried to question his apparent retailing alchemy were warned off with furious outbursts. In 2003, *The Guardian* asked Ian Griffiths, a chartered accountant and former City editor of *The Independent*, to scrutinize BHS's finances and see if it was really worth £1 billion. Over the course of several days, Green called Griffiths 'some dickhead, ex-*Independent* journalist that can't read' and ranted, 'For fuck's sake. Jesus Christ. Robin Saunders and Chris Coles [of Barclays Capital] are on my board. Allan Leighton is my chairman. I've got a fucking audit committee that I am not on. And Ian Griffiths, some old cunt from *The Independent*, knows more than all these people.' Green claimed *The Guardian* was insinuating that BHS's profits were 'fictitious'. The encounter reached its nadir when Green said of *The Guardian*'s financial editor, Paul Murphy, 'He can't read English. Mind you, he is a fucking Irishman.'

The Guardian ran his comments verbatim on its front page. The Irish Centre accused Green of 'a truly deplorable piece of racism that is breath-taking in its arrogance'. He was forced to apologize to the Irish community. 'It was said in the heat of the moment,' Green insisted, adding that 'some of my best friends are Irish'. He listed Michael Smurfit, Dermot Desmond and J. P. McManus – all multi-millionaire members of the country's business elite.

The Guardian's attempts to penetrate BHS's accounts annoyed Green, but questions about Richard Caring touched a particularly raw nerve. Chris Blackhurst, City editor of the *Evening Standard*, once made the mistake of suggesting to Green that Caring was his business partner. 'He's not my fucking partner,' Green said. Blackhurst, a plump, bald man with glasses, had lunch with Caring at Harry's Bar in Mayfair shortly afterwards. The waiter brought over a boiled egg with spectacles drawn on in black felt-tip. Caring was bemused. 'It's from your special friend, sir,' the waiter told him. Caring asked who exactly that might be. 'Mr Green, sir,' the waiter said. Blackhurst muttered, 'It's a warning.'

Those who probed deeper received a less humorous response. In August 2002, Robert Winnett, an investigative journalist on the *Sunday Times*, received a credible tip that Richard Caring held a secret stake in BHS. The implication was that, by supplying clothes to BHS at below-market prices, he was helping to drive up its valuation, allowing Green to borrow more money and pay bigger dividends, which they shared offshore. Winnett's source pointed out that Caring and Green also jointly owned Whistles, the women's fashion chain. On 19 September 2002, Winnett and a colleague knocked on the door of an accountant they believed was involved with BHS. When Green realized what was afoot, he went nuclear.

He called Winnett that evening. 'It's really lucky your name's Robert, because the next name on my phone is Rupert,' he snarled, referring to Murdoch, the *Sunday Times'* ultimate owner. He said that suggestions of Caring's ownership were 'bollocks' and threatened to smash Winnett in the face with a baseball bat. Next he called Rory Godson, the *Sunday Times'* business editor, who was emerging from a theatre in the West End. 'Sober up, Paddy,' Green growled at the Irishman. 'Who is this fucking cunt, Rob Winnett?' Godson told him, 'Philip, you're lucky it's me you're speaking to and not John Witherow [the *Sunday Times'* editor at the time].'

The next day, Green faxed a long, garbled letter to Godson. He was clearly still furious. It began, 'I have been in business some 25 years and experienced along the way some rather extraordinary things none more so than what happened yesterday. I am still trying to tell myself that last night was all a dream, but sadly it was not.' Green said he had tried to forge 'a good open and fun working relationship' with Godson 'built on trust, honesty and friendship'. 'Taking the situation I have laid out, it is incomprehensible that two journalists from your newspaper could therefore doorstep some-one's house last night and make some of the most vulgar and seriously damaging allegations without foundation I have ever heard,' he wrote. 'Can this journalist [Winnett] read?? Does he act on his own? Does he have someone he has to report to? Can people just phone a journalist out of the blue, make something sensational up and the actions that have taken place just happen?'

BHS's owner continued, 'Last night will live long in my memory as an act of evilness, underhanded behaviour and pure jealousy that is incomprehensible whichever way I turn it over in my head.' He said that he had gone from running a single shop in 1979 to almost 2,000 stores 'against odds of a million to one' and despite 'a system and a country . . . [that] does not encourage or like winners'. 'If I could turn the clock back three or four weeks when I was on holi-day with Tina and the kids and thought that anything like this could happen to me again I would have never taken or made another corporate move in the UK for the rest of my life,' Green said. 'I would have stayed on the beach and enjoyed the fruits of my labour.'

Green's references to evil and jealousy were interesting. Appar-ently, he thought the only motivation a journalist could have for wanting to look into his affairs was envy of his wealth. Despite the tycoon's passionate denials, Winnett continued to dig. By early 2003, he had established that Caring held at least 17 per cent of BHS through Dar Jenna in the British Virgin Islands. He had also been reliably told that Dar Jenna was controlled by John Macaulay, a finance director who was on the board of numerous Caring compa-nies including International Clothing Designs and Whistles. By then, Godson had left for Goldman Sachs and been replaced by Will Lewis, former news editor of the *Financial Times*. It fell to Lewis to confront Green by phone.

Lewis put it to Green that 'this bloke Caring' owned almost

20 per cent of BHS. 'Well, he doesn't,' Green shot back in a strained voice. 'We'll produce all the share certificates at your office after the weekend if [Winnett] wants to see them.' Green insisted that Tina was the owner of Dar Jenna and said he had never heard of John Macaulay. He warned Lewis there had been 'a big blow-up' a few months previously, and said, '[Winnett's] making accusations that we use Caring 'cos we want to inflate our profits, da-dee-da-dee-da. It's not the case.' When Lewis pushed harder on Caring, Green exploded, 'It's got nothing to do with him. It's a lot of bol-locks . . . This guy [Winnett] is going to get a smack in the mouth from me. He's getting me annoyed. If he's got a piece of paper that says on it anybody else, then fucking print it! He hasn't got a piece of paper . . . This guy's been on our case for six or nine months. I threatened to punch him in the fucking mouth last time, so I'll come down to your building and you can watch. Because the fel-low is a cunt . . . He's been on a fishing expedition for ages.'

Faced with the brick wall of Green's denials, and unable to persuade his source to provide any documents to disprove them, Winnett was forced to shelve the story. Green marked his card nonetheless. When Winnett moved from the *Sunday Times* to the *Daily Telegraph* four years later, the tycoon unsuccessfully lobbied for the newspaper to rescind his job offer.

Caring enjoyed hereditary non-domiciled tax status thanks to his father's American birthplace. Despite that, and despite the BVI addresses of the companies used to hold his 22 per cent BHS stake, he always insisted that he had paid full tax on the £93 million of dividends he banked. When I asked for clarification, his lawyers at Carter-Ruck said, 'Our client paid very substantial (and indeed all) requisite UK tax on the dividends deriving from BHS.'

Several years later, in 2015, *The Guardian* and other media outlets received a huge data leak from HSBC's Swiss private bank. Among the many stories to emerge was a *Guardian* report that Caring had withdrawn £2.25 million in cash from HSBC's Geneva office in September 2005. The intriguing point was the source of the money. Caring had arranged for £2.5 million to be transferred to Geneva from Tina Green's account in Monaco. An HSBC file note recorded, 'As we know, until now [Caring] has hesitated from holding the vast majority of his cash assets in his own name, preferring to accept the offer of Mrs Green that she holds them in trust on his behalf.' The note implied that the financial links between Green and Caring went far deeper than BHS. In fact, it was not clear where Green's fortune ended and Caring's began.

In September 2006, as he was dealing with the fallout of Jane Shepherdson's resignation from Topshop, Green was shaken by an abrupt deterioration in BHS's performance. Its pre-tax profits tumbled by two-thirds to £31 million. Green blamed his womenswear department for ordering the wrong styles – 'wrong fashions, wrong shapes, wrong sizes', he told *The Guardian* – but that didn't make sense given that its sales for the same year declined by just 3.3 per cent to £851.9 million. Perhaps more significant was the end of Richard Caring's close involvement. In 2005, Caring sold his shareholding back to Green and abandoned his office at BHS's Marylebone headquarters. The Quota King later suggested that his view on life had changed after he and his two sons survived a tsunami while scuba diving in the Maldives on Boxing Day 2004. One of his family friends thought he and Green drifted apart for a more prosaic reason. He said their original plan had been to increase BHS's profits and float it on the stock market for a huge gain, but that Green had grown greedy and come to see BHS as a 'milch cow' – a reliable machine that would pump out endless dividends. Caring was said to have become frustrated with his business partner's short-termism and walked away.

Almost overnight, Caring turned himself from a shadowy figure operating in Hong Kong's textiles undergrowth to a prolific buyer of British trophy assets. His father, Lou, had been a determined individual who learned to play as a scratch golfer in the space of a year. Lou, who lived as a Jewish man despite his Italian-American descent, played at a club in Potters Bar, Hertfordshire, in the days when Jewish people were blackballed from many of London's best courses. Lou had occasionally taken Richard to father-and-son tournaments at Wentworth, the exclusive golf club in Surrey. In May 2004, Wentworth was put up for sale by its owners, the property company Chelsfield and a group of wealthy entrepreneurs including Eddie Shah, founder of the *Today* newspaper. Caring entered a bidding war and clinched Wentworth for £130 million in October 2004 after warning his rivals – a self-made Indian hotelier called Surinder Arora and an Irish tycoon called Seán Quinn – that he would pay any price. Arora, who already owned a home on the Wentworth estate, took a minority stake in Caring's deal.

Caring bought Camden market, followed by a group of upmarket restaurants including The Ivy, Le Caprice and J Sheekey (he later half-joked that it was cheaper than paying them to run concessions in Wentworth). He added the Mayfair fish restaurant Scott's, the mid-market eateries Belgo and Strada and the London members' clubs Annabel's, George, Harry's Bar and Mark's Club. A stake in Soho House came next. Caring also co-founded the chains Côte and Bill's. Within a few years, he had spent close to half a billion pounds amassing one of the most prestigious dining empires in Europe. At least some of the money came from Tina Green. The HSBC files disclosed that £23.5 million was moved from her bank account in Monaco to help pay for Caring's acquisition of Belgo and Strada from the entrepreneur Luke Johnson.

Tina also paid for the construction of Caring's superyacht, according to a source who was closely involved in the project. Caring stipulated that *Silver Angel* should be a foot longer than the Greens' *Lionheart*, which it was – 211ft versus 210ft. Tina oversaw the decoration, fitting out the interior in black, cream and silver, with Lalique crystal glassware perched on almost every surface. When her husband inspected the results, he apparently exclaimed, 'Are these the only fucking colours you can do? It's exactly the same as our boat!'

Caring's office, on the top floor of an unremarkable building near Great Portland Street Tube station, was a cross between an art gallery and a Bond villain's lair. As he became more outwardly successful over time, he stuffed it with an impressive collection of treasures. The first sight greeting visitors was an oil painting of a cherubic David holding aloft the grey, severed head of Goliath. There were charcoal Edgar Degas sketches of ballerinas, a bar decorated with a neon Tracey Emin sign ('With you I breathe') and a giant Henry Moore sculpture of a mother and child, which Caring claimed to have bought while drunk at an auction, and which had needed to be lifted into the building through the roof terrace using a crane. There was also a Fabergé egg, a nest of gold-painted turtles and several Picassos, one of which was sometimes left leaning casually against a wall.

In 2009, Caring threw a spectacular wedding party for his son Ben, transforming the ornamental lake in the garden of his Palace of Versailles mansion in Hampstead into a floating ballroom where the Bolshoi Ballet performed scenes from Act II of *Swan Lake*. More than 400 guests – among them, Liz Hurley, Sir Michael Parkinson, Kevin Spacey and David Walliams – dined on Royal Beluga caviar from Annabel's served on plates of ice, halibut from Scott's and white chocolate spheres from Harry's Bar, finished off with chocolate truffles from Le Caprice. Green was heard muttering to fellow revellers that it was 'a waste of money'.

Green and Caring's relationship was becoming impersonal and focusing more on the financial, but their shared history occasionally drew them together. Scot Young, the property developer who had met Green through the loan shark Tony Schneider in the 1980s, went through a bitter divorce from his wife, Michelle, who accused him of secreting £400 million in a web of offshore companies and going bankrupt to avoid paying her a settlement. In 2010, it emerged that Green, Caring, Sir Tom Hunter, Harold Tillman and Stephen Kay, the Intervision video wholesaler who was involved in the Amber Day saga, had made payments totalling £1.3 million to the couple, almost £1.2 million of which had gone to help Michelle with rent and school fees for their two daughters.

Michelle alleged that her husband was using his tycoon friends as conduits to feed her crumbs from his hidden fortune. They said they were simply trying to help because she was destitute. In November 2013, Michelle was awarded a £26 million settlement, but she never saw a penny. Scot Young, who was believed to have had links to Russian organized crime as well as the Adams family in London, was found impaled on railings beneath his fourth-floor Marylebone penthouse on 8 December 2014. A coroner decided there was insufficient evidence of his mental state to rule Young's death suicide, but said that there were 'no suspicious circumstances'.

BHS's decline was not due to Caring's departure alone. Green had loaded the business with interest charges and siphoned off hundreds of millions of pounds of dividends at a time when the retail market was fundamentally changing. Amazon was making inroads into electricals and home furnishings, and George by Asda, Matalan and Primark were producing better-quality clothes at lower prices. Having been starved of investment since Green took over in 2000, BHS's stores began to show embarrassing signs of decay. Emma Matthews, who joined the Luton branch in 2002, said, 'We never really got anything new. Even the mannequins were hand-me-downs from bigger BHS stores. We had a manager who used to do everything himself, literally – screw things on the wall, get staff in to paint . . . There was an awful lot of structural issues with the roof. Water was leaking through the ceilings and we would have to clear it up. They'd get people in to look at it, the quote would be too much, they'd do a patch job and it would leak again – and we were losing stock because it was going everywhere. Nothing ever got done.'

BHS's pre-tax profits slid from £38.5 million in 2007 to £21.7 million in 2008. In 2009, as recession hit, the chain crashed to a loss of £62.1 million. It never made a profit again. Realizing he needed to take action, Green decided to fold it into Arcadia. The deal was codenamed Project Footprint. In 2009, he bought out minority BHS shareholders, including Sir Tom Hunter, for a mere £22 million and brought the department store under the umbrella of Topshop's parent company. The rationale was that it would improve BHS's finances by creating efficiencies, but in practice Green used the merger to suck out more money from the weakening company. He installed concessions for Arcadia brands such as Dorothy

Perkins, Evans and Wallis in BHS's stores, making an extra £400 million in sales for Arcadia and costing BHS about £33 million compared to the rates normal concessionaires would have paid. BHS also paid expensive management charges to Arcadia for services like accounting and HR, amounting to £75 million above the standard industry rate. The combination of bond interest, dividends, rental income, management charges and concessions took the Green family's total drawings from BHS to almost £530 million.

BHS had been a lucrative building block, but its billionaire owner was increasingly ashamed of its disintegrating stores and falling sales. And an even bigger problem was gnawing away at the back of his mind – one that would eventually come to threaten his entire empire.

9.

The Pension Problem

Dr Margaret Downes had blazed a trail in Irish business. Born in County Mayo in 1932 to a family of shopkeepers, she became the first female partner of the accountancy firm Coopers & Lybrand, which was later subsumed into PwC. She was one of the first women to sit on the board of the Bank of Ireland, and she managed the delicate balancing act of simultaneously chairing Bupa, Ireland's biggest healthcare company, and Gallaher, its biggest tobacco producer. Downes went on to serve as a trustee of the Chester Beatty library and a director of the Douglas Hyde art gallery in Dublin. She had moved through the male-dominated decades of the 1970s and 1980s with a firm manner and an upper-crust accent, but despite her early achievements she seemed to evolve into a daffier, gentler character over time. Downes happened to be chairman of BHS's pension trustees in the twilight years of her career, between 2000 and 2013. It was she who was responsible for representing the pensioners' interests to the owner, Sir Philip Green.

Green's parsimonious treatment of BHS's pension-fund members was in stark contrast to his generosity towards its shareholders, including his family. While hundreds of millions of pounds flowed offshore to BHS's owners, its two retirement schemes – one for shop-floor workers, one for senior managers – were allowed to wither on the vine. When Green took over in 2000, the pension funds showed a combined surplus of £43 million. By 2006, when Richard Caring left and BHS's performance slumped, that surplus had turned into a deficit of £73 million – on the most optimistic measure. On the most pessimistic measure, which included the cost of outsourcing the payment of benefits to an insurance company if

BHS ceased to exist, the deficit was £281.6 million. From that point on, the situation grew steadily worse.

Some of the later deterioration in BHS's pension funds could be blamed on the strange market conditions that persisted after 2009. In an attempt to jump-start the economy following the financial crisis, the Bank of England slashed interest rates to almost zero and printed money – a process known as quantitative easing. The Bank did this by creating money electronically to buy huge volumes of government bonds, known as gilts. One side-effect was that returns on gilts fell to near-zero as demand increased. Pension funds' liabilities are calculated using gilt yields – the lower the yield, the higher the liabilities – so the Bank of England's move to rescue the economy inadvertently ruined their funding positions. (Many pension funds were heavily invested in equities, and although markets rallied after 2009, the rise was generally not enough to make up the gap between assets and liabilities.) By March 2015, when Green finally offloaded BHS, the Pension Protection Fund estimated that 80 per cent of traditional retirement schemes were in the red, with a combined deficit of almost £250 billion. As well as the downward movement in gilt yields, a number of longer-running issues had contributed to the problem, such as Gordon Brown's removal of tax relief on dividends in 1997.

That said, many of BHS's woes undoubtedly resulted from the behaviour of its tycoon owner. Green extracted huge sums from the company, leaving it unable to invest in its business model and in turn make higher pension contributions. As the deficit widened inexorably over the fifteen years of his ownership, minutes of meetings charted a journey from complacency to concern and then panic – on the part of both Green and the trustees themselves.

When he took over in 2000, Green dispatched his loyal lieutenant Paul Coackley to deal with the trustees. That September, Coackley set out the company's proposed contributions to the main pension fund for shop workers. The trustees, who thanked him, were soft enough to offer Green a 'holiday' from payments into the second scheme for senior staff, saying it was so well-funded that 'no company contributions would be requested at this time'. The following month, the trustees said they were 'reasonably comfortable' with a review of the funds' assets. It didn't take long for their relaxed attitude to come back and bite them. In 2003, the surplus fell from £43 million to £28.3 million. The trustees blamed 'poor inter-valuation investment returns and the impact of the company contribution holiday', although they made a point of noting that 'the company's prospects of becoming insolvent are unlikely'.

In 2005, the trustees flagged a 'significant deterioration' in the funds' financial position. BHS's pension savings had plunged into deficit for the first time, and the trustees commented that 'a surplus no longer exists on any acceptable basis'. Coackley wrote them two letters recommending several cost-cutting measures, including closing the pension funds to new joiners and introducing cheaper versions. That November, Downes told the others that she had written to Coackley 'seeking reassurances from the company about its future commitment to the schemes'. The following March, the trustees 'speculated about requesting a cash injection from the company to help clear the deficit', and in November 2006, Downes and her colleagues confronted Coackley about the possibility of securing higher contributions from BHS to fill the shortfall. Green's functionary 'responded that the deficit was not huge in the context of the value of the business' and said he 'felt the company could do better by investing the additional money in the business'. Coackley had already vetoed the idea of putting money into escrow accounts for the funds on the basis that 'he did not feel that constraining the company's trading activities . . . was an appropriate route to follow'. He made optimistic noises about BHS's future, saying the business was 'very cash-generative, prudently managed and risk-averse'.

In 2007, after the Pensions Regulator took an interest in the growing problem, Coackley 'accepted that any unplanned dividend announcements [by Green] would not be viewed positively in this climate'. He continued to reassure the trustees that the business was 'in a good shape stock-wise' and was being run on a 'tight rein'. His tone darkened a year later, as the sub-prime crisis moved from

America to Britain and BHS's sales slid. 'The middle market is having a very tough time and we are very much "in the eye of the storm",' he told the trustees in November 2008. Coackley ominously warned of 'a challenging couple of years' ahead. Having previously talked up BHS's financial strength, he now said the company would be unable to 'sustain any increase on the current level of [pension] contributions'.

BHS's payments became the battleground between the trustees and the company. In 2009, the results of a three-yearly pension revaluation came through. They were ugly. On the most optimistic measure, known as the 'ongoing' basis, the BHS funds were £162.9 million short of being able to meet their liabilities. On the most pessimistic measure, known as the 'buyout' basis, the deficit had widened to a staggering £401.9 million. In other words, BHS's pensioners would be almost half a billion pounds out of pocket if it were to go bust the next day. Despite the grave situation, Coackley insisted on Green's behalf that the company could not 'countenance' paying more than £6.5 million a year into the two funds. In a letter, Coackley said the 'hoped-for recovery in the company's trading position had not materialized' and that the business would have to 'take serious steps to reduce expenditure wherever possible'. He urged the trustees to cut costs further by stopping the pension funds' existing members accruing further benefits. For the first time, he suggested that BHS's long-term survival was at stake.

Downes and her colleagues asked if the pension funds could take security over some of BHS's assets to give them peace of mind. Coackley said that idea would 'not find favour' with its bankers. The trustees then agreed among themselves that they were 'loathe [sic]' to accept his offer of £6.5 million a year. They noted his view that paying any more would 'jeopardize opportunities to return the business to profitability and, in all likelihood, would result in further redundancies and job cuts'. In a 'full and candid' face-to-face encounter in May 2009, Coackley said that 'if there was more money available', he would be 'happy to let the trustees have it, but the fact is there are no such surplus funds'. He described how BHS was being 'stripped to the bone' to keep costs down and said, 'The business is facing a rocky three years ahead and cannot accept any restraints or shackles.' At a subsequent meeting in June, Coackley said the financial outlook would be 'very severe' if BHS continued to trade at its current rate, and warned that 'standing still is not an option'. He told the trustees about Project Footprint, the plan to merge BHS into Arcadia. At a further meeting that month, Downes, who was growing worried, asked what would happen if BHS were to collapse in five years' time. Coackley said the future was impossible to predict, but he admitted that the worst-case scenario would not make for a 'pretty picture'. An argument raged for months over whether BHS could afford to pay more than £6.5 million a year. With the Pensions Regulator watching, the two sides eventually agreed on a recovery plan of twelve and a half years, with BHS's contributions to rise from £4.5 million a year in 2009 to £10 million a year from 2012, and by 10 per cent a year after that.

There was another battle in 2012, when the next triennial review put BHS's pension deficit at £232.5 million, or £514.5 million on a buyout basis, the most pessimistic measure. This time, the offer from Green was even less generous – and he made it personally. In October 2012, accompanied by his son, Brandon, whom he was trying to induct into the business, Green told Downes he would pay £10 million a year into the funds, and not a penny more. There would be no 10 per cent uplifts. That arbitrary figure resulted in a recovery plan of twenty-three years – an incredibly long time given the industry average of twelve years. By this point, Coackley had retired. In December, Downes sent his successor a message saying that the trustees were 'disappointed and actually quite concerned at the lack of progress and the absence of any meaningful engagement by the company/its advisers in relation to the March 2012 valuations'. The Pensions Regulator intervened more forcefully than before. It presented the trustees with a fistful of concerns, ranging from the length of the recovery plan to the drop in contributions and the deterioration of BHS's financial strength. As it turned out, events outran the lumbering watchdog.

It would have been difficult to imagine two more different organizations than Arcadia and the Pensions Regulator. Arcadia's billionaire boss worked from a black and cream office behind Oxford Street, where he hung a photo of Gordon Gekko, the 1987 film character who declared that 'greed is good', signed by Michael Douglas, the actor who portrayed him. He declined to use a computer and asked his secretary, Katie, to print out every email. The Pensions Regulator was based in a bland building near Brighton station, its office desks curved in a style described by one visitor as 'trendy civil service'. From 2015, its chief executive was Lesley Titcomb, a stern chartered accountant. Titcomb, a portly woman with wavy brown hair and glasses, was a typical member of the modern establishment. The daughter of a policeman and a priest, she had read classics at Oxford, where she was a Conservative Association contemporary of Andy Street, the future boss of John Lewis and mayor of Birmingham. She was married to the Tory MP Mark Prisk, who was minister for business and then housing in David Cameron's first government. On her desk was a mug that said 'I am silently correcting your grammar' – a leaving gift from friends at the Financial Conduct Authority, the City regulator, where she had been chief operating officer.

There are broadly two types of pension scheme: defined contribution, the newer model, where a company pays a certain percentage of an employee's salary into their retirement pot every year, and defined benefit or 'final salary', the older kind, where a company promises to pay an employee a fixed amount based on their career earnings. Defined benefit pensions are sometimes called 'gold-plated'. They are potentially far more generous than defined contribution pensions, and most companies have stopped offering them because they are so expensive to run. But there are still thousands of legacy schemes in existence, many of them carrying heavy deficits because of their huge liabilities. The two BHS funds were defined benefit. As well as more humdrum duties such as making sure smaller employers automatically enrolled staff in defined contribution schemes, the Pensions Regulator was tasked with protecting members of defined benefit funds from unscrupulous owners who might try to evade their responsibilities. Unfortunately for Green, Lesley Titcomb was determined to toughen up in this area. Over the next few years, the rotund regulator would become his nemesis.

Green had been closely involved with the BHS funds. As he had tried to interfere in the football transfer market and advise Simon Cowell on his TV contracts, so he was unable to resist telling the pension trustees how they should be investing their money – in contravention of normal practice. In June 2002, following two years of poor returns from the stock market, he ordered them to deliver 'no surprises'. That sparked several weeks of discussion among the trustees, who decided to cut back on risk by switching some of the portfolios from shares into bonds and property. Green pointed out there were 'adequate supplies of bonds available in the market' yielding 6 per cent a year (which was the pension funds' return target). He also arranged for the head of property to meet his favourite agent, Malcolm Dalgleish, who had sold off the Sears and Allders empires and helped orchestrate the fruitful BHS sale-and-leaseback.

The trustees eventually decided that Dalgleish lacked the right experience, but Green approved the selection of another property agency, Fletcher King. The following April, the tycoon introduced his contact from Barclays Capital, Chris Coles, even though he was not a pensions expert. Coles said he was 'bearish on overseas markets – particularly the US and Japan', and that he would prefer to see 'someone based in the UK managing UK stocks'. Coles' advice was questioned by one of the trustees' investment managers, Merrill Lynch. It was unusual for a company's owner to take such a granular interest in the performance of its pension funds. Green seemed to be intent on making sure they met their return target so he could keep his payments as low as possible. For their part, the trustees sought Green's approval for even the smallest changes. In May 2004, they made sure he was 'happy' with minor tweaks to the pension funds' European property investments. A nod or a shake of his head could apparently determine the movement of anything in the BHS kingdom.

Green's interventions were not always helpful. In 2006, he persuaded the trustees to place some of the BHS pension money with Goldman Sachs, his preferred investment bank. They initially planned to allocate £20 million, but Green encouraged them to put in £40 million. The trustees' minutes from November 2006 recorded that Goldman had 'got off to a poor start'. The following October, they noted that Goldman had lost 22 per cent over a three-month period and that its performance continued 'to severely worry and disappoint'. In November 2007, less than eighteen months after it had been hired, Goldman was sacked 'with immediate effect' and its allocation of BHS pension money was moved to two other investment companies.

It was obvious that Paul Coackley and Ian Allkins, the BHS executives put in charge of dealing with the pension trustees, were little more than tools through which Green exercised his will. In April 2008, Allkins relayed his boss's views on a wide range of topics, from the prospects for the Far East and emerging markets ('positive') to corporate bonds ('worthy of consideration'). Between July and August 2009, Coackley found himself unable to respond to three letters from the trustees because Green was away on his summer cruise. On occasions when the billionaire descended in person, his switch was more often set to transmit than receive. In October 2012, when he brought his son in tow and refused to pay more than £10 million a year into the gaping pension hole, he ranted about the levy placed on BHS by the Pension Protection Fund, an insurance programme paid for through a tax on 'final salary' schemes (the older type of pension that promises to pay fixed benefits based on an employee's earnings). He was 'very aggrieved' about the £2.4 million paid by BHS that year and vowed to take the PPF's calculation methodology 'to the top of the government'. Green had already unsuccessfully complained to the pensions minister, Steve Webb, about the increase to BHS's PPF levy, in a manner that Webb later described as 'rather aggressive'.

By that point, almost every light on the BHS dashboard was flashing bright red. Its pension funds were somewhere between

£232.5 million and £514.5 million in deficit, but the more immediate danger was the dramatic slump in trading. In 2010, the first year after the merger of BHS and Arcadia Group, the chain's sales fell below £800 million and it made a pre-tax loss of £7.2 million. By 2012, sales had dropped to less than £700 million and losses had rocketed to £116 million. Once the proud cornerstone of Green's empire, BHS was turning into a financial disaster – although Arcadia was pumping in tens of millions of pounds to keep it afloat and the published accounts (entirely legally) did not show anywhere near the true extent of the pension problem.

City analysts missed the extreme level of distress because BHS was sheltered within Arcadia, but it was easily visible in the stores. Jean Costello, who worked in the South Shields branch from the day it opened in November 2005, said, 'It was the lighting I noticed first. It was harder to get them to replace bulbs that went out and the shop started getting duller and duller. Then the painting had to get done by the staff. Young 'uns – sixteen-and seventeen-year-olds – aren't used to painting, and they used to make a mess of it. They cut back on the cleaning and the staff toilets didn't get cleaned properly. There was always something.'

The days when Green would beat BHS into shape and retire exhausted to Les Ambassadeurs casino for dinner were long gone. Other than the Oxford Street and Milton Keynes stores, which Tina was said to visit occasionally, Green rarely took a personal interest – and when he did, the shabbier shops were usually spruced up forty-eight hours before his arrival. The king of the high street was losing his appetite for the gritty realities of retailing. By 2012, he was more likely to be seen with the *Vogue* editor Alexandra Shulman than the journalist Jeff Randall, and he was increasingly fixated on expanding Topshop in America – a far more attractive task than turning around BHS for the second time. An old friend thought that he became 'dazzled by his own success' as he flew around the world, opening stores and rubbing shoulders with celebrities. 'It was highly damaging to what little he had in terms of understanding the environment in which he traded – by which I don't just mean his customers, but the political and social environment,' he said. 'Philip became completely detached from that.'

BHS's billionaire owner had turned down opportunities to sell out for a whacking profit in the past. Before his sidekick Terry Green resigned in 2002, he made an offer for BHS backed by PPM Ventures, a private equity firm. Philip Green initially demanded £500 million, then £550 million, then more. When Terry Green finally produced a cheque for £600 million, his boss told him, 'Actually, it's not for sale.' In 2007, before its fortunes dived, Green rejected a £700 million bid from his then chairman, Allan Leighton, who was being financed by Goldman Sachs. In 2002, greed seemed to be the driver. 'If a better offer came along, I'd think about it,' Green said. In 2007, it was more about competitiveness and pride. Green told the *Sunday Times* he had 'no intention of engaging in selling this very valuable footprint to another retailer'. Leighton left a few months later and Green bought out his shareholding for a nominal sum.

Green must have realized all too late that he had made a terrible mistake by holding on to BHS for so many years. In 2011, he and Goldman Sachs drew up a convoluted plan to get rid of all his retail brands apart from Topshop by taking over Argos in partnership with Morrisons, the supermarket chain. It would have involved Morrisons buying Argos, then Green selling his weaker brands to the enlarged group in return for an equity stake, but the idea proved too fiddly and it never went beyond the planning stage. In 2013, he flirted with a deal to sell BHS to a group of US tycoons including Jay Schottenstein, head of the clothing company American Eagle Outfitters, but the suitors demanded an indemnity on the pension funds, and he got cold feet. Green also held talks with the South African billionaire Christo Wiese, who was working with a former boss of Asda, Andy Bond. Wiese, who had been among the potential bidders for BHS before Green took it over in 2000, said they would need a 'dowry' of up to £300 million to cover the pension problem and the cost of asbestos removal. Green refused.

In public, Green put a brave face on BHS. At the November 2013 press breakfast where he humiliated his nephew with his 'I'll take the house back' jibe, the tycoon tried to draw attention away from the department store's losses by announcing a plan to start selling food at its sites. I nervously asked who would provide the products. 'We have a supply,' he said menacingly, snuffing out the question.

In private, Green was becoming desperate. He turned to one of his oldest allies in the business establishment. Neville Kahn was a balding, imposing insolvency practitioner with rectangular glasses. He had a commercial nose and a surprisingly deft social style. Kahn had known Green since 1992, when he was one of the administrators to Parkfield Entertainment, a failed video distributor whose stock of 21st Century Fox and Warner Brothers films was bought by Green's Intervision friend, Stephen Kay. By 2013, Kahn had risen to be one of the most senior figures in the London office of the accountancy firm Deloitte. The BHS pension deficit was hanging around Green's neck like a lead weight. He told Kahn that he needed to get rid of it. Deloitte started work on a radical restructuring codenamed Project Thor.

Project Thor was a plan to slash the BHS pension funds' liabilities by reducing the 20,000 members' benefits to levels only slightly higher than those offered by the Pension Protection Fund, the lifeboat that would bail them out if BHS went bust. Members with pension pots of less than £18,000 would be encouraged to take cash lump sums and forgo their future payments. Project Thor would particularly help senior staff with bigger pensions. In years gone by, BHS had been a generous employer, and some of its former bosses were drawing retirement incomes of up to £100,000 a year. The PPF imposed an annual cap of about £35,000, meaning anyone receiving more than that would have their benefits cut if BHS went under. Project Thor would involve more pain for shop workers than the top brass. It would be a tough proposal for the trustees to endorse, but Green believed he had leverage. Arcadia had pumped almost £180 million of loans into BHS to keep it on life support since 2009, partially offsetting the tycoon's bumper gains in the early years. Without Arcadia's help, BHS would collapse immediately. Deloitte put together a report warning that Green could not consider stom-aching any more losses unless the pension problem was resolved.

In January 2014, Margaret Downes stepped down as chair of the trustees. She was replaced by Chris Martin, a decent but meek man with close-cropped grey hair who had chaired other troubled schemes. Martin signalled his willingness to explore Project Thor, although he warned Deloitte that he would not be 'bumped into agreeing' anything. As so often with Green, the first sticking point was money. Deloitte, on his behalf, thought he should inject about £50 million as a one-off payment to make the restructuring work. KPMG, working for the trustees, argued that the number should be closer to £85 million. Green was adamant that he would pay no more than £50 million – and for that price, he wanted permanent closure.

That desire led to the second sticking point. In early July, Chris Martin called the Pensions Regulator to run through Project Thor. Among the first words to come from the other end of the line were 'moral hazard'. It was a technocrat's phrase that would come to bear nightmarish significance for Green. Moral hazard is financial jargon for a situation when someone is encouraged to take danger-ous risks because they know another party will pick up the pieces if it goes wrong. After the financial crisis, it was regularly applied to bankers who made wild loans in the hope of earning bonuses, knowing they would be bailed out by taxpayers' money if the worst came to the worst. In this case, the regulator was drawing a con-trast between the amount of money Green had extracted from BHS in the past and the diminished state of its two retirement schemes. If Project Thor failed and BHS went bust, he knew the funds' members would be rescued by the Pension Protection Fund.

The watchdog was acutely interested in this angle. Notes of a phone call between Chris Martin and a colleague in August 2014 recorded, 'TPR [the Pensions Regulator] stressed the importance of moral hazard provisions and said the company needs to appre-ciate this aspect is critical. In virtually the same breath, TPR referenced Arcadia's £1 billion dividend and speculated about the acquisition of Arcadia being "supported" by the ownership of

BHS – [it] also mentioned BHS was bought for £200 million and had "grown into a £1 billion business".' The regulator was keen to delve beyond the dividends Green had taken and look into areas like the management charges BHS was paying to Arcadia. Unsurprisingly, Green was sensitive about the idea. Notes of a further phone call between the trustees and their advisers said that he was 'reluctant to engage in this aspect', perhaps because 'at the end of the day Taveta [Arcadia's holding company] has loaned BHS £200 million which it has little if any prospect of recovering'. On the same call, it was said that Green had asked whether putting BHS through a form of insolvency might be an alternative to dealing with the regulator. He was told, 'No.'

Green's team, the trustees and their respective advisers continued to bat Project Thor back and forth. In August 2014, Chris Martin was informed that Green wanted to delay its launch until the New Year to concentrate on Christmas trading. At that point, the two sides were further apart than ever in their views on the amount he should inject to restructure the pension funds. Green's advisers thought it was less than £50 million. The trustees' advisers said it was more than £100 million. On 28 August, the regulator warned Green he would need to put in a significant amount – more than the pension funds would recoup if he were to tip BHS into administration and have its assets sold off. A week later, the watchdog sent a detailed letter asking for more information on the £423 million of dividends taken out by Green and his partners, plus management charges and property transactions. The same day, one of Green's lieutenants emailed Neville Kahn, their lead adviser at Deloitte, telling him to put his 'pen down for [the] time being'. The following day, Green's camp told the trustees that Project Thor would be put on hold for three months. According to notes of a conference call, they gave a number of reasons, ranging from the looming Scottish independence referendum to political tension in Russia, Ukraine and the Far East, plus the more obvious need to focus on Christmas sales. A cynic might have suspected that Green's reluctance to engage with the regulator was the real reason.

Adam Goldman, Green's company secretary at Arcadia, emailed Kahn just over a month later to say that his boss was 'determined to "deal with BHS" one way or another in the first quarter of next year'. Project Thor was looking difficult and expensive. By then, two charming strangers had come into Green's life, offering to solve the problem for free.

10.

Enter the Fraudster

One overcast lunchtime in September 2011, a Rolls-Royce Phantom pulled up outside Virginia Withers' farmhouse in rural Somerset. An overweight, ruddy-cheeked man in a navy jacket and shiny shoes clambered out and gave her a warm handshake. Paul Sutton was a friend of Virginia's ex-husband, Dick Withers. Virginia and Dick, both pig farmers who had gone into racehorse breeding, had been childhood sweethearts, and they had remained on good terms despite separating twenty years earlier. The previous year, Dick Withers had met Paul Sutton through a plan to redevelop a stud farm in Newmarket, near Cambridge. Sutton had presented himself as a Monaco-based millionaire who was experiencing short-term cash-flow problems following a tax investigation. The stud-farm idea had fallen through because they failed to raise enough money, but Sutton wanted to pitch a new investment.

As Virginia prepared a beef casserole in the kitchen, Sutton described Snoozebox, a pop-up hotel operator that provided temporary accommodation for music festivals and sporting events using stackable freight containers as rooms, complete with hot and cold running water and free Wi-Fi. Snoozebox had been set up by Robert Breare, a shambolic serial entrepreneur with a magnetic personality, and its president was David Coulthard, a former Formula One racing driver. Coulthard had arranged for the company to erect forty rooms at Silverstone for the British Grand Prix that summer. Sutton said he was helping Snoozebox to raise a round of private funding ahead of a potential stock market float. With his East End stockbroker's patter, gold watch and neat white hair, Sutton looked plausible. Virginia thought he was 'very smart and sort of sounded as if he knew what he was doing'. To Dick, he was 'very, very nice, but also very persuasive'. Over the next week, Sutton bombarded the pair with calls, urging them to invest. Virginia and Dick were in their sixties, and they were concerned about the risk, but Sutton promised that they would receive three times their money back within three years.

Virginia had already drawn down £100,000 against the value of her farmhouse through an equity release scheme in anticipation of the abortive stud-farm plan. Sutton asked her to hand over £75,000 for Snoozebox. In the early hours of the morning allotted for one of his assistants to drive down and oversee the bank transfer, Virginia panicked and called Dick to tell him she had a bad feeling about it. Dick spoke to Sutton, then rang back at 2.30 a.m. to soothe her doubts. Sutton's brother-in-law, Neil Burns, collected the money and gave Virginia a handwritten statement guaranteeing repayments of £1,100 a month. He asked her to sign a non-disclosure agreement to keep the deal confidential. Dick then sold his 115-acre farm overlooking the Blackdown Hills and sent Sutton the £600,000 proceeds, followed by a further £250,000, including a lump sum from his pension. Two of their friends, a vegetable farmer called Richard Clarke and a professional footballer called Scott Rogers, also invested £50,000 between them. Sutton said that all their stakes in Snoozebox would be held by his intermediary company, B52 Investments. He distributed home-made B52 share certificates.

Over the next two years, Virginia received sporadic repayments totalling about £15,000. Then the money stopped. She sent Sutton a series of increasingly desperate letters, which he mostly ignored. She sold antique furniture and jewellery to meet her mortgage payments, until she was finally forced to sell her four-bedroom farmhouse, along with its twenty stables and sixteen acres of land. Luckily, Virginia was able to buy a smaller property with help from her son. Dick lost almost everything. Financially ruined, he ended up living in a caravan in Devon. At the time of writing, HM Revenue & Customs was preparing to make him bankrupt over an unpaid capital-gains tax bill relating to the sale of his farm, and he was contemplating putting down some of his remaining horses because he could not afford to keep them. Clarke and Rogers also lost most of their money, although they were young enough to shrug it off.

Unfortunately for the Withers and their friends, Sutton was a convicted fraudster and one of Britain's most prolific con men. He raised more than £5 million through B52 Investments, of which just £720,000 was invested in Snoozebox shares. Sutton kept his name off all the paperwork, but his fingerprints were everywhere. In 2016, one of Sutton's creditors managed to put B52 into liquidation. Edge Recovery, the firm of insolvency practitioners appointed to comb through its records, reported 'major concerns' with the way the company had been run. Edge said the entire £5.3 million invested into B52 had flowed out again, with Sutton and his brother-in-law Neil Burns receiving 'a large amount of money for what appears to be personal expenditure'. Among other things, investors' cash had been used to buy an Aston Martin, a Fiat and a Maserati – all of which were missing. Edge said, 'Although large amounts appeared to be utilized by Mr Burns and Mr Sutton, both of these parties have since been made bankrupt. Accordingly, any recovery of monies from these parties would not be possible.' The firm added that B52's shares in Snoozebox had been transferred – apparently for free – to a number of people, some of whom were connected to Sutton and Burns. The liquidator's report suggested that Burns, through his association with Sutton, had serious questions to answer.

In any case, Snoozebox turned into a disaster. Robert Breare had come up with the idea after being caught short in the middle of the night during an uncomfortable camping trip to the Le Mans 24 Hours motor race. According to one of Breare's family, 'the awful Mr Paul Sutton' inveigled his way into a shareholding early on. 'Robert hit very bad times at one stage, and every now and again [Sutton] would slip Robert an envelope of money,' she said. After Snoozebox was listed on the stock market in April 2012, the shares initially shot up as Breare gave effusive interviews suggesting that its containers could one day be helicoptered to the front line by the

Ministry of Defence. The price crashed in April 2013 when problems emerged with a contract to accommodate security staff for the London Olympics, and Breare, who once declared that he wanted to 'drive a Ferrari like the next person', was ousted in May. Two months later, he was found dead at home in Ascot by his ex-wife, Susie. Breare, who was severely diabetic, had suffered a massive heart attack. He was just sixty. Snoozebox limped along until it went into administration in 2017.

Virginia Withers was stoic and sturdy. She had almost died at the age of forty-two when a racehorse suddenly reared up and kicked her in the face. She lost sight in one eye, where a fragment of bone pierced the optic nerve and caused a haemorrhage, and she spent fifteen days on life support before undergoing a nine-hour operation to save the other. Despite the heartbreak of Sutton and B52, she saw herself as 'lucky to be alive'. B52's other victims ranged from an insurance broker to a group of single mothers, and not all were able to be so philosophical. Madeleine Legwinski, who was divorced from the former Ipswich Town and Fulham midfielder Sylvain Legwinski, invested a total of £550,000 after meeting Sutton's girlfriend, Nicola Tarrant, outside the gates of Hill House, a private prep school in Knightsbridge where their children were enrolled. Legwinski thought Tarrant was 'a beautiful, very charming woman'. She said that after her divorce settlement came through, Sutton stood in the kitchen of her home in Chelsea and declared, 'I'm going to make you a deal because you're family, and we love you and the kids.' Sutton promised she would get back three times her investment and that the interest would cover her rent and her two sons' school fees.

Like the Withers and their friends, Legwinski received homemade share certificates for B52 rather than Snoozebox. Like Virginia, she saw her repayments dry up without explanation after a couple of years, leaving her in a state of constant financial panic. When Legwinski challenged Sutton and Tarrant over her investment, they blamed Robert Breare and Snoozebox's poor performance, although in reality most of her money had been used to fund their opulent lifestyle. A letter from B52 said, 'The share price collapse was a shock to all of us and the price now sits at circa 10p per share, creating a loss for everybody. None of this was our fault and we were ignorant of any issues with the business until Robert Breare told us at the eleventh hour, which is all public knowledge.' It went on to suggest that Legwinski was actually in debt to B52 because of the share price fall. However, it said, 'As you are a friend, the intention is still to get you a return on your money.' With hindsight, Legwinski said, 'They didn't take my life, but they took everything my boys could have had. I look back today, I'm sitting here on my own and it's like a different life for me. It's like living in a nightmare.'

Sutton was a bizarre character. He was capable of spontaneous acts of kindness, such as when he drove one of his girlfriend's sisters around pharmacies in London for hours to find the right medication for her mastitis, but he could also be utterly cold and ruthless. Wherever he was, asleep or awake, he liked to have the TV or radio crackling in the background, unable to spend time alone with his thoughts. He struggled to relax and was prone to attacks of obsessive compulsive disorder that would compel him to rush around a house unplugging electrical items and throwing away brand-new phone chargers. His life followed a long trail of destruction and dishonesty that led him, through a strange twist of fortune, to Sir Philip Green.

Paul Sutton's early years are shrouded in mystery. According to his birth certificate, he was born in Barking hospital on 30 August 1956, to Richard, a stockbroker, and his wife, Bessie. The family lived in a small, shabby house on Kempton Road in East Ham. Some of Sutton's business acquaintances thought he followed his father into the City and became a successful commodities trader, working in London and New York before retiring to Monaco as a millionaire while still in his twenties. Others said he was never more than an East End wide boy. According to a former employee, he was 'always looking for acceptance' from his parents. 'If there was a deal done, no matter how small or stupid, his dad had to know,' the acquaintance said.

The first indisputable record of Sutton's activities is a High Court judgment in a case between Conister Trust, an outfit on the Isle of Man specializing in vehicle finance, and London Trust Bank, a small corporate lender. In late 1993, a Barclays bank manager on the Isle of Man made an 'informal approach' to the boss of Conister to say that his friend Paul Sutton wanted to buy a rental company there, Cleveland Car Hire. Sutton, who was looking for finance, sent Conister a business plan and an 'extravagant' CV mentioning multimillion-pound property deals in Paris and New York, ownership of land near Deauville in Normandy and a stud farm. When Conister asked Sutton to demonstrate that he could handle a loan of £500,000, he provided a reference from someone called Terry Riches at London Trust Bank. Riches wrote, 'We feel he would not enter into any business arrangement he could not see his way clear to fulfil and therefore we believe he can be considered good for the amount mentioned.'

Conister went ahead and lent Sutton a total of £470,000 over the course of a year. The judge said that, within months, 'both Mr Sutton's personal account and the company account were beset by dishonoured cheques', and towards the summer of 1994 'arrears of instalments were beginning to mount up'. Conister pulled the plug, appointing receivers from KPMG Peat Marwick. Their report made for 'disturbing reading'. 'Payments from Cleveland funds totalling £371,480 had been traced to Mr Sutton, his relatives or friends,' the judge wrote. 'A further £399,671 was unidentified spending, and included large cash withdrawals. A total of £771,157 had gone missing.' The receivers found seventy cars, although Sutton had pledged more than a hundred as security to two other lenders. As a result, Conister's loss was 'almost total'.

It transpired that Sutton had been made bankrupt in 1982 at the age of twenty-five. He had not been discharged for at least a decade because of his 'non-compliance' with the rules, meaning he was bankrupt for the entire time he was running Cleveland. The judge said it was 'significant' that Terry Riches received a free Alfa Romeo Lusso TS2.0 in November 1993, the same month that Conister approved its loans to Sutton. 'To put it at its lowest, Mr Riches was not acting in the best interests of his employers, LTB,' he wrote. Riches later went to work for Sutton.

Sutton's next known escapade was a strange property deal in Paris. In July 1995, he and an Irish business partner bought the head-quarters of the industrial group Bouygues for 30 million francs (£4 million at the time) – although the seller, a company called SBT Immobilier, had paid 180 million francs for it less than two years earlier. Sutton's associate, Sam MacCormick, had a relationship with Anglo Irish Bank, which agreed to lend them 46 million francs. As part of the deal, they paid 7 million francs to a company based in Liechtenstein called Minar Establishment, which had been granted an option over the building by SBT. Sutton and MacCor-mick ran the property through a company called Clamart III, which went bust in 1997 after it stopped paying bills. The Tribunal de Commerce in Nanterre, north-west Paris, accused Sutton of stripping Clamart III's assets before it collapsed by taking 3.6 million francs in personal expenses and making Clamart III pay for work on the yacht he co-owned with MacCormick, *Leave Me Alone*.

Three judges found Sutton guilty of corporate negligence and misusing company assets, and said he had 'acted with a particular dishonesty'. The court fined him 8 million francs and made him bankrupt for fifteen years. MacCormick was banned from running any company in France for eight years. Two years later, Nanterre's Tribunal de Grande Instance convicted Sutton of further charges of abusing company assets and corporate theft. This time, he was sen-tenced to three years in prison to reflect 'the nature and seriousness of the facts'. Sutton did not turn up to the hearing. A private inves-tigator's report commissioned by one of his creditors said that he fled Monaco in 2001, before the judgment was made public, leaving €20,000 in unpaid rent (£13,300 at the time). The investigator's report said he had lived in Le Formentor, Sir Philip Green's family home, and Le Roccabella, where Green would later take a pent-house. Sutton's ex-wife stayed behind with their two daughters, whom he liked to call 'the ladies'.

Sutton was a deal machine. 'He couldn't go on holiday and lie there for two weeks, having a good time,' said one of his girlfriend's sisters. 'It always had to be work. He had to have a project and be on the phone. He absolutely hates Christmas because no one's available on the phone. Hates the weekend.' A separate private investigator's report commissioned by another creditor listed the boggling collection of assets Sutton bought using bank loans between the late 1990s and the late 2000s, ranging from garages and petrol stations to property developments around the world. A former employee of the accountancy firm PwC's Bermuda office, who was persuaded to join Sutton's team, told one of the investigators, 'In the five years I worked for him, I spent the first two and a half pretty busy, trying to push his deals through, but the last two and a half were spent spinning my wheels. I had caught onto the fact the guy is smoke and mirrors – and smoke and mirrors only. There is nothing behind the façade. He spends his whole time trying to raise money – and everything he owns is either on 100 per cent financing, or as close to that as possible.'

In 2002, while the fallout from his Parisian deal was still ongoing, Sutton was introduced to James Broughton, one of the sons of Lord and Lady Fairhaven, owners of a 2,000-acre estate called Kirtling near Newmarket. James had inherited a parcel of land north-east of Bury St Edmunds in Suffolk, and Sutton helped him negotiate the sale of an option to the renowned housebuilder Berkeley Group, which wanted to build 1,250 homes. Impressed, James took Sutton for afternoon tea with his parents at Anglesey Abbey, the family's stately home. It was an invitation he came to regret bitterly. Sutton arrived in a Rolls-Royce and bowled over Lady Fairhaven with his easy charm and reassuring manner. She opened up about their financial problems. Kirtling was a classic aristocratic estate, built around a sixteenth-century tower with ornate gardens, and the Fairhavens had the classic aristocratic conundrum: they were asset-rich but cash-poor. In the past, the family had been forced to bridge the gap between income and outgoings by selling properties, which shrank their estate and created capital-gains liabilities. Sutton had a solution. He said the Fairhavens should borrow against the value of their estate from their bank, Hoare & Co., and invest the money in his projects, which would produce a guaranteed annual return of 18–20 per cent.

Sutton became the Fairhavens' trusted adviser. In November 2003, six months after that fateful Sunday meeting, they gave him their precious Blue Book, which contained sensitive details of all their financial affairs. Over the next four years, Sutton persuaded Lord and Lady Fairhaven to raise £8 million and send the money to various companies under his control, often with minimal paperwork. As well as borrowing from Hoares, they sold their beloved farm in New South Wales. Another of the Fairhavens' sons, Henry Broughton, had been to Cass Business School in north London and wanted to become a property developer. He began working as Sutton's assistant, driving him around and listening to his tales of the big time. At first, Henry was star-struck as they flew to Monaco and the Caribbean to negotiate deals. One of Sutton's grand ideas was a hare-brained scheme to redevelop a hotel in St Lucia, the Caribbean Jewel, into a $1 billion Monaco-style resort. Henry smelled a rat in 2008 when he heard that Sutton had stopped paying the labourers. When the Fairhavens investigated their investments with Sutton properly for the first time, the house of cards tumbled and he disappeared. They sued the law firm Wilsons for negligence, accusing their solicitors of failing to protect them from a 'fraudster' who had abused the 'trust and confidence reposed in him'. The Fairhavens settled out of court in 2009, recouping almost 90 per cent of their losses from Wilsons. Sutton escaped from the wreckage and tiptoed away to do his next deal.

There was more in the same vein. The billionaire brothers David and Simon Reuben sued Sutton over an outstanding loan to one of his service station companies, Anglo Petroleum, which he had bought from the Spanish energy giant Repsol for £1. They were awarded £4 million damages after a seven-year battle, but Sutton never paid. By that point, Anglo Petroleum was in receivership and the Reubens were unable to find him to serve bankruptcy papers.

There was also a fiasco with the former boss of Rover cars, Kevin Morley, who accused Sutton of agreeing to buy his yacht for £1 million, then sailing away without paying. 'He conned me into thinking he had money to pay me for my boat,' Morley told the *Sunday Times* in May 2009. 'He didn't have the funds, and even if he did he had no intention of paying.' Sutton's solicitors, Stockler Brunton, insisted that Morley had been given a £100,000 deposit and said a dispute had arisen over the boat's condition. Sutton changed its name from *Golden Horizon* to *Elephant Walk* and had it refitted, but he neglected to pay the boatyard in Gibraltar. Morley eventually received £650,000 after the yacht was seized and auctioned by the French courts.

By 2013, Sutton had angered an incredible number of investors. Under pressure from some of his savvier B52 clients, who were worried about the share price slump at Snoozebox, he began to cast around for new ideas. Sutton and his cronies initially came up with Containasuite, a cheap knock-off of Snoozebox. They drafted a glossy thirty-two-page PowerPoint presentation for potential backers, promising there would be high demand for its pop-up hotel rooms from the oil and gas sectors and listing a set of fanciful forecasts predicting pre-tax profits of £28.7 million by June 2015. Then, just when he was in need of a shinier bauble to placate his critics, life dropped one of its funny opportunities into Sutton's lap.

Robin Saunders, the American banker who had helped Green buy BHS, had seen her career at WestLB burn brilliantly but briefly. After its headline-grabbing bond issue for Formula One in 1999, her department had gone on a spree. Saunders, a former cheerleader who still found time to take hip-hop dance classes, was a natural beacon for publicity. In June 2002, she held a three-day party in Florence for her 40th birthday at a cost of £400,000, with an 'Italian medieval' dress code. She was also attracted to high-profile deals. WestLB bought the Pubmaster group, backed a management buyout of the Whyte & Mackay whisky company, financed the redevelopment of Wembley stadium and led a syndicate that took over Odeon cinemas. Saunders' aggressive approach put her into competition with Guy Hands, a curly haired whizz-kid who was engineering deals at the Japanese bank Nomura, and it transformed WestLB's financial performance. Despite the mild embarrassment of failed bids for the Wolverhampton & Dudley brewery group and the rail network operator Railtrack, at the end of 2002 Saunders' bosses in Germany decided to put €5 billion (£3.1 billion at the time) behind her 'principal finance' division, as it was by then known, based on a recommendation from the management consultancy McKinsey.

Saunders' downfall was precipitous. In the spring of 2003, one of her early deals unravelled. WestLB had organized a bond issue for the TV rental business Box Clever secured against customers' future payments, but the advent of cheap flat-screen TVs destroyed the rental market almost overnight. WestLB suffered a massive write-down, which contributed to a €1.7 billion pre-tax loss in May 2003. BaFin, the German financial regulator, launched an initial investigation into the Box Clever deal, followed by a second into the personal stakes Saunders and her colleagues had taken in companies such as BHS. Saunders found herself splashed across the tabloids as well as the broadsheets when the wife of Marco Pierre White, the alpha-male chef, discovered a string of text messages from her on his phone and announced to his entire contacts book, 'Marco Pierre White has left his wife and three children for Robin Saunders.' (Pierre White, Saunders and her husband, Matthew Roeser, all denied there was anything more than a friendship.) A former colleague said that Saunders started coming into work in dark glasses, looking 'as thin as a sparrow'. It was all too much for her state-owned bank's bosses, who were being savaged by local politicians for risking taxpayers' money on trophy foreign deals. WestLB decided to close her department. By the end of the year, she was gone.

Saunders reappeared six months later with a low-profile advisory firm, Clearbrook Capital, and from then on she stayed out of the limelight. In late January 2013, a mutual contact introduced her to Paul Sutton. Sutton told Saunders that he wanted to merge a temporary power company with Snoozebox. Saunders was uninterested, but Sutton produced a letter stating that he had £400 million on deposit in Monaco, so she agreed to keep him in mind for any other deals that might come up. They became friendly enough for Sutton to start renting desk space for his small team at Clearbrook's offices on Grosvenor Street in Mayfair.

Saunders and Sir Philip Green had begun to drift apart even before her exit from WestLB. They had been fellow travellers for a short time in the debt-fuelled takeover years of the early 2000s, but Saunders had become uncomfortable with the way he routinely reduced other bankers to tears. She was also aware that rival billionaires would tease Green about her, saying that he had only made money because of her generosity. Saunders knew that the insecure tycoon would badmouth her in return, unable to resist rising to the bait. Nevertheless, Green still called for the occasional chat. A few months after Sutton arrived, Saunders happened to see the Topshop boss for one of their infrequent coffees. Green mentioned how much he would love to get rid of BHS, so Saunders suggested a meeting with her new millionaire tenant. Green apparently replied, 'All right, let's do that.'

In mid-April 2013, Saunders shepherded Sutton into Arcadia Group's headquarters on Berners Street, off Oxford Street. Sutton was in no way intimidated by the prospect of meeting the king of the high street. In fact, with their Estuary accents and voluminous bellies, he and Green seemed like long-lost brothers. According to someone familiar with the conversation that ensued, they 'got on like a house on fire'. As the two men chatted away, Sutton boasted that he was about to buy a $25 million yacht. Green offered Tina's services as an interior decorator. The meeting went on for an hour, and they parted on warm terms. Saunders lost touch with Sutton soon afterwards as Clearbrook moved out of its offices on Grosvenor Street, leaving him behind, but a spark had been struck. A chain of events had been set in motion that would eventually bring devastating consequences – both for BHS's staff and for Green.

According to Sutton, he and Green spoke by phone two weeks

after that meeting, then sat down again for a shorter session. Sutton said, 'Look, I can put together some people to have a look at it.' Green told him, 'Fine, carry on.' Sutton claimed that Green promised to resolve the deficit in the pension funds himself with the words, 'I'll take care of that.'

Sutton concocted a rudimentary takeover codenamed Project Albion. His first forty-nine-page business plan, apparently produced using information provided by Arcadia and material scraped from the internet, said his company, Swissrock Holdings, would 'acquire 100 per cent of the share capital of Albion Group [BHS]'. It said that Peter Graf, the former boss of a Swiss clothing retailer, Charles Vögele, would be chief executive, and it noted the possibility of raising £100 million from BHS's property portfolio. Green engaged with Sutton even while he dismissed approaches from far more respectable suitors like Jay Schottenstein, the head of American Eagle Outfitters, and Christo Wiese, the South African billionaire. In fairness to Green, he was under the impression that Sutton had £400 million in the bank, although he clearly didn't try very hard to verify the claim. Sutton was not bothered about the pension funds or the need for a dowry: he was just desperate for a deal. The convicted fraudster made sure that news of his talks with Green percolated through his network of investors to give them hope of recovering their money. Virginia Withers, the farmer who was persuaded to put £75,000 into B52, said that Sutton repeatedly told her he was going to buy BHS for £1 and 'strip it right out'.

In August 2013, two victims who particularly hated Sutton tried to blow up his BHS deal. They flew to Monaco and delivered a brown envelope to the concierge on the ground floor of Green's luxury apartment block, Le Roccabella. It contained a dossier on Sutton's toxic past, including his 2002 French fraud conviction. Green received it and digested the contents, but – incredibly – continued to work on a sale to Sutton. In late January 2014, Sutton went into Arcadia's headquarters to meet Green and his finance director, Paul Budge, who had replaced Paul Coackley at Green's side. They had a wide-ranging discussion about Sutton buying everything in

Green's empire other than Topshop and Topman. It was serious enough for Budge to contact PwC, an advisory firm trusted by Green, and ask one of its senior partners to begin high-level work looking at how they would separate the businesses. Steve Denison, the PwC partner in question, relayed via email to his colleagues that 'SPG may have a buyer for everything except TS/TM (an entrepreneur called Paul Sutton who has been sniffing around for a while)'.

In March, Sutton saw Budge again, this time with Neville Kahn, Green's lead contact at Deloitte. They discussed how the separated BHS and Arcadia balance sheets would look. Sutton told them he was almost ready to make a formal bid. According to an email from Green's PA, Katie O'Brien, which Sutton's team forwarded to one of his investors as proof of the impending deal, Sutton was then invited to see Green in May (although the tycoon later claimed that meeting was arranged by mistake and cancelled). Abruptly and without explanation, the talks between Sutton and Green fizzled out. The dirty dossier could not have been the sole reason: Green had been in possession of its contents for nine months. A source close to Budge suggested that Sutton had been 'discredited' by a yacht broker in Monaco, who had a chance conversation with Green. Perhaps it was also the fact that Sutton had been made bankrupt yet again, in February 2014, at Bournemouth and Poole County Court. Whatever the reason, it was unimportant. Unknown to all except Green's inner circle, a neat solution to the problem of Sutton's poisoned reputation had already presented itself.

Enter the Charlatan

The figure trudging through Mayfair towards Paul Sutton's rented mews house in December 2013 looked unimpressive to Madeleine Legwinski, the footballer's ex-wife who had put her divorce settlement into B52 Investments. Legwinski was stepping out of the front door with Sutton and his girlfriend, Nicola Tarrant, when Dominic Chappell approached in a jacket and jeans, carrying an overnight bag. A brown-haired, jowly man in his late forties, he resembled an overfed version of the actor Hugh Bonneville. 'He looked scruffy,' Legwinski said. 'I didn't pay any attention to him at all. It was not like, "Oh, wow, this is a businessman."'

As Sutton would later tell Parliament, Chappell was 'down on his uppers'. His last project of any note, a property development on the Isle of Wight called Island Harbour, had gone bust, triggering massive losses for his lender, Anglo Irish Bank. After that he had effectively been sacked from an oil-storage depot in Spain for allegedly misappropriating more than €360,000 (£300,000). Chappell had been made bankrupt at least twice. He and Sutton had first met on the Isle of Wight in 2007, although they later disagreed as to the exact circumstances. Chappell, who was trying to build luxury holiday homes around a marina on the River Medina, said that he 'didn't know him from Adam' until Sutton 'literally just turned up, wanted to buy a house, then four or five houses, then he wanted to buy the whole project. He pissed me around for a few weeks and we put him down as a timewaster.' Sutton claimed he had put down a deposit of £160,000 for some of Chappell's properties and lost the money. 'I looked at suing him, gave up and put it behind me,' he said.

Whatever the truth, Chappell repeatedly tried to get in touch with Sutton between 2010 and 2013, when he sent a string of Facebook messages to Natalie Tarrant, the sister of Sutton's girlfriend, Nicola. Chappell later said that Sutton was 'a contact, and I heard he was doing great guns [sic]'. In truth, Chappell was desperate for any kind of work. He was fighting to keep his small terraced house in Dorset from the clutches of his most recent bankruptcy trustee, and he had a wife and two young children to support. He looked up to Sutton, whose Mayfair home had a swimming pool in the basement and a Rolls-Royce parked outside. After meeting Sutton for coffee in December 2013, Chappell started working as the fraudster's dogsbody, driving him to meetings and answering his emails (like Sir Philip Green, Sutton distrusted computers). Sutton was later less than complimentary about his understudy. He said, 'He would wait . . . outside BHS or outside wherever I was, and he gradually got more and more involved with me and the team.' To Sutton, Chappell was useful at first 'as long as he could drive a car and go into meetings. With the greatest respect, he wasn't that important in what I was doing.'

Having been educated at Millfield public school in Somerset, Chappell was blessed with a more polished exterior than Sutton. He had a kind of country squire's charm and a plummy accent, but the two men's family backgrounds were not so different. Chappell's paternal grandfather was a bricklayer. His father, Joe, was a rough diamond who was born in Shepherd's Bush, west London, and grew up in Shepperton. In the early 1970s, Joe was part of a crowd of self-made businessmen who used to drink at the Peggy Bedford, a long-since-vanished pub near Heathrow airport. One of the group described him as 'a dealer in everything' and 'a ducker and a diver . . . He gave himself these airs and graces, but as far as I could see he was into all sorts of things.' Joe had property interests, and he was later said to be involved in the oil trade in Libya. He married Alexandra, the well-heeled daughter of a manager at the Jack Barclay Bentley dealership in Mayfair, and they had two sons – Dominic, born on 28 November 1966, and Damon, born on 26 June 1968.

The brothers grew up in Sunbury-on-Thames, a leafy commuter

town in Surrey. Both boys went to Millfield, but they took diverging paths. Damon went into the City and worked as a broker at the Rothschild Partnership. He developed a cocaine addiction, ran up thousands of pounds in debts and ended up in court after going on a four-day crime spree in an attempt to pay off his dealer. In July 1998, Southwark Crown Court heard how Damon had spent £13,266 on a cloned American Express credit card provided by his tormentor, including £4,800 on a watch and £1,480 on a dress from Harrods. He had apparently been caught after a suspicious shop manager called the police while he tried to buy a £2,900 Rolex. According to the *Birmingham Post & Mail*, Damon's barrister said his behaviour was 'completely out of character' and explained, 'He was a City boy leading a typical City lifestyle – staying out late, going to clubs, drinking champagne and snorting cocaine.' Damon was given a two-year suspended sentence on the condition that he promised to repay the credit-card company in full.

Dominic stuck close to Joe and tried to follow him into business. Father and son were made bankrupt together at Slough County Court in June 1992, when Dominic was twenty-five. The *London Gazette* listed his occupation as 'car salesman'. (Chappell later claimed those bankruptcies were annulled. The official receiver could not absolutely confirm that, although he said all the costs were paid and the petitioning creditors had their deposit returned.) In 1993, Chappell joined the board of his father's property company, and between 1994 and 1995 they ran a service station between Heathrow and Slough, which was later closed. Chappell was also an amateur racing driver. He took part in the Le Mans 24 Hours race four times as a factory works driver in the 1990s, and competed in Formula Two and Formula 3000 with his own team, Apache Racing. In 2001, in the wake of the first dot-com boom, Chappell tried to launch a breakaway championship that would stream live camera feeds from inside the cars to viewers. He raised £800,000, but the Interactive Sportscar Championship folded after its first race at Donington Park. A technical glitch meant there was no cockpit streaming. Almost half the cars failed to arrive, and there turned out to be no prize money.

The failure of Chappell's subsequent Isle of Wight property development, which saw Anglo Irish Bank (and ultimately Irish taxpayers) lose roughly half the £24 million it lent, was followed by the Spanish oil debacle. In 2009, Chappell and two partners bought an oil-storage depot in Cadiz out of administration through a new company called Olivia Petroleum. The facility, Istamelsa, owed about €8.5 million to creditors ranging from crew members and suppliers to social security and tax offices. Chappell and his backers planned to pay off the debts at a discount and end up with a valuable asset, free of claims. But he was pushed out in 2012 after €368,000 of allegedly unauthorized payments came to light. Internal documents showed that Chappell, a keen sailor, had spent €23,855 on the company's credit card at places such as Desty Marine and X-Yachts in Southampton. He also appeared to have sent thousands of pounds to his wife, Rebecca, an attractive blonde almost twenty years his junior. In November 2011, the company removed his power of attorney, and in April 2012, one of his partners, Stephen Rodger, emailed him, 'You cannot deny the level of your deceit as we have very clear evidence of this . . . I am sorry that this has ended in this way but you have just run yourself out of time and you have deceived Rob [the other partner] and I at every turn.'

(When the story finally came out in 2016, Chappell denied having misappropriated any funds from Istamelsa. He said the credit-card payments to yacht companies had been for 'safety gear for the dock workers – things like lifebuoys, lights, fluorescent jackets, blah blah'. He said of Rodger, 'I did a very, very good job down there and I've been fucking shafted by this fat cunt who I will severely deal with when I see him.')

By the time he arrived in 2013, Sutton's new driver barely had a better CV than his scandal-ridden boss, but Chappell was nothing if not self-confident. It ran in the family: his father had social aspirations too. Joe claimed to have been an extra in the 1976 war film *Shout at the Devil*, and he bought an obscure aristocratic title to use on business cards, calling himself 'His Excellency Count Joseph Chappell de Lys et Marino'. The Chappells pronounced their surname 'Chappelle', with more than a touch of Hyacinth Bucket, the *Keeping Up Appearances* character who insisted her last name was a homophone of 'Bouquet'. Alongside his chauffeuring duties, Sutton put Chappell in charge of developing a business plan for Containasuite, the B52 subsidiary set up to mimic Snoozebox. Soon he was doing more. 'He's a very personable person, and before we had got a long way down the road he was very much involved with the guys who were working for me,' Sutton later said. 'It just snow-balled from there.'

One of the 'guys' working with Sutton was Eddie Parladorio, a balding hard-man libel lawyer who looked like a nightclub bouncer and once dated the TV presenter Ulrika Jonsson. Parladorio had known Sutton for about a decade, and Parladorio's law firm, Manleys, had sometimes stepped in to threaten Sutton's victims with legal action when they became vocal about their losses. Sutton referred to him as 'a good chap'. Keen to be involved in the BHS takeover, Parladorio offered the use of his office near Oxford Street as a bunker. Parladorio would become the crucial thread linking Chappell to Sutton as the story unfolded.

Green told Sutton that he would need to find a well-known retailer to front the transaction, so Sutton approached LEK, a firm of management consultants. A log of meetings kept by three partners at LEK showed how Chappell gradually supplanted Sutton as the person calling the shots. The first meeting took place in June 2013, before Sutton and Chappell came together. According to LEK, Sutton came alone and 'claimed to have known the Green family for many years, having initially been involved in helping facilitate their move to Monaco'. Sutton said their children 'went to the same schools' and boasted that he 'was viewed as a safe party for Sir Philip to do business with in the context of this sensitive proposal, based on his long relationship with Lady Green and the family'. Sutton apparently also told LEK that Green was under pressure from Leonard Green & Partners, Topshop's American private equity investor, to get rid of his weaker Arcadia brands. If BHS could trade for a few years under a new owner, Sutton explained, it would absolve the Green family 'of responsibility for any future failure, and associated reputational damage'. Chappell was first introduced to LEK as Sutton's 'business associate' in February 2014. He went along to LEK's offices again in April.

By that point, Chappell and Sutton were almost equal partners. They stalked the high street like a pair of tubby vultures, looking for dying companies to feed on. In May, they tried to buy parts of Paul Simon, a furniture retailer that had gone into administration. Sutton asked Chappell to lead the bid, which failed. Sutton also urged Chappell to deploy his public-school charm on B52's disgruntled investors to dissuade them from going to the press while the BHS talks were at a tentative stage. When they received complaints from Virginia Withers, the farmer in Somerset, Chappell paid her £1,000 from a joint account with Sutton. Chappell also posted a blank cheque from his Halifax account to Withers' friends Richard Clarke and Scott Rogers, promising that they would be able to fill it in for an unbelievable amount as soon as the BHS deal closed. When Madeleine Legwinski kicked up a fuss, Chappell forwarded her an email from Green's PA, telling her: 'Conformation [sic] on the BHS deal with SPG.' He sporadically paid her children's school fees, although his cheques sometimes bounced, and he paid part of the rent on her Chelsea maisonette for a month. Chappell also put smaller payments directly into Legwinski's bank account.

Chappell later said that he made these payments because the likes of Withers and Legwinski were driving Sutton 'nuts' and he wanted to 'keep the whole show on the road', but he was distinctly less generous after he bought BHS. In September 2015, as Legwinski continued to pester him, Chappell demanded the return of more than £48,000 and ordered her to 'CEASE AND DESIST' from all contact, adding, 'Failure to do so will result in legal action.'

In January 2014, Chappell and his father set up a company called Containa Ventures. In April, they changed its name to Swiss Rock Plc – almost the exact same name as Sutton's BHS bid vehicle. Chappell and Sutton's roles in the deal were about to switch. In May, Green pulled the plug on his talks with Sutton. The convicted fraudster later blamed the envelope delivered to Green's Monaco apartment, claiming that it was part of a blackmail plot by his girl-friend's family. Chappell said it was because Topshop's boss had heard that Sutton was 'hoodwinking a lot of people that he was a big-time property player and that he had a very close relationship with Philip Green'. The end result was the same. Sutton said he took Chap-pell in to see Paul Budge, Green's finance director, and told Budge, 'I have to stand down. The whole team is there. You've met all my guys. Dominic is coordinating it and you'll be working with them.'

The fraudster stepped into the shadows and the charlatan stepped forward.

The summer of 2014 went quiet as Green and his advisers worked on Project Thor, the radical plan to restructure BHS's two pension funds. On 4 September, the Pensions Regulator demanded details of Green's BHS dividends. On 5 September, Project Thor was put on hold for three months, with the trustees given the strange mix-ture of excuses ranging from the Scottish independence referendum to geopolitics and Christmas trading. Within a fortnight of that decision, Adam Goldman, Arcadia's company secretary, gave Dom-inic Chappell a non-disclosure form to sign so he could enter talks to buy BHS. Chappell had never even been into one of its stores. 'I actually knew nothing at all about BHS,' he later told the BBC.

There was a wobble almost immediately. Paul Budge, who was leading the sale process for Green, thought that Chappell might have leaked news of the talks to a third party. They had what Chap-pell called a 'straight no BS discussion', which he followed up with an email saying, 'I was very put out that my integrity has been put in question at this early and delicate stage with you and SPG, and can ensure [sic] you of Swiss Rock Plc best intention at all times.' Budge replied, 'Thanks for this. My PA emailed to set up a time for a catch up.'

Chappell changed the takeover's codename from Project Albion to Project Harvey, but he essentially copied the business plan laid down by Sutton. An early briefing note said that his intention was to appoint the Swiss retailer Peter Graf to the board and draw on the expertise of BHS's existing management team. Through one of his father's friends, a foppish Swedish businessman in his late fifties called Lennart Henningson, Chappell met a financial advisory firm, RiverRock Securities, which agreed to act for him. Paul Sutton accompanied Chappell to the first meeting with RiverRock in October. Eddie Parladorio recruited two non-executive directors – Mark Tasker, head of the commercial department at the law firm Bates Wells Braithwaite, who happened to be a childhood friend, and Stephen Bourne, former head of corporate finance at the accountancy practice BDO Stoy Hayward. Parladorio, Tasker and Bourne agreed to negotiate huge fees from Chappell for their services, including success bonuses for completing the deal, annual salaries of £180,000 for one day a week and a free Range Rover Vogue 4.4 each. The total came to almost £1.5 million, to be paid by BHS. Bourne emailed the other two to say that it did seem 'a huge amount for three non-execs – invaluable as we are, but if you don't ask, you don't get'.

It was agreed that Tasker and Bourne would take stakes of 2.5 per cent each in the BHS bid vehicle. Parladorio would receive 5 per cent in recognition of three years' unpaid work that he had done for Sutton on various projects. A sense of camaraderie developed among the motley crew as they set out on their unlikely quest to buy BHS from the king of the high street. Tasker, a bald, mole-like lawyer, joked on email that he would like Hugh Grant to play him in the Hollywood version of their adventure. He said Parladorio would be played by Russell Brand, Bourne by Dame Judi Dench and Chappell by Russell Crowe or Dolph Lundgren '(if still alive)'.

Also in October, Chappell replaced Sutton as the main point of contact for the consultants at LEK, and in November his Swiss Rock bidding team hired the accountancy practice Grant Thornton and the law firm Olswang as further advisers. Bourne, who handled the first meeting with Grant Thornton, told Chappell on email that its lead partner, Paul Martin, was 'very excited'. Bourne said he had explained to Martin that the deal was happening 'because of your [Chappell's] relationship with PG, no competition and a desire to see the business go to good hands'. Tasker reported that David Roberts, the lead Olswang partner, was 'tingling' with excitement. On Olswang's recommendation, Swiss Rock engaged the PR firm Bell Pottinger to handle press inquiries. Bell Pottinger was tasked with developing a 'script' on Chappell's dubious background. All the advisers agreed to work on a 'contingency' basis, meaning there were no upfront fees – which was just as well, because Swiss Rock had no money.

Green made a discreet call to Mike Sherwood, who was by then joint chairman of Goldman Sachs in Europe. The tycoon told the banker he was planning to sell BHS. Perhaps sniffing trouble, or perhaps because it was simply too small, Sherwood declined to act as a formal adviser. But he offered Goldman Sachs' informal vetting services. Sherwood delegated the job to his right-hand man, Anthony Gutman, a slim, urbane investment banker with a neat salt-and-pepper beard. Paul Budge directed Chappell 'to start the process with Goldman first'. Gutman told Budge that he would 'await the call with eager anticipation!' On 24 November, Chappell emailed Budge to announce that Swiss Rock was ready to make a formal approach. Budge had been through the gruelling and ultimately fruitless process of Project Thor, and he knew how valuable it would be for an unknown buyer to carry BHS's pension nightmares away on his shoulders. At that point, Green was seriously considering putting BHS into administration as an alternative – a worst-case scenario that would have drawn immediate attention from the Pensions Regulator in terms of Green's responsibility for the funds' deficit. Budge emailed a group of colleagues, including Neville Kahn at Deloitte, 'We have a prospective Father Christmas!' From that moment, Arcadia codenamed the sale Project Rudolph.

Eddie Parladorio was suspicious of Goldman Sachs. 'My instinct remains that GS will do what they want (which will likely not suit us) and the quicker they are out of the picture the better,' he wrote in an email to the Swiss Rock team. But Stephen Bourne jotted down reassuring words from Anthony Gutman in his notebook, 'We are the gatekeepers and we are here to open the gate.' As its opening bid, Swiss Rock offered £1 for BHS, the ten Carmen properties and Marylebone House, one of the store chain's two headquarters buildings. It promised to invest £120 million by raising money secured against the property portfolio. On 12 December, Gutman warned Budge that Swiss Rock had no retail experience, that the proposal was 'lacking in detail' and that Chappell 'had a history of bankruptcy'. Budge instructed Gutman to reject the approach. But he added, 'No doubt they will be in touch!'

Chappell immediately called Gutman, who relayed the conversation to Budge via email, 'Spoke to him. Pushing v hard – saying can go faster, put more money in etc!' Chappell also sent a desperate text to Budge, saying, 'We just need a steer on what SPG wants . . . We are willing to work closely with SPG to ensure all are happy.' The rejection caused dismay inside the Swiss Rock camp, which had been labouring under the impression that Chappell had a special relationship with Green. Parladorio described the news as 'extremely disappointing'. He apportioned the blame to RiverRock and its boss, Joseph Dryer, a tubby American with slicked-back grey hair. Parladorio thought Dryer had been under-prepared before presenting the proposal to Goldman Sachs. Dryer thought Chappell had exaggerated his closeness to Green. In an email to Lennart Henningson, Dryer accused Chappell of 'changing the facts + forgetting what he has agreed to + not telling the truth'. RiverRock resigned as Swiss Rock's merchant bank on 15 December. The news was greeted with satisfaction by Parladorio, who emailed Chappell, 'Damn good riddance to the shambles / rip off clowns.'

Before Christmas 2014 melted into New Year 2015, Chappell reassured his team that Gutman had told him, 'I am here to help and guide you to ensure that we all get what we want.' He sent email after email to Gutman, promising to find £35 million of equity and £100 million of debt for BHS. Chappell had so little money he could barely afford to pay his own household bills, but he fancifully hoped the former Charles Vögele store boss, Peter Graf, would stump up the equity and cover the transaction's £5 million costs. Chappell formalized his next offer on 8 January, but Green rejected it a week later because he was unwilling to throw the ten valuable Carmen properties and BHS's Marylebone House building into the deal for free. He was also concerned about the lack of a 'creditable' (sic) retail leader. Chappell was back chasing the next day. His secretary told Budge that he was 'prepared to peruse [sic] any opportunity necessary to reach an agreement'. Budge remarked to Gutman, 'They won't go away easily!'

As he tried to turn the thumbscrews on Chappell, Green called in a favour from the *Sunday Times*. One day in late January 2015, Dominic O'Connell, the business editor, took me aside in the newsroom and explained that Green had phoned in with a scoop: after years of speculation, he was ready to put BHS up for sale. At the time, we had no inkling of the drama unfolding behind the scenes with Chappell, or the true extent of the pension problem, which was at least partly driving it. Green demanded an unusual quid pro quo: in return for the exclusive, we had to agree not to mention BHS's pension deficit. I checked the Companies House accounts. They showed a shortfall of £109.3 million – not ideal, but far from disastrous. Green's sensitivity struck me as odd, and I noted it mentally, but I wrote the story as agreed. It ran on 25 January under the headline, 'Philip Green Puts Struggling BHS Up for Sale'.

A few days earlier, unknown to us, Green had given the deal's goalposts 'a sharp eleventh-hour tug', in the words of Eddie Parladorio. Having previously said that he would 'take care' of the pension funds, BHS's seller now wanted Swiss Rock to make a contribution. He also wanted the buyers to pay millions of pounds for the Carmen properties and Marylebone House rather than receive them for free as part of the £1 purchase price. Chappell was already desperate to get his hands on BHS, and the press leak put him under new competitive pressure. It flushed out approaches from the private equity firm Sun Capital, the former Asda boss Andy Bond, a Turkish retailer called Cafer Mahiroglu and Tony Brown, a former Green lieutenant who was working with Apollo, a US hedge fund. Jason Kow, the head of a private property company called Queensgate, also expressed an interest. Chappell became frantic.

The news also caught BHS's pension trustees and the regulator on the hop. Chris Martin, the trustees' chairman, had been left thinking that Green was going to relaunch the Project Thor restructuring that month. He emailed a link of the sale story to Neville Kahn at Deloitte, asking, 'Neville – I assume that this is just press speculation?' Kahn replied that he 'knew it was under consideration' and added, 'Have to say given the losses why wouldn't he explore [it].' The Pensions Regulator chased Martin, who sent a stream of increasingly anxious messages to Kahn and Paul Budge. Green's acolytes were well aware of what was going on. 'We have started down a road,' Budge meaningfully emailed a group of colleagues ten days before the *Sunday Times* story appeared. But Martin was mostly kept in the dark as Project Rudolph hurtled forward. On the tricky issue of pensions, so too was Chappell. Green was 'adamant' that Chappell's advisers at Grant Thornton should not be allowed to look at detailed information on the pension funds, speak to the trustees or sound out the regulator. Grant Thornton observed internally that this did 'not bode well'.

Based on what they had been told by Budge, Chappell and his friends believed the pension problem would be fixable for a sum of £50 million, whereas in reality it would cost far more because the deficit had widened to an astonishing £571 million. Budge boasted to Anthony Gutman at Goldman that he 'did not enlighten them re current values', and when Chappell finally met Chris Martin, the trustees' chairman was 'surprised' that due diligence on pensions was not 'the focal point anticipated – particularly considering the schemes' funding positions'. Chappell obviously did not understand the nature of the teetering liabilities he was about to take on.

After the *Sunday Times* story, events moved at a bewildering and breakneck pace. Green was suspicious that Sutton was still lurking in the background, pulling Chappell's strings – or as Eddie Parladorio put it in an email to the group, 'floating around in our midst'.

For weeks, Parladorio had been trying to get Sutton to sign a statutory declaration promising that he would have no further involvement with BHS. Sutton finally signed it. If Green's team had looked closely, they would have noticed that his given address was a cottage in the village of Winterborne Clenston in Dorset – inside the grounds of the Grade I-listed manor house Chappell had started renting (the first six months' rent was covered by a loan from the landlord). Chappell continued to send updates marked 'For your eyes only' to ps@swissrockplc.com – an email address that looked distinctly like Sutton's – and the fraudster rang Parladorio constantly for news.

By 3 February, Chappell thought Swiss Rock was back on the front foot, and he emailed his colleagues to say the BHS deal was 'ours to loose [sic]'. Parladorio doubted they were 'getting anything even remotely approaching a straight bat from SPG and his motley crew of merry men', but as the dance carried on, both sides softened their positions. On 12 February, Chappell went in to see Green at Arcadia's offices. Until that point, 'SPG' had directed the action through his functionaries, although he and Chappell had been in constant contact over the phone, often 'going at it hammer and tongs', as Parladorio put it in an email to several of the bid team. Now Green descended from the clouds and agreed the outlines of a deal with Chappell face-to-face. Paul Budge emailed Chappell that evening, 'SPG confirmed as far as he's concerned the handshake cemented this and he's done . . . Look forward to working with you to a successful outcome.'

The document that emerged, headed 'Points of Principle', required Chappell to run BHS as a going concern for at least three years, and promised him first refusal over Arcadia's other non-Topshop brands in return. It asked Chappell to invest £10 million of new equity into BHS, although it simultaneously said that he would be allowed to buy the Marylebone House headquarters building from Green for £35 million. Marylebone House was owned directly by the Green family through a company in the British Virgin Islands, Wilton Equity. It was worth a lot more than

£35 million. Chappell had already lined up a buyer who was prepared to pay £45 million, so Green was effectively providing Chappell with £10 million of equity for free by allowing him to keep the profit. Grant Thornton referred to this internally as a 'gift'. Green had apparently dropped his two main objections to Chappell's bid: Swiss Rock still had no money and no credible retail leader. But, significantly, Chappell had agreed to take on BHS's pension liabilities.

On 26 February, Green ordered Chappell to 'lose the Swiss reference', perhaps because the newspapers were full of headlines about tax evasion following a huge leak from HSBC. Swiss Rock became Retail Acquisitions. The level of scrutiny applied to Chappell by Green's lawyers at Linklaters was captured in a handwritten note of a phone call with their opposite numbers at Olswang. Linklaters faithfully jotted down Olswang's descriptions of Chappell as an 'honest guy + entrepreneur' whose only fault was that he was an 'eternal optimist'.

Over the next fortnight – despite cries of alarm from BHS's pension trustees, the regulator and some of Chappell's own advisers – he and Green pushed the deal forward. On 6 March, Chappell threatened to walk away as a glimmering of uncertainty broke through, but Green hauled him back, then pushed him across the finishing line in a ferocious meeting that evening. The goalposts were given another sharp last-minute tug. Chappell had tried to line up £120 million of debt from a hedge fund called Farallon Capital, but he had failed. Green turned to HSBC and its head of commercial banking, Ian Stuart, an old friend whom he sometimes saw for dinner in Barbados when they were both there for the Christmas break. Green organized a £70 million loan from HSBC so Chappell could buy the Carmen property portfolio. He also promised to set up a separate £25 million HSBC overdraft for BHS. Green suddenly changed his mind about selling Marylebone House to Chappell – in typical fashion, because he thought he could get a higher price than the £45 million Chappell had obtained. Green's reversal meant that Chappell's £10 million of equity evaporated.

The tycoon said he would split the increased profit from the property with BHS's new owner at a later date. Paul Martin, Grant Thornton's lead partner, emailed a colleague, 'One of those "legendary" meetings you get in a career. Wonderful theatre. Basically put a deal together that should get done on Mon/Tues.'

Five days later, on 11 March 2015, Sir Philip Green sold BHS to Dominic Chappell. As they gathered in the boardroom on Marylebone Road, Green contemptuously turned to Chappell's lawyers from Olswang and asked, 'Why are you all here? I can fucking do this deal myself.' Eddie Parladorio wonderingly emailed two friends: 'Just to let you know we are sitting with Sir Philip Green at this moment signing off and acquiring BHS Group.' The final completion statement was handwritten on a single sheet of A4 paper. In the end, the deal was completely funded by Green. Chappell was literally buying the department store chain for £1 – although he jauntily gave Green £2, 'just so he could show a profit'.

12

Keys to the Plane

June 2000, just after the first dot-com bubble burst, should have been a daunting time to launch a web business, but Nick Robertson was not the type to fret. The great-grandson of the tailor Austin Reed had grown up in comfortable Surrey and left Canford boarding school in Dorset with three A levels (two Ds and an F). Robertson, a boozy, bantering man's man with a Cheshire Cat's grin and a love of Chelsea, had worked in advertising sales and co-founded a product placement company, 'putting cans of Pepsi on *EastEnders* and so on'. In 2000, he and his business partner, Quentin Griffiths, spun a new venture out of their interest in celebrity. 'I came across this statistic in a TV guide,' Robertson later explained. 'A lamp appeared in *Friends* and NBC got 28,000 calls or something ridiculous about where the lamp came from.' The business born from that moment of inspiration was AsSeenOnScreen, a website that connected viewers with products featured in their favourite films and TV programmes. You could type in 'Mission Impossible' or 'Pulp Fiction' and find Oakley sunglasses or Samuel L Jackson's 'Bad Mother Fucker' wallet. At first, Robertson and Griffiths hoped the brands would be prepared to pay for the publicity, but 'of course they weren't' because 'that was the early days of the internet and nobody was willing to pay anything for anybody [sic]'. Robertson owed a profound debt to the company's first buyer, Lorri Penn, who came from Topshop. Penn set him up on a blind date with her best friend, Jan, who eventually became his wife. She also guided AsSeenOnScreen towards fashion.

Asos, as the company soon became known, transformed itself from a tacky online version of *Heat* magazine, where shoppers could copy the looks of Victoria Beckham and Coleen McLoughlin, into a credible destination where mid-market brands such as Superdry and Tommy Hilfiger sat alongside Balenciaga and YSL. A self-described 'armchair sportsman' who proudly said that he owned only one suit, Robertson was an unlikely clothing tycoon, but he gave shoppers what they wanted: choice and easy delivery. 'We weren't retailers and we weren't fashion people,' Robertson told an interviewer in 2014. 'We weren't even internet builders. We were entrepreneurial and we were solving a very different problem – how do customers want to shop online? Well, they want as much choice as they can have.'

Asos was set up with less than £3 million of seed funding from Robertson's Monaco-based brother, Nigel, who had made £29 million from co-founding the online phone book Freepages, and some of Nigel's friends, including Andrew Regan, a corporate raider who once tried to break up the Co-operative Group. A little more than a year after its creation, it floated on the stock market valued at £12.3 million. In 2004, Asos turned a maiden profit and launched its own womenswear range, and in December 2005 it survived the worst fire in Europe since the Second World War when an oil depot exploded near its warehouse outside Hemel Hempstead, destroying most of that Christmas's stock (luckily, it was comprehensively insured). Asos launched online catwalk videos in 2006 and moved into an art deco former Carreras cigarette factory in Camden a year later. The pub opposite, the Lyttelton Arms, became known as the Asos Arms thanks to the stream of fashionable twentysomethings heading to the bar from 3 p.m. in the summer months, when Robertson instituted a policy of 'doss Fridays'.

Sir Philip Green told anyone who would listen that it would never work. 'Do you know how high their returns rate is?' he would scoff. 'It's 40 per cent. It'll kill them.' But in 2005, Asos poached Miss Selfridge's merchandising director, Rob Bready. A stream of others followed him from Arcadia Group. Green refused to put Topshop clothes on the Asos platform as long as the poaching continued, and Robertson refused to stop poaching. Green would ring him and shout, 'Stop nicking my cunting staff, you fucking cunt.' Robertson, who was happy to play the belligerent retailer at his own game, would tell Green to fuck off and hang up. Their rivalry was not always particularly serious. When Green heard about the Hemel Hempstead fire on one of his morning calls with the City analyst Richard 'Ratty' Ratner, he gave Robertson the name of his favourite insurance assessor to help Asos negotiate the maximum possible payout. (As well as being altruistic, Green might well have been hoping for a cut of the proceeds.)

By 2008, when the old-fashioned high street was reeling from the recession, Asos was valued at £200 million. With sales of £81 million, it was still smaller than Topshop's Oxford Street flagship store, but the website had 3.4 million monthly visitors and it was growing quickly. In 2015, the year Robertson stood down at the age of forty-seven, its sales crossed the magic £1 billion mark. By then, the business he had co-founded a decade and a half earlier was valued at more than £3 billion.

Asos was among a wave of new companies that operated without costly store estates and shop-floor staff, allowing them to offer sharper prices than their traditional rivals (Robertson estimated that Asos was 25 per cent cheaper than Topshop on comparable products). They were also able to change ranges and react to trends quicker. The leader was Amazon, founded in Seattle by the Princeton graduate and former hedge-fund analyst Jeff Bezos. Having started life as an online bookseller, Amazon morphed into a distributor of everything from car parts to pet food, pioneering cloud-computing infrastructure along the way with Amazon Web Services and producing inexpensive digital devices such as the Kindle e-reader and the Fire tablet. Like Robertson, Bezos was an entrepreneur rather than a retailer who had earned his spurs on a market stall and spent a lifetime painstakingly building contacts in the supply chain. Amazon's powerful shareholders were happy to make short-term losses in the interests of long-term market-share gains. By 2015, consumption in Britain was stagnant, so every pound spent online was a pound taken away from the high street.

Over the same period, value retailers like Matalan and Primark had become more aggressive, forcing the likes of Marks & Spencer and Next to drop their prices. Department stores such as Allders, C&A and Littlewoods had already perished under the squeeze. If Green, the king of the high street, was unable to protect BHS from these formidable new predators, how would anyone else?

On the morning of 12 March 2015, six and a half weeks after the *Sunday Times* announced BHS's impending sale, I was on a flight back to London from a conference in France. As the plane dipped down on the descent into Gatwick, my iPhone went berserk with text messages. Then it rang. 'Have you fackin' seen this?' said the grainy voice on the other end of the line. 'It's a joke. He's losing it, I reckon.' It was one of my favourite contacts, an old-school broker who knew Green well and even sounded like him. He relayed the news that was flashing up on websites everywhere: Green had sold BHS for the token sum of £1 to an unknown consortium called Retail Acquisitions. As the wheels touched onto the tarmac, a text message arrived from Dominic O'Connell, my boss at the *Sunday Times*. He had secured an exclusive interview with the tycoon that afternoon to explain the deal. 'I think he's nervous,' he said. I asked if I could come. 'Subject to negotiation!!' O'Connell replied. 'I'll let u know.'

I raced from the airport to BHS's faded headquarters on Marylebone Road, scanning the Arcadia press release along the way. It was light on detail, particularly about Retail Acquisitions, but it quoted Green as saying, 'One of my clear objectives in identifying a purchaser was ensuring their desire to take the business forward.' O'Connell was waiting outside the boardroom on the second floor, his usually inscrutable expression tight with tension. We both had the sense this was going to be an awkward encounter. After what seemed like an eternity, the double doors to the boardroom swung open and Sir Philip Green stood before us, arms outstretched, a showman's grin on his face. 'The boys!' he called out.

Green led us inside and barked to his PA for a pot of tea. BHS's boardroom was a monument to the past. There was a wall covered with yellowing newspaper cuttings celebrating his bygone glories ('Arcadia's Place in Green's Dream'; 'High Noon on the High Street'; 'King Phil'). There were framed photographs of Green receiving his knighthood and posing with Kate Moss, miniature models of his private jet and helicopter, and bookshelves lined with folders of more articles. The tycoon reached for a doughnut from a plate in the middle of the table and leaned back. Silhouetted by the pale light streaming in through a huge window, he looked like an old bull at rest. Green was about to turn sixty-three. He said he was feeling 'sort of happy-sad', but I had the feeling the balance tipped towards the former. 'I think my birthday present was a disposal as opposed to a purchase,' he said with an indulgent chuckle.

We began on a reflective note. 'Fifteen years, right?' Green remarked about his time owning BHS, in a low voice that implied we were being drawn into his confidence. 'I left school at sixteen and started work. So that's too long ago – forty-seven years ago. This has been owned for a third of my whole working life. It's a long time.' O'Connell remarked that BHS had made him wealthy. 'It wasn't about that,' Green corrected him. 'It's nice to pick things up, make them work. On the back of BHS, enabled me to do Arcadia. On the back of Arcadia, enabled me to raise the money for M&S. So I think each building block, if you like . . . You know . . . And with hindsight or foresight we'd all be doing something different, wouldn't we? Buy, sell, swap.' He nodded laconically towards the recorder on the table. 'We'll come to that further on in your tape.'

The interview was textbook Green. He descended into riddles and vagueness whenever he wanted to avoid answering questions. He meandered off constantly into politics and showbiz, boasting about his connections. There was a story about a dinner featuring Ed Miliband, the Labour leader, who was two months away from his first (and last) general election. 'He's the speechmaker, so he gets all these papers out of his pocket,' Green recounted. 'I said, "You can't make a speech without writing it all down?" He sort of looks at me. I said, "Come on, son, I'm confiscating all those notes." And I did, and to be fair he actually spoke OK.' Somehow that strayed into Green's views on the dearth of talent in the business world. He said that Tidjane Thiam, the outgoing chief executive of the Prudential, was 'the shrewdest man in this country'. 'Nice, quiet, goodbye, fuck off, I'm off to the hills,' Green said. 'Bravo. I sent him a text to say, hey' – he clapped four times – 'good for you. Tripled the share price. No big noise. You look at all these other jokers. Couldn't hold a candle to the guy, could they?'

At this point, Green was still immensely powerful. He expected interviewers to be deferential, and he repeatedly steered us away from details of the BHS deal. Dominic Chappell's name was not yet in the public domain. The only figure attached to Retail Acquisitions was its chairman, Keith Smith, a former stockbroker (and, as it later transpired, Chappell's uncle). Smith had played a walk-on role in one of the most infamous stock-market stories of the mid-2000s, when a company called Langbar collapsed in a £365 million fraud involving non-existent bank deposits in Brazil and the Netherlands. (At the time, Smith said he did not know about the wrongdoing, and he was not implicated in any subsequent investigations.) Green was hazy about the individuals operating behind Smith. 'They're people, and they've been sitting with the management for the past three weeks, four weeks, working through different scenarios,' he said. Green insisted BHS had been cleaned up in advance of the sale and that the buyers were 'not walking into a shipwreck'. 'Yesterday was D-Day,' he said, 'so I said to my team, are we buying or selling? And there was a split vote. Because when we actually saw what we were selling and the shape it was now in, it's the sort of thing I've bought all my life.'

It got more interesting when O'Connell asked about BHS's pension funds. Green turned staccato. '[The buyers] met with the chairman during the process,' he said. 'Everybody's calm. There's no dramas. But you can take any pension fund at a moment in time and crystallize what the loss could be. You know, it's only a loss if you crystallize it.'

Remembering his sensitivity about the January story, I tried to provoke him further. I asked what would it mean for his reputation if the chain were to go bust under its new owners. The question had the desired effect. The mood immediately darkened. 'Am I really going to get into that debate?' Green snapped, shooting O'Connell a warning look. 'You can say that about anything. If you buy my house and it falls down, is it my fault? As far as I'm concerned, in terms of the actions we've put in place, there's no reason they should get in trouble. Now, where they get to – I'm not the driver. If I give you my plane, right, and you tell me you're a great pilot and you crash it into the first fucking mountain, is that my fault? If you get lucky and you cross the mountain in the first fucking six months but one night you fall asleep and hit the wall, is that my fault? I know what they're getting today is 100 per cent clean. No skeletons. Tidy. Clean.'

O'Connell pointed out that newspapers might choose to see it differently. By now, Green was exasperated. 'People buy companies,' he growled. 'Some they win, some they don't. I can't have something wrapped around my neck. I can't not sell anything in case somebody gets into trouble with it. I can't take BHS back to Storehouse now, can I?'

As we left, Green's long-suffering head of PR, Tania Foster-Brown, stressed that Sunday was his birthday. 'You'll make PG happy on his big day, won't you?' she said pointedly.

There was no doubt in my mind that something was wrong. The retail analyst Richard Hyman provided an astute quote. 'So with all his skill and nous, [Green] has thrown in the towel,' he said. 'It is not a matter of finding someone with more money and management skills than Philip. This is not a turnaround. Its natural constituency no longer exists.' One of the more credible BHS suitors spurned by Green told me, '£1 is way too much for that business. It's worth about minus £300 million.' And the contact who had called as my plane landed that morning made a prophesy that reverberated in my mind for a long time. 'If he had put a proper retailer in there it would have a semblance of a chance,' he said. 'But as it is, it's hopeless. Philip Green's power base will wane from now on. If he doesn't watch it, he will be in front of a lot of people for a long time trying to explain what he's done here, because he does have a responsibility.'

There was back-slapping and celebration on both sides immediately after the deal. Paul Martin of Grant Thornton described it as a 'great result' for the accountancy firm. Having stayed up for two nights straight with their lawyers, Chappell's exhausted team went for a bottle of champagne at the Landmark hotel across the road from BHS's head office. Green called Chris Martin, chairman of the BHS pension trustees, and berated him for 'jeopardizing' the sale by telling Chappell the company's contributions might have to rise. Green then congratulated himself for having 'put the ball in the net on [my] own without twenty-seven advisers'. Tina Green was so delighted she personally gave a special bonus to Paul Budge, Arcadia's finance director, as a gesture of appreciation for the long nights he had spent away from his family. Just over a fortnight later, Anthony Gutman, the Goldman Sachs banker, sent an ingratiating email to Chappell. 'Congratulations on getting the deal done,' he said. 'You deserved it – you were consistent throughout and stuck to your word.'

The warm messages belied the chaotic way the deal had clattered through its final stages. Chappell's lack of money had started to rattle his advisers at Grant Thornton and Olswang in late February, but they decided to press ahead with their due diligence because stopping might have threatened the timing of the transaction. On 3 March, Eddie Parladorio remarked that 'the pressure on fees is becoming intense', and on 5 March, Paul Martin of Grant Thornton complained to Chappell that 'a sizeable team' had spent three weeks analysing BHS with no sign of a fee arriving. 'This has now become a point of principle and trust,' he typed. Martin warned that unless some money materialized the following morning, he would walk away. 'I am very disappointed that we have reached this position,' he added. 'It is a first for me.' The next day, with still no fee in sight, Martin warned Chappell that he would boycott an important 11 a.m. meeting unless Grant Thornton was paid. Chappell managed to whip Martin on by promising his accountancy firm an enormous success bonus a few days later. On 13 March, after the deal closed, Grant Thornton and Olswang were still waiting to be paid. Stephen Bourne, one of Chappell's non-executives, urged the others, 'We cannot pretend that this is not damaging all of our reputations . . . Things are kicking off, we don't need this grief and will be in a stronger position when this is done.'

Green had come under a different kind of pressure. Chris Martin, the trustees' chairman, had reacted badly to the initial news of a sale in January, describing it as 'not entirely consistent' with Green's previous plans. Martin chased Green's advisers throughout February. On 4 March, a few days before the sale to Chappell, the Pensions Regulator called an urgent evening meeting at BHS's Marylebone Road offices. The watchdog sent a team of five, led by Geoff Cruickshank, its head of intelligence. They wanted to know who was behind Retail Acquisitions, and they again mentioned the phrase Green dreaded – 'moral hazard'. The regulator had no power to block the deal, but Green knew it could open a retrospective investigation that would cause him a serious headache. The meeting was a disaster. In the conservative language of the regulator, it 'broke up with Sir Philip Green requesting time out to discuss matters with his advisers'. In the words of another source, the tycoon 'started screaming and shouting and stormed out'. The regulator sent Green a follow-up letter the next day, which he ignored. They had no further contact until the sale news broke.

As late as 5 March, less than a week before the Chappell deal, respectable bidders were still making approaches for BHS. Alteri Investors, an offshoot of the US hedge fund Apollo, wrote a polite letter to Green. Alteri's team included Tony Brown, Green's erstwhile lieutenant, Clem Constantine, a former head of property at M&S, and Jonathan Feldman, the brother of David Cameron's chief fundraiser, Lord Andrew Feldman. (The Feldmans were big suppliers to BHS and Arcadia through their family's textiles company, Jayroma.) Like Retail Acquisitions, Alteri offered £1, but it wanted substantial upfront funding from Arcadia to cover several years' losses and working capital. Green said no. He rushed onwards with Chappell.

Stephen Bourne captured the madness of the first few days in his notebook. At 8.30 a.m. on Thursday 12 March, the morning Retail Acquisitions' takeover was announced, the new owners had fifteen minutes of quiet with 'SPG before he started talking to staff'. They regrouped at the Landmark hotel, then returned at 10 a.m. for the 'mass chaotic arrival of all and sundry'. At 2 p.m., there was a meeting at the Landmark where Chappell tried to cut the fees for his three non-executives (they 'all resisted'). Bourne then stayed behind with BHS's incumbent management team 'to discuss [the] shambolic first day – they want to know who all these people are!' He 'left with SPG after watching him abuse [an] *FT* journalist on his mobile'.

By the second day of Chappell's ownership, Bourne was already getting worried. He noted that Chappell had immediately ordered ten new Apple Macs when there weren't even ten people in his team – making a 'terrible impression in a cash-strapped business'. Bourne complained in his notes about 'erratic behaviour', a 'cast of weird advisers swimming around' and a 'lack of clarity on all sorts of issues'. Over the weekend, he told Chappell his priority should be 'to recover from [the] bad impression made so far' and warned him that 'everything he says or does is being watched intensely'. Chappell was an hour late for their 8.30 a.m. meeting the following Monday. 'I don't think I can work with this guy for long,' Bourne wrote.

The theme developed as the second week progressed. Retail Acquisitions was shaken by a couple of negative press stories – first by a 'disastrous' interview with its chairman, Keith Smith, who told the *Sunday Telegraph* that 'it will be at least two years before we will see it coming back to profit', then by an 'appalling' *Property Week* article about potential store closures. Chappell reacted badly. Bourne noted that Retail Acquisitions' boss 'lost it' on a conference call with Bell Pottinger, his PR firm, insisting that 'he was giving no information and we should reply to nothing'. Chappell stormed out of the room. Bourne stayed behind and 'calmed things'.

The other pressing issue was credit insurance. Suppliers to retail companies like to insure their goods in the months between accepting order and receiving payment in case the retailer goes bust. In very risky cases, credit insurers refuse to provide cover for a particular company's suppliers. Two of the biggest insurers, Coface and Euler Hermes, had pulled cover for BHS in the run-up to Green's £1 sale, meaning that a number of suppliers were refusing to ship products without upfront payment. A company can limp on in that situation, but having to pay for goods in advance puts severe strain on its cash flow – and BHS's finances were already stretched. Chappell had been under the impression that Green would use his clout to bring the credit insurance back online – if necessary, by providing some kind of bond – but according to Bourne's notepad, it was 'all [Dominic's] problem now' and Green had 'walked away'. The tycoon also seemed to be insisting that Chappell put up some of BHS's best properties, including its Oxford Street store, as security for the HSBC overdraft he was arranging. That meant Retail Acquisitions would be unable to use them to obtain any other loans. The billionaire seemed to be keeping Chappell on as tight a leash as possible.

Instead of focusing on these problems, Chappell appeared to be 'desperate' to get his hands on cash to pay unspecified 'costs'. He did not seem to understand the restrictions Green was placing on him. Bourne described watching Chappell 'cheerfully' announce that he had agreed to give HSBC security over BHS's Oxford Street flagship store, assuring the room that Green would 'sort out' HSBC when they needed to sell the property. 'Everyone looked incredulous,' Bourne wrote. 'I asked him what he meant exactly. He babbled the same line.'

Bourne was an experienced corporate financier. On Friday 20 March, eight days after the champagne celebration in the Landmark hotel, he jotted down his multiplying doubts about the deal. He went through a list of troubling facts and concluded, '[Green] knows [Dominic] needs the properties, just like he knows BHS needs credit insurance. Makes no sense.'

Bourne asked himself, 'Is it all a set-up? But who gains?'

★

The seeds of an epic row between Sir Philip Green and BHS's new owners had already been sown. The tycoon's restrictive attitude towards credit insurance and the property portfolio were the first visible shoots, but the roots went back to the point of the sale. Green's decision to hold on to Marylebone House rather than sell it cheaply to Retail Acquisitions had stripped Chappell's team of the £10 million profit they had expected to use to pay their advisers' fees.

The buyer that Chappell had lined up for Marylebone House was Alex Dellal, a secretive and sharp thirty-one-year-old property dealer with cold brown eyes. Dellal was the grandson of 'Black Jack' Dellal, the late trader who had known Green in his Amber Day incarnation. Chappell had been introduced to Dellal by his father's friend, Lennart Henningson. The connection was tenuous: Henningson had once been married to a cousin of Dellal's aunt. The Swedish businessman had occasionally brought deals to the patriarch Black Jack in years gone by.

To recap: the original agreement had been for Green to sell Marylebone House to Chappell for £35 million, then for Chappell to trade it on to Dellal for £45 million, creating £10 million of 'equity' for Retail Acquisitions to invest in BHS. Two days before the deal closed, Green abruptly changed his mind. He thought he could get £53 million for Marylebone House from another well-known property player, Sir John Ritblat. He promised to split the upside with Chappell at a later date, but in the meantime he still wanted Chappell to put £5 million of equity into BHS. Chappell had no money. In desperation, he begged Dellal for a short-term loan of £5 million. Dellal's offer was eye-wateringly expensive. He said he would lend the money for two months. The total repayment would be £6 million, including a first instalment of £2 million within just a week. The loan was to be secured against BHS's distribution centre in Atherstone, Warwickshire – so Chappell would effectively be buying the chain using its own assets. Eddie Parladorio, Retail Acquisitions' legal adviser, told Chappell he thought Dellal was 'ludicrously and disgustingly greedy'. Parladorio also warned that 'the proposed structure will be transparent to SPG because of the requested property charge'. But Chappell had no other options. He took Dellal's money.

Dellal had placed £35 million in an escrow account with Olswang in February (Chappell needed to show Green that he had the funds ready to buy Marylebone House). When Green withdrew Marylebone House from sale, Chappell suggested that Dellal use the money to buy BHS's second headquarters building, North West House, instead. Dellal later described it as a 'silver medal'. It was next to Marylebone House and it was a similar size. On 11 March, Dellal paid £32 million for North West House, granting BHS a two-year grace period before it had to leave. BHS desperately needed the cash, but it only ever received £25 million of the proceeds. Chappell diverted £7 million to Retail Acquisitions. He used the money to pay success fees of £1.2 million each to Grant Thornton and Olswang. He also paid himself and his team generous bonuses. Chappell took £1.8 million, Parladorio received £460,000 and Mark Tasker and Stephen Bourne got £387,500 each. The rest went on interest payments to Dellal and other fees. Rather than invest money to help revitalize the ailing chain, Chappell and his friends ripped out cash straight away. Tasker and Bourne, who by then had decided to help with the acquisition stage only, stood down as directors as soon as the deal went through.

Dellal did very well out of Chappell. BHS defaulted on his £5 million 'equity' loan almost immediately and suffered a penalty charge when it finally sold the Atherstone distribution centre. And having paid the cheap price of £32 million for North West House, Dellal traded it on for a £6.5 million profit two months later. A week after Dellal told him of the profit, Chappell texted, 'Just in case you forget. Rolex yacht master 2 stainless steel with white face blue bezel.' A few days later, Chappell texted Dellal again, 'Did you find the shop?? Begins with Ro and finishes with ex.' Dellal texted back, 'Ha. Not yet. You're ruining the pleasure of giving you a gift! It was on my list either way only now I know what you want. I want a gift too!'

In his *Sunday Times* interview on the day of the deal, Green had said there were 'covenants' that meant Chappell's crew were 'not allowed to take any money out'. BHS's £7 million loan to Retail Acquisitions obviously broke those covenants – although David Roberts, Chappell's lead lawyer at Olswang, seemed to think Green himself had suggested that BHS should bear the cost of advisers' fees. 'SPG said that we should merely invoice BHS,' he wrote in an email. Green later told Parliament that he was under the impression the £7 million had been deposited with the Bank of China to help Retail Acquisitions secure a line of credit. Whatever Green's level of knowledge about the murky transactions taking place, he must have developed a nasty feeling about Chappell when some of Paul Sutton's victims started contacting him, asking for restitution. Madeleine Legwinski, one of B52 Investments' creditors, sent an email to Green's PA, Katie O'Brien, explaining how she had been 'financially ruined' and forwarding correspondence showing Chappell boasting about the BHS deal. Green quickly grew uncomfortable.

In return, Retail Acquisitions began to feel bitter towards Green. His blatant disregard for the Pensions Regulator rapidly backfired. The watchdog immediately launched an investigation into his £1 sale of BHS, sending more than 120 aggressive legal notices to the various parties involved under Section 72 of the Pensions Act. The regulator's enforcement team demanded the disclosure of thousands of documents. The Section 72 targets ranged from Tina Green to Joe Chappell and included every conceivable adviser and counterparty.

Eddie Parladorio believed that Retail Acquisitions had been treated like 'mushrooms' by Green over the extent of the pension deficit ('kept in [the] dark and fed shit'). He complained via email about how they had been 'forced to do the deal at breakneck speed with all the SPG special twists and turns', leaving them dealing with 'painful and distracting firefighting' on problems including relations with an 'angered Pensions Regulator who was clearly smarting from historic issues'. An atmosphere of paranoia and mistrust rose up between Green and BHS's new owners. At one of the first BHS board meetings under Retail Acquisitions, a lawyer friend of Eddie Parladorio's called Dominic Chandler passed around a handwritten note warning that Green's team might have left 'covert listening devices' in the conference rooms. It suggested they adjourn to another location. According to minutes of the session on 25 March, when they were outside, Chandler told his colleagues he had met a security specialist who had said 'that it had been widely understood within his industry that SPG had for some years employed a covert security team, and that he had, inter alia, installed listening devices in his business in order to listen in on staff discussions'. Retail Acquisitions paid £7,500 to have Marylebone House and North West House swept for bugs left by the tycoon's aides, but they found nothing.

None of this angst was visible to the outside world. Green had ostensibly sold BHS to a group of wealthy entrepreneurs who were committed to turning it around. The initial press reaction to the unconventional deal was muted, and apart from a smattering of articles trying to explain the backgrounds of the buyers using publicly available information, the story soon faded away. No doubt the billionaire used his media contacts to smooth its path.

BHS's new owner, Retail Acquisitions Limited, was a shell company incorporated less than four months earlier. Its 90 per cent shareholder was a forty-eight-year-old called Dominic Chappell. None of my contacts had ever heard of him. Bell Pottinger, Chappell's PR firm, said that he would be unable to provide a CV 'at short notice due to other commitments'. However, it sent over a paragraph on his career highlights, which apparently included overseeing 'a €20 million, four-year turnaround plan' at a Spanish oil depot, 'heading up the property and construction division of his family business' and 'acting as the [managing director] for the media-based start-up IMI Group', the business behind the Interactive Sportscar Championship.

Chappell's Companies House record was clean: he had no previous directorships. However, a deeper search showed this was because he had created a new record for himself. Under his old identity was a string of collapsed businesses. The most recent, Island Harbour, looked like some kind of property development on the Isle of Wight. On a whim, I typed Chappell's name into Twitter. I spotted a lone message from an anonymous account questioning his credentials to buy BHS. I contacted the sender, who called me. By a stroke of luck, he had been closely involved in the financing of Island Harbour. 'You get some borrowers who start out with good intentions and manage to get into trouble,' the source said. 'Chappell was just a different kettle of fish entirely. This is the first time I've heard of him since then and I nearly spilled my coffee. He struck me as a great bullshitter but I don't think he has the credibility to pull off this kind of deal. He's not in that kind of league whatsoever.'

My skin began to tingle with the feeling that turns all journalists into hopeless addicts: the intuition that there was a big story brewing. I suspected there was a direct relationship between the BHS pension deficit – the very mention of which made Green so twitchy – and Chappell's obvious unsuitability to run a business of 164 stores and 11,000 staff. With no other leads, I decided to go through the phone book and cold-call addresses near Island Harbour Marina on the Isle of Wight. The breakthrough came in the form of a salty voice down the phone. 'The most important thing you need to know about Dominic Chappell,' it said, 'is he's a sociopath.' My pulse quickened and I strained to jot down every word. 'I didn't know what that word meant until I met him,' the voice continued. 'If you Google it, you'll find twenty points. Dominic Chappell ticks all the boxes. He's a Walter Mitty, a Svengali.'

I had stumbled across the old harbourmaster who had managed the disastrous Island Harbour scheme for Chappell and his partners. As soon as possible, I caught a train to Southampton, crossed the Solent by ferry and took a taxi from Cowes to a marina on the Medina river.

It was a cool March day. Boats creaked and sighed in the dry dock. Sounds of sanding and tapping drifted through the air. Henry Hector was waiting for me in a quiet café decorated with cut-away pencil schematics of yachts, overlooking the marina. The harbourmaster was a whiskery, weather-beaten man in an old anorak. He spoke in a hoarse East End whisper.

'I've ducked and dived, but I've lived an honest life,' he said, by

way of an introduction. Chappell, in contrast, was a 'total repro-
bate'. The story came tumbling out: Hector had met Chappell
through his brother, Damon, whom Hector had employed at a boat
restoration business in Antibes while Damon was recovering from
his cocaine affair. In 2005, Chappell and his father had come up
with the idea of building luxury holiday homes around a marina.
They alighted on a site being marketed by the property agency
King Sturge on an offshoot of the River Medina, which cleaves
between west and east Cowes. Island Harbour was not a prime
location. It was almost a mile south of the Folly Inn pub, the point
beyond which 'anything on the Medina is considered Timbuktu', in
the words of a local. Back then, Hector said, it looked like 'a swamp
full of tiddly boats'. But in 2006, the property boom was nearing its
peak, and unrealistic projects were all the rage. In June that year, a
few days before The Prodigy, Foo Fighters and Coldplay headlined
the nearby Isle of Wight festival in Newport, Chappell and his
father agreed to buy Island Harbour from a local landowner, Syd
Cavner.

Chappell partnered with an Irish builder, Kevin Clancy, who
brought in Tom Barry, a former head of corporate banking at Allied
Irish Bank. Chappell owned 50 per cent through Olivia Investments, his father's holding company in Gibraltar. Clancy and Barry
took 25 per cent each. Unknown to his partners, Chappell was an
undischarged bankrupt at the time. Nonetheless, he became a director of their development company and played a lead role in its
affairs, in breach of insolvency rules. Chappell 'didn't have a shilling', Hector said, but the presence of Barry, a respected figure in
Dublin, persuaded Anglo Irish Bank to lend the trio £24 million to
buy the site and fund the development. Island Harbour came with
planning permission for forty-eight holiday homes, seven of which
had already been finished. Chappell's team sought permission for a
further 119 flats. They also wanted to build a restaurant and dredge
the marina to put in new pontoons. Hector excitedly moved to the
Isle of Wight and took up his new job as harbourmaster.

It was an expensive plan, and contractors on the island tended to charge a premium because the closest competition was on the mainland, but Chappell didn't seem interested in controlling costs. The moment Anglo Irish's loan arrived, Hector said, Chappell bought several Range Rovers. He leased a Eurocopter EC120 helicopter, which he flew back and forth from Dorset, and bought an X-41 racing yacht to sail at Cowes Week and the Rolex Fastnet. 'He just blew the money,' Hector said. 'It was overspending – stupid beyond your wildest dreams.'

Chappell was charming and confident. He told the *Daily Mail* that buyers would benefit from 'a sense of tranquillity' at the marina, and he spun the locals tall tales about flying helicopters for the SAS. But Anglo Irish started receiving complaints from contractors who said they were not being paid. When the bank investigated, it found serious accounting irregularities. Money earmarked for contractors had been siphoned off for personal spending. Chappell's mismanagement was compounded by the financial crisis of 2008, when the market for second homes dried up. Anglo Irish put Island Harbour into administration in 2009 – by which point just eighteen of the first forty-eight homes had been built. The bank considered pursuing Chappell, who had given a personal guarantee for the full £24 million, but he was saved by the scale of the economic crash. Anglo Irish was nationalized and the Island Harbour loan was transferred to Ireland's 'bad bank', known as NAMA. Accounts for Island Harbour subsequently filed by the administrators showed that Irish taxpayers eventually suffered a 'significant shortfall'. Kevin Clancy and Tom Barry lost several million pounds, and small contractors wrote off £885,000.

Bruce Avey, an investigation officer from the Department for Business's enforcement unit, looked into Island Harbour's failure. Although nothing came of his work, the wider fallout was messy. Air & General Finance, the leasing company behind Chappell's helicopter, tried to reclaim the aircraft when his payments stopped, but realized it had gone missing. The Eurocopter was eventually found at Redhill aerodrome in Surrey, minus its rotor blades. In October 2009, Chappell was made bankrupt by a particularly angry contractor. The

Island Harbour administration also brought down the Chappell family's sixty-two-year-old property company, Eyot (Walton-on-Thames), which had given some kind of cross-guarantee.

Hector had been amazed to hear the BHS news. 'What's concerning is that Dominic seemed totally incapable of running any company at all,' he said. 'My view is that he couldn't run a penny machine in a toilet door.' His view was corroborated by others who were involved with Island Harbour. John Peck, who ran a construction firm on the island, was owed £1.3 million for his work on the housing element when the development went bust. He was eventually paid by the administrators, who decided to finish the work. He remembered Chappell as a 'smooth-talking guy' who could 'charm the pants off a nun'. 'There were a lot of island businesses that fell foul of his spending,' Peck said. Of Chappell's miraculous reinvention as BHS's new owner, he added, 'How he manages to bumble from one thing to another amazes me – but then people must let him. If people are going to be foolish enough, he's going to take advantage and asset-strip it or whatever, because I can just see that's his style.'

When I returned to London, I tracked down the contractor who had bankrupted Chappell. Steve Frankham picked me up from Sidcup station in a peacock-blue Aston Martin Vanquish Volante. 'It took me thirty-four years to afford it,' he said as I climbed in. 'If it wasn't for Dominic Chappell it would have been twenty-five years.' He cackled and put the pedal down. With his self-made tycoon's tan, thick build and silver hair, Frankham was a jolly cove, but he was also obviously hard as nails. As we drove to his headquarters on a business park in south-east London, he advised, 'He won't be able to stop himself spending the money from BHS when he gets it – you watch. He's flash. It'll be boats, cars, helicopters all over again.' Over tea at his office, Frankham explained how his eponymous building consultancy had been persuaded to lend Chappell £150,000 to help him clinch the purchase of Island Harbour from Syd Cavner. Chappell had only ever repaid £30,000. He had also failed to pay some of Frankham's consultancy fees for work on the marina. Frankham, an ardent Chelsea fan, had been furious enough to spend a further £30,000 bankrupting Chappell on a point of principle.

Frankham's finance director, John Gardner, rooted around in some paperwork and pulled out Chappell's final bankruptcy report, drawn up by the accountancy firm BDO. It was dated 6 March 2015 – less than a week before he had bought BHS. It made for an astonishing read. Chappell had debts of £24.5 million, including the loan from Anglo Irish. According to his own pleadings, he had no assets at all. BDO had tried to seize his £300,000 terraced home in the grounds of Bryanston public school in Dorset. The house carried a £233,879 mortgage from Birmingham Midshires. In March 2013, Chappell had offered BDO a sum of £5,000 to walk away. Given the hassle involved, BDO had accepted. But Chappell hadn't paid. The report said, 'The trustee reluctantly concluded that it would be disproportionate to continue the action to trial as, even if it was successful, it would not result in a realization for creditors.'

Frankham provided a lethal quote. '[We] undertook considerable design work for Chappell and his companies in good faith and he reneged on his promises to pay us,' he said. 'We eventually proceeded to bankrupt him when other creditors [with claims] totalling over £25 million came forward in support of the petition. No creditor recovered a penny.'

The coup de grâce came from an Insolvency Service search. Chappell turned out to have been made personally insolvent three times. In 1996, at the age of twenty-nine, he had entered into an individual voluntary arrangement (IVA), an alternative to bankruptcy where a borrower agrees to repay fixed amounts to their creditors over a period of time. He had then been made bankrupt by the London estate agency Foxtons in 2005 over an unpaid fee on the sale of a £1.2 million riverside flat in Fulham, and again by Steve Frankham in 2009. Those facts would prove troublesome for Chappell when they emerged because he had given his advisers a signed assurance that he had only been made bankrupt once, in 2009. The professional firms had apparently not bothered to check their client's claim with a simple search on the insolvency register.

Chappell sounded almost blasé when I finally got hold of him. 'If you want to write a character assassination piece such as the piece you're planning, c'est la vie,' he said. Green was less sanguine. In an attempt to neuter criticism of Chappell in the *Sunday Times*, which he knew would rebound badly on him as BHS's seller, he set up a last-minute interview with the new owner. Eddie Parladorio remarked in an email to some of the Retail Acquisitions team that the meeting was 'not ideal', but he accepted it was 'probably the best way to try and take the sting out'.

It felt strange shaking hands with Chappell in BHS's boardroom, now cleared of Green's newspaper cuttings and trinkets. He was porky and unremarkable-looking, dressed in jeans and a navy jumper, but he had a public-school accent and the affable manner of an upmarket estate agent. He struck me as a deeply improbable saviour of a loss-making department store. Sitting on one of Green's black leather sofas, Chappell said he wanted to 'set the record straight'. 'I've made some mistakes,' he said. 'I've really cocked a couple of things up on the way through but I'm an entrepreneur – we've got involved in businesses.'

Chappell tried to explain away the IVA (a personal guarantee to a Formula One team), the 2005 bankruptcy (a 'stupid' mistake) and the collapse of Island Harbour (Anglo Irish's fault). He said the bank had illegally switched the £24 million loan from sterling to euros, causing a default, and added, 'We were 90 per cent of the way through before bloody Anglo Irish started pissing around. We were on time, on track and on budget, and if Anglo are saying any different I'll sue them.' Retail Acquisitions' leader said his team had put £10 million of their own 'cold, hard cash' into the BHS deal, including £5 million from Chappell himself – a 'bonanza' from his oil business in Cadiz. My ears pricked up when he mentioned that Anthony Gutman, co-head of UK investment banking at Goldman Sachs, had vetted them 'to make sure we were correct and decent people'. As I turned to leave, Chappell called me back, grinning nervously. 'Oliver, don't be too hard on us, OK?' he said. For a moment, I was almost won over by his charm.

Green rang that evening. His tone was somewhere between matey and menacing. I could hear glasses clinking in the background and imagined him having a sundowner in Monaco. 'Why are you beating up my guy?' he said, half-joking. He initially denied that Gutman had been involved, then relented when I mentioned what Chappell had told me. 'Yeah, so what if he was?' Green snapped. 'I wouldn't lie to you, would I? But do not print that. I do not want Goldman's name appearing.' He left me with a typical Green bon mot. 'I'll say to you what I always say to my lawyer at Linklaters,' he grunted. 'DFU. Right? You can work that out.'

The exposé ran on 29 March 2015, under the headline, 'Revealed: The Trail of Disasters Behind Mystery Buyer of BHS'. I made sure that Goldman Sachs was mentioned prominently. The way Grant Thornton, Olswang, Goldman and ultimately Green had fallen for Chappell struck me as a remarkable example of groupthink. The most cursory investigation suggested he was thoroughly unfit to run a big business, yet they had all persuaded themselves the deal would work. Grant Thornton and Olswang were obviously desperate for fees. I expected that Goldman was trying to cosy up to Green, who wanted to rid himself of BHS's losses and pension deficit. Chappell came across as a chancer looking for a way to fund his extravagant lifestyle. In the middle were BHS's 11,000 employees and 20,000 pension-fund members.

The article met with stunned silence from Monaco, but it stirred up Chappell's neighbours in Dorset, where he turned out to be nicknamed 'ConDom' for his tendency to borrow money and bounce cheques. After Millfield school, Chappell had lived in London, then moved to the Hampshire town of Lymington, where he was part of the yachting community. According to a former girlfriend, he left Lymington 'owing money left, right and centre' and set up home in Blandford Forum in the early 2000s. She said he had tried to embrace the country lifestyle, buying a horse and joining the Portman hunt in north Dorset, but his subscription payments had lapsed and he had gradually lost interest. One of his neighbours, a sculptor called George Bingham, rang out of the blue and told me that, prior to

BHS, Chappell hadn't had 'a brass farthing'. Bingham recounted his own story about ConDom. Bingham was trying to sell his six-bedroom house in the Dorset village of Shillingstone in the autumn of 2011 when Chappell swept up the drive in a black Range Rover. After looking around, Chappell grandly offered £2.2 million on the spot. It was £300,000 less than the asking price, but Bingham conferred with his wife and – to Chappell's surprise – they accepted. Bingham put down a £2,000 deposit for a rental property so that he and his wife could move out and complete the sale by Christmas, but Chappell missed the dates for exchange and completion, then went silent. In irritation, Bingham spent the first half of 2012 pursuing Chappell through the small-claims court for the £2,000 he had lost. Chappell missed the first hearing, but turned up at the second and told the judge he had been away working on an oil rig. Bingham eventually recouped his £2,000 from Olivia Investments, the holding company in Gibraltar run by Chappell's father.

Other than calls from Bingham and a few other neighbours, the trail went cold for a week. Sometimes in those situations you have to pray for a new piece of information to arrive from left field. That is exactly what happened. The weekend after the first Chappell exposé, my uncle got married by Loch Lomond. As I staggered to bed in the early hours of the morning, I scrolled through my iPhone and spotted an intriguing email. The subject line was, 'Chappell/Sutton/BHS'. The message said, 'We can help you to know the real story behind it and who is the mastermind and what is going to happen.' I Googled the sender's name. He seemed to be a hairdresser based in Knightsbridge. It looked odd, but at that point I was open to any lead. A few days later I was sitting in the Capital hotel bar in Knightsbridge with George Vallossian and his wife, Melissa. Mrs Vallossian's maiden name was Tarrant. She was a sister of Nicola Tarrant, the fraudster Paul Sutton's girlfriend. Melissa, who was clear and straightforward, described Nicola as a brassy, good-looking blonde in her early fifties. She explained that Nicola had acquired a taste for money at a young age: in her early twenties she had been the mistress of the boxing promoter Frank Warren, who had showered her with couture from the designer Azzedine Alaïa and bought her a Porsche 911. Nicola's name had come up in the attempted murder trial of Terry Marsh, the former prize fighter who was accused of shooting Warren outside the Broadway theatre in Barking in 1989. Marsh's barrister, who was trying to suggest that a rival lover might have had a motive to shoot Warren, referred to her as 'the flower girl' because of the popular stall she ran at Romford market. (Marsh was acquitted at the end of the trial.) Nicola eventually married another man, Bradley Wetenhall. She reverted to her maiden name and became Sutton's girlfriend when she and Wetenhall divorced.

Nicola Tarrant was Paul Sutton's groupie. She had even helped him take money from members of her own family, including Melissa, who was owed about £130,000 from B52 Investments. Like others among Sutton's victims, Melissa had received threatening letters from Eddie Parladorio's law firm, Manleys. She and her husband, George, who spoke with a thick Lebanese accent, felt a moral obligation to stop Sutton. It was they who had delivered the dossier on his past to Green's apartment block in August 2013. Now they handed me a brown envelope containing the same material. It was dynamite. The most important document was the 2002 French fraud conviction, which described how Sutton had siphoned off millions of francs from a company called Prestige and spent it on travel, restaurants, salaries for his children's nannies and staff in villas in Monaco and St-Tropez. It also said he had sent millions of francs from Clamart III, the company that had owned the Bouygues building, to an Irish bank account 'without justification'. Sutton had been found guilty of stealing or concealing corporate assets and sentenced to three years in jail, but the judgment said he was 'en fuite' – on the run. The dossier included a picture of Sutton looking puce-faced and shifty. Even the idea that Sutton had introduced Chappell to the BHS deal would be devastating.

George and Melissa Vallossian struck me as entirely honest people, motivated by a desire to expose what was happening. They explained that Sutton rarely put his name to deals, usually choosing to operate through puppets. They believed he was still pulling Chappell's strings. 'It's wickedness, when you think of all those poor people's pensions,' Melissa sighed.

When I called Green and mentioned Sutton's name, he immediately saw where it was leading. It was my first experience of his hair-trigger temper. 'Bollocks!' he shouted. 'Total bollocks. He has no role. None. The first piece you wrote has already done enough damage.' Chappell also tried to distance himself from Sutton. 'In my view he's a grade-A scumbag,' he said. 'I came to know him a year ago when he was talking directly to Philip. He owes me a huge amount and I'm suing him.' Green's denial was undermined by Bell Pottinger, Chappell's PR firm, which sent over Sutton's signed promise that he would have no further involvement with BHS. Green had clearly been concerned enough by Sutton's presence to ask for it.

Retail Acquisitions instructed the law firm Harbottle & Lewis to send my employers an aggressive, four-page letter accusing me of 'operating under a grave misunderstanding'. Green also leaned hard on my editor, Dominic O'Connell, to kill the story. O'Connell retreated into a private room to take the tycoon's call on his mobile phone. When he emerged half an hour later, O'Connell sent me a Google Chat message saying the piece was 'fundamentally flawed' and that it would be scrapped. I argued and begged until O'Connell changed his mind again. From that moment on, O'Connell backed the BHS story with increasing resolve. As soon as he heard the article was going to run, Green called me back. 'Take a look in the mirror!' he screamed. 'There are 11,000 jobs at stake here. This is going to get very ugly, Oliver. I've never had a fight with the *Sunday Times*, but I'll fight if that's what you want.' He conveniently seemed to have forgotten about his shouting match with John Jay in 2000 and his out-of-court settlement with the paper over the story of Tina's Marks & Spencer share-buying the same year.

The scoop, 'Fraudster's Links to the £1 Sale of BHS', ran on 12 April 2015. I awoke on Sunday morning to a missed call from Green. It seemed cowardly to avoid him, so I rang back and submitted myself to ten minutes of uncontrolled rage. 'What is your fucking ambition here, apart from being a smart arse?' he shouted. 'You are going to fucking bankrupt this company, and when you do I'm going to sue you and the *Sunday Times*.' Green added, 'If I was Chappell I wouldn't bother with lawyers. I'd come round to your office and punch you on the fucking nose.' Then he abruptly changed gears and became almost friendly. 'Anyway, why did you use an old picture of Sutton?' he demanded. I couldn't help laughing.

'We are where we are,' Green concluded with a sigh. 'I know it's not personal. I know it's the game. But leave it. Leave it, seriously, or this is going to get ugly.'

The next week, Green tried to contact Martin Ivens, the *Sunday Times'* editor, but was told that he was too busy to speak. 'He will be busy when I've finished with him,' Green promised. 'I'm gonna call Rupert [Murdoch] . . . because this is unacceptable. This has got to stop.'

Bell Pottinger resigned as Retail Acquisitions' PR adviser a few days later. Chappell had lied to the firm about his bankruptcy record. On top of that and the Sutton revelations, one of Bell Pottinger's partners happened to be friendly with George Bingham, Chappell's neighbour-cum-enemy. Bingham had warned the PR man, 'I wouldn't touch him with a barge pole – with a dead rat tied to the end.' Bell Pottinger stepped down with a terse statement saying that its work was now 'complete'.

The trail went cold again. But Steve Frankham, the contractor who had bankrupted Chappell, quickly proved to be accurate in his prediction. Unseen by anyone beyond his immediate circle, Chappell was splashing money around like water. One of his first actions as BHS's new owner was to buy a dark green Range Rover. Less than three weeks after picking it up, he made inquiries about buying an SE Tech Discovery from the same dealership, Hunters in Southampton. When in London, he stayed at the five-star Landmark hotel opposite BHS's headquarters, where he spent almost £1,000 over three nights alone in April 2015. He took his wife, Rebecca, skiing in the Austrian resort of Kitzbühel and bought a Swan 42 racing yacht, which he called *Maverick 5*. Chappell had team polo shirts made with BHS's logo on the back. Grant Thornton and Olswang were so eager to curry favour with him that they agreed to sponsor the boat with £65,000 and £50,000 respectively. David Roberts of Olswang also invited Chappell and his wife to watch Madonna at the law firm's box at the London O2 arena.

Chappell paid £8,000 for lifetime membership of 10 Castle Street, a new private club near his home in Dorset, where he spent £4,442 in a single day for a BHS board lunch. He organized races for *Maverick 5* at Round the Island and Cowes Week, bantering on email with his teammates, 'Great crew for this one, so let's not get to [sic] pissed the night before (like last time).' There were shooting weekends with friends in the Scottish Borders and Wales and trips to events such as Royal Ascot. Despite its distressed finances, BHS's new owner seemed to think he was entitled to a tycoon's lifestyle – and he was egged on by his colleagues. A typical email from Eddie Parladorio to Chappell in June 2015 said, 'Hope First Class treated you kindly, that the champagne flowed and the pillow was fluffy.' In the same message, Parladorio mentioned that he was about to have breakfast with Paul Sutton.

These extravagances might have remained secret had a surreal coincidence not given the BHS story a new lease of life. One of my contacts was a banker who occasionally gave me advice and tips on stories. One evening in March 2015, he was sitting in the bar of a hotel in central London when he got chatting to an attractive woman in her early thirties. Rebecca Chappell explained that her husband was about to buy the BHS department store chain from Sir Philip Green. They stayed in touch, and over the next few months she excitedly relayed how Dominic had paid himself enough to buy them two Range Rovers, a long-overdue family skiing holiday and a yacht. I happened to tell this contact the story of my emergency interview with Chappell in the BHS boardroom, and how he had cut the meeting short because he needed to fly off and meet suppliers. My banker friend spluttered with laughter. 'Yeah, suppliers of snow, maybe,' he said. That was the weekend the Chappells had gone to Kitzbühel.

The information he gave me formed the basis of the third scoop, published on 7 June 2015, 'New Owner of Loss-Making BHS Enjoys a Life on the Ocean Wave'. It included a quote from Chappell, who said, 'There's no difference in my pattern of behaviour since I bought BHS, and if you're trying to suggest I've had a lot of money from BHS, that's not the case.'

Green was incandescent yet again. 'What do you expect him to do, ride a bike to work?' he bellowed down the phone on the Friday before publication, when I mentioned Chappell's new Range Rover. 'I'm gonna come round there and smack you in the fucking mouth!' A few hours later, another threatening letter arrived from Harbottle & Lewis. Retail Acquisitions' aggression was being fuelled by Eddie Parladorio, its legal director. He had already remarked in an email to Chappell that he would like to 'put a dent in Shah'. He approved the Harbottles letter, saying that he was itching 'to teach this chap (and his employers) a lesson'. Chappell forwarded a copy to Green's PA, Katie O'Brien. Parladorio then reassured Chappell, 'They know we are watching them with machine guns ready.'

The letter was full of the usual bluster. 'Our clients are tasked with turning around a once-great British brand,' it said. 'You should allow our clients to pursue that aim.' However, one section stood out. Headed 'Your Communications with Third Parties', it included comments I had made to Green about Chappell being a 'liar' and a 'spiv'. The billionaire had clearly filleted our conversation and passed bits out of context to Chappell's lawyers for ammunition. I felt a red mist descend. I texted Green, 'Surprised you didn't mention your repeated threats of violence to me down the phone.' I went out for a run to relieve the stress. When I came home, my phone was glowing with a string of missed calls from a hidden number. I rang Green back. It was the only time I ever heard him sound contrite. 'Oliver, I apologize,' he said, his gravelly voice suddenly warm. 'You know, I only lose my temper because I care.'

13.

Take-off

Darren Topp had spent his entire career working in retail, and it showed: with his stocky build, square glasses and colourful ties, he was the friendly store manager from central casting. The working-class son of a lorry driver and a cleaner from Salford, Topp had left education at eighteen despite getting three A levels. He went straight into a trainee job with Marks & Spencer and rose up the ranks, eventually becoming regional manager for Wales and south-west England. In 2008, he told his boss, Sir Stuart Rose (who had been knighted that year), that he was planning to leave for a role at BHS under Rose's old frenemy Sir Philip Green. Rose told him, 'There are two things you need to know about Philip. One is he's a brilliant dealmaker. The other is he's an absolute wanker. If you have any trouble with him, call me.'

Topp was reliable and solid. He learned to handle Green's caprices, and he was second in command at BHS by the time Dominic Chappell's £1 takeover went through. Richard Price, BHS's incumbent chief executive, left for a job at Tesco. Stephen Bourne, Chappell's short-lived non-executive director, advised him to make Topp the interim leader. 'The management team is good, serious and can turn this business,' Bourne judged. Topp was promoted a few days after the deal and made permanent chief executive a month later.

Many of BHS's rank-and-file head-office staff were unconvinced by Chappell. 'The first time he stood in front of us you could tell he didn't know what he was talking about,' said one. Some of its shop workers were astonished when he landed in a rented helicopter on a whistle-stop tour. But Topp, a mild-mannered forty-seven-year-old, was initially excited about the change in ownership. He hoped the separation of BHS from the Arcadia Group mothership would help persuade some of its landlords to cut rents – something that had proven impossible under Green because of his billionaire status. Topp warmed to Chappell, who openly told him, 'I've been bankrupt in the past and let me tell you, I don't want to go there again. I've bet my shirt on this business.' Topp's wife, Helen, met Chappell at a function and warned her husband that he was a 'wrong 'un' based on an instinct she couldn't quite explain. But Topp chalked up Chappell's new Range Rover and weekend yachting trips to the natural trappings of a successful entrepreneur. BHS's new owner assured Topp that Retail Acquisitions was a crack team of finance and property experts who would raise the cash necessary to save the company.

'DC1', as Chappell became known, installed himself in Green's old office and assumed an imperious air. 'DC2' was Dominic Chandler, Eddie Parladorio's friend from the law firm Manleys. Chandler was a barrister who had worked for Paul Sutton. He came in to help on the legal side. Parladorio, the brightest but also the jumpiest, was Chappell's right-hand man. Chappell hired a financier, Michael Morris, a property director, Mark Sherwood, and a project manager, Paul Wareham. Sherwood, a partner at Vail Williams, a small building surveying firm, was nicknamed 'Lord Sherwood of Andover' on their frequent shooting trips. Wareham had been the best man at Chappell's wedding. The members of Retail Acquisitions had two things in common: they were all on generous pay deals, and they were all Chappell's friends or family. In the brief window before he left, Stephen Bourne noted that Chappell was 'surrounding himself with weak people' because they happened to be his 'pals'.

That was not immediately apparent to Topp, who was rolled out to give media interviews defending Retail Acquisitions against the *Sunday Times'* stories. In April 2015, after the Sutton revelations, Retail Acquisitions' new PR firm managed to place an article in *The Times*, its daily stablemate. Headlined 'BHS Boss Takes on Primark and M&S', it quoted Topp describing Chappell as 'a force of good in the business'. Eddie Parladorio emailed Topp that morning to say it had been 'very helpful'. 'Let's continue to keep the news agenda on the positive side and get away from the negatives from Oliver Shah at [the] ST,' he said.

Topp had never held a board-level position before. BHS was a baptism of fire. He had a business with £700 million of sales that was losing altitude quickly, a group of unproven new owners and a former proprietor whose attitude towards its future was at best puzzling. The loss of credit insurance was an issue that brought all three elements together quickly. Chappell and Green were unable to persuade insurers like Coface and Euler Hermes to restore cover for BHS's suppliers. Green, for whatever reason, was unable or unwilling to underwrite a bond. The alternative was for BHS to arrange letters of credit from a bank, which would promise to reimburse suppliers if BHS went under. That would mean tying up millions of pounds of BHS's much-needed cash in security deposits with the bank. At the end of April, after a meeting with Green, Grant Thornton put the unexpected drain on resources at £32 million. BHS had £13.5 million in its account. It needed several big windfalls to make up the gap. Less than two months after Green's sale, the chain was already at serious risk of going bust. Topp remarked gloomily, 'We are not in the last chance saloon, but we are getting our hair done next door.'

Green understood the severity of the situation, yet he only seemed prepared to help within limits. Where Arcadia and BHS shared suppliers, Green encouraged the factories to carry on shipping to BHS or face a 1 per cent discount on their Arcadia bills. The tycoon kept £500 million on deposit with HSBC in Monaco, giving him huge sway over the bank, and he was close to its head of commercial banking in Europe, Ian Stuart, who had been among the mourners at Green's mother's funeral that January. (Not every senior banker at HSBC was so keen on Green: one remarked in an email that he was as 'slippery as a Vaseline-coated eel in a pool of grease – not that he'd ever let his best buddy Ian down of course!')

Green made sure that HSBC kept providing some credit insurance to BHS suppliers, and he arranged the £25 million overdraft he had promised Chappell. But he maintained a tight control over Chappell's ability to draw down the money. On 26 March, Paul Budge, Arcadia's finance director, emailed Chappell to say that Arcadia had provided letters of guarantee worth £8 million to several BHS suppliers. Green apparently planned to restrict £8 million of Chappell's HSBC overdraft in return, meaning that BHS would still be gasping for breath.

The Topshop billionaire kept his fingers around Chappell's throat in another way. By the time he sold BHS, Green had pumped in £240 million of loans from Arcadia to cover its losses. He wrote off £200 million when Retail Acquisitions took over, but he kept £40 million in place, secured by a charge over BHS's stock and its store at Cribbs Causeway shopping centre near Bristol. The debt made Green BHS's biggest creditor and gave him the power to push it into administration at any time by calling in the money, which the company would be unable to repay. The £40 million charge was also intended for a more interesting purpose. Green realized that Chappell would have to deal with BHS's unsustainable pension burden at some point – ideally, by restructuring the funds along the lines of Project Thor. The 'Points of Principle' document drawn up by Green and Chappell for the outline of the BHS deal in February had stipulated that Swiss Rock, as Retail Acquisitions was then known, should 'use its endeavours to reach a settlement, as soon as reasonably practicable'. Green knew the Pensions Regulator would force him to make a contribution towards any deal. He hoped it would be in the region of £40 million. On the day of the £1 BHS sale, he wrote Chappell a side letter confirming that the £40 million would be held to guarantee Arcadia's obligations towards the pension schemes.

But Green's relations with the regulator were at an all-time low. Its investigation into BHS had spread discomfort through his network of contacts. Each Section 72 notice demanding disclosure of information reminded the recipient in bold type that failing to hand over documents could be a criminal offence. The notices had gone far beyond Green's family to include his trusted advisers at Deloitte, Goldman Sachs, HSBC, Linklaters and PwC. Green moaned to Chris Martin, chairman of the pension trustees, that he was 'being tortured' by the watchdog. According to Martin's notes of a call in October 2015, Green felt the regulator was 'trawling through bullshit from ten years ago'. At some stage, Green said, they would 'all need to get round a table and sort it out', but for the moment he insisted that 'the contributions are still being paid' and 'the bloke [Chappell] is doing OK and paying what he owes people'.

If the Section 72 notices sent discomfort through Green's team, the feeling in the Retail Acquisitions camp was closer to panic. The Pensions Regulator wanted to know the details of any money taken out of BHS. The unexploded bomb was obviously the £7 million Chappell had creamed off from the proceeds of North West House's sale to pay bonuses and fees. Olswang, Retail Acquisitions' law firm, consulted a specialist pensions barrister, Paul Newman, who confirmed what they all feared: if the watchdog decided that Chappell and his crew's payments had weakened the company's balance sheet, and therefore its ability to service the pension funds, it would have the ability to pursue them for compensation. It was decided to present the transfers as loans rather than payments, although Olswang pointed out that the regulator would see through the technicality because the loans carried no interest and there was no security. There was a month of fevered debate as to how they should reply.

Olswang sent Retail Acquisitions' response to the Pensions Regulator on 1 June 2015. Darren Topp had not been party to its preparation. He asked Dominic Chandler, the Manleys barrister, if he could see a copy. Chandler had not been involved either, so he obliged. Topp commuted weekly from a small village in Lincolnshire, so one weekend he took the document home. On a warm Saturday morning in June, Topp went out onto the patio with a mug of coffee and settled down to read it before his family woke up. The Section 72 response was long and detailed, but Topp only made it to the fourth page. Two words froze in his mind, '*Oh fuck.*' Chappell had told him that Retail Acquisitions had invested £10 million of equity into BHS – supposedly the fruits of his profitable time running the oil storage depot in Cadiz. The document revealed that no real equity had gone into the business at all. Chappell had put in £5 million, but that had come via a loan from Allied Commercial Exporters, Alex Dellal's family company (which was often referred to as ACE). Far from injecting money into BHS, Retail Acquisitions had taken money out. On top of the success bonuses for the deal, the Section 72 response showed that Chappell was drawing a salary of £540,000 a year.

Topp was troubled. He had trusted his own instincts about Chappell's wealth. He had also trusted Green. Before the sale to Retail Acquisitions, he and Ian Grabiner, Green's most capable lieutenant, had even asked if they could do a management buyout of BHS themselves. Green had discussed it with his board but said no because they would have needed to put it through some kind of insolvency to reorganize the property portfolio. The headlines would apparently have been too much for the king of the high street to bear. Topp was certain that Green must have realized Chappell was buying the company using its own assets.

On Monday morning, Topp confronted Chappell about the £7 million missing from North West House. The reply was short-tempered. 'Darren, this is how private equity works,' Chappell snapped. 'I had a stack of fees to pay. I was on the hook for millions of pounds. You've not done a deal. You don't get it.' Topp told him, 'I might not have done a deal, Dominic, and I might not get it, but I know the difference between putting £10 million in and taking £7 million out.'

The dynamic between Topp and his new boss had changed. Chappell became suspicious of his chief executive. An 'us and them' culture developed between members of Retail Acquisitions, whom Chappell called his 'home team', and the BHS staff. There were reasons for Topp to be concerned about Chappell other than the money. The BHS turnaround plan was predicated on leveraging its property assets to raise crucial funding, yet Chappell was inexplicably interested in taking over Charles Vögele, the Swiss retail chain. 'We're going to clap those two businesses together,' Chappell told Topp repeatedly. 'It's going to generate significant efficiencies. It'll cost £20 million to buy but it's got net assets of £100 million.' Topp had to explain, 'We haven't got £20 million, Dominic. Let's focus on trying to get the business we have got working.' It was like dealing with a child. Topp told friends that Chappell was 'living in fantasy land'.

Topp was unaware, but buying Charles Vögele was another harebrained plan dreamed up by the fraudster Paul Sutton. He wanted to act as the middleman and take a fee, which he offered to share with Chappell. Sutton set up a company in Panama, Clarberry Investments, which would broker the Charles Vögele deal and receive the commission. Chappell secretly took a 50 per cent stake in Clarberry in May, a month after telling the *Sunday Times* that Sutton was a 'grade-A scumbag'. They then engineered a farcical situation whereby someone called André Plassard made contact with BHS on behalf of Clarberry and asked Chappell to sign a non-disclosure agreement. Chappell returned it, saying there were 'some potentially interesting synergies' between BHS and Charles Vögele. He offered to pay Clarberry 5 per cent of the deal value. Chappell even flew to Geneva to meet Plassard between 12 and 14 May.

Unsurprisingly, the idea went nowhere. As well as BHS's obvious lack of money, as pointed out by Topp, it was scuppered by Sutton, who could not resist brandishing Clarberry paperwork as proof of his connection to BHS whenever he was trying to raise funds from new punters. A month after Clarberry's 'approach' to BHS, Eddie Parladorio emailed Plassard to say there had been 'a serious breach of confidence and misrepresentation'. Parladorio asked Clarberry to 'cease and desist from any misrepresentation' over its relationship with BHS.

Chappell seemed to think he could replicate Green's dealmaking and lifestyle as long as he occupied the billionaire's old office. He dropped into BHS stores at weekends and fired off angry emails about the availability of garden furniture and the cleanliness of tables in the canteens. He spent time online browsing for new cars and luxury properties. In June, while BHS was going through a particular cash squeeze and Grant Thornton was questioning whether it would be able to pay its quarterly rent bill, Chappell inquired about converting its entire fleet of 150 vehicles to his favourite brand, Jaguar Land Rover. In July, he and his wife spent £4,400 on a christening party for their son, complete with a marquee in their garden. The same month, Chappell paid £25,600 for a grey Volkswagen Crafter minibus.

Attention from the *Sunday Times* was the only impediment to some of this free-and-easy spending. When Tony Perks, Chappell's IT director, forwarded him a link to a 'D1 BHS' personalized licence plate priced at £999, Chappell replied, 'Nice plan, but I think a certain shit head reporter would have a field day.' On another occasion, he sent around an image of my head Photoshopped onto a chesty woman's body, asking, 'Gents. Any update on what the prick below is planing [sic] this Sunday?' Eddie Parladorio replied, 'Hilarious!'

I had no idea at the time, but Chappell also considered engaging private detectives to investigate the sources of the stories. Quintel, an intelligence firm based in Mayfair, gave Chappell a quote on a piece of work codenamed Project Mayen. The pitch said, 'The investigative focus will commence with Mr Oliver Shah to understand, through his associates and pattern of life, who is providing him with information and why.' Chappell appeared to lose interest, because he did not reply to Quintel and he never heard from the firm again.

Meanwhile, Green continued to rain down criticism of the *Sunday Times'* coverage. After the latest article, he texted my boss, Dominic O'Connell, 'How sad oliver shah cant [sic] find a new script just the same as written before. I have never understood his agenda.'

While the Retail Acquisitions soap opera carried on, BHS lurched from one cash crisis to another. At the end of June, Green finally came good on his promise to give the buyers £10 million compensation for scrapping the Marylebone House property deal at the outset. Arcadia wired Retail Acquisitions £6.5 million in cash and £3.5 million through an interest-free loan, which Chappell's crew called 'the Tina Green soft loan'. The £10 million was used to pay down BHS's HSBC overdraft, meaning the bank agreed to release its charge over several properties. Chappell then used the Oxford Street and Manchester stores as security to borrow a further £25 million from Alex Dellal's company, ACE. Before he could, though, he had to defuse a row between Dellal, who was making millions of pounds out of BHS, and Green, who was apparently making 'controversial' comments in the market about Dellal's sharpness. On 25 June, Chappell emailed Bernie Berman, Dellal's lieutenant, and said, 'I really feel strongly that for whatever reason you think Sir Philip is upset or annoyed with ACE, it is simply not the case.'

The £25 million from ACE was so expensive it became known as the 'Wonga' loan. BHS had to repay £31 million in three months' time. The implied annual interest rate was 107 per cent. ACE clearly saw Chappell and his team as gullible idiots who could be milked for cash. A few days after they extended the loan, Berman advised Dellal in an email, 'Don't be too aggressive with them just yet and let's be calm and relaxed as we really can fuck them so hard.'

Darren Topp had already decided he needed an adult reinforcement to help keep an eye on Retail Acquisitions' profligate toddlers. Odgers Berndtson, a headhunting firm, put forward Michael Hitchcock, the former head of Beales department stores. A balding, bespectacled cynic with a hawk's eye for detail and the pedantic manner of a ticket inspector, Hitchcock was the ideal man for the job. Topp asked Hitchcock to unravel Retail Acquisitions' existing transactions with BHS and stop Chappell taking any more irregular payments. Hitchcock later told Parliament the task was like 'being given a thousand-piece jigsaw puzzle and being told to make the picture up'. Within two weeks, he had decided that Retail Acquisitions 'just did not smell right' and amended BHS's banking arrangements to stop Chappell or his friends taking money out without a second signature. They snuck the change past Chappell by handing him a thick sheaf of papers, hoping he wouldn't bother to read them. Topp told him they contained routine bank instructions. Chappell cheerfully signed everything.

Hitchcock was astonished to find that Topp had been spending '90 per cent of his time trying to govern what was happening above him and not focusing on what was happening in the business'. As interim finance director, he brought a degree of financial rigour to BHS for the first time since Chappell's takeover four months earlier. He clashed repeatedly with Retail Acquisitions. Paul Wareham, Chappell's best man, was the first to feel the sting of Hitchcock's acid tongue. BHS's financial plight was such that even electricity suppliers were demanding hefty security deposits. Wareham sent Hitchcock and Topp a rambling email setting out the two best offers from Npower, which involved either a £2.75 million down payment for seven months on a normal direct debit or £260,000 upfront for seven months, with all bills to be paid seven weeks in advance. Hitchcock replied, 'Paul, this is one of the worst emails I have ever received. It is full of issues with no solutions. I ask myself what I am paying you for.'

While Wareham tried to defend himself, Chappell was busy ordering £20,000 worth of equipment from Aztec Marine in Southampton for his sailing yacht, *Maverick 5*, including an autopilot system, speakers and a Wi-Fi router. He also accepted an invitation to race with his friend Andrew 'Willo' Wilson at the Silicon Cup, the IT industry's charity regatta, on 17 and 18 September. Willo emailed Chappell, 'On the Thursday evening there is a dinner in Cowes and the theme is Super Heroes so we expect you to come suitably attired!!'

In August, BHS's Atherstone distribution centre was sold for £15 million to one of Chappell's old friends, Mahmood Ismailjee, with some of the proceeds used to repay Alex Dellal for the £5 million emergency loan he had given Retail Acquisitions for the BHS takeover. Hitchcock questioned why a £400,000 fee was being paid to Vail Williams, the property agency that was part-owned by Mark Sherwood, Chappell's property director. Hitchcock emailed Chappell, 'There is a blatant conflict of interest here with MS being an equity partner in VW. I am concerned that you are paying MS a not inconsiderable amount of money and yet paying his own firm an even greater fee on a project that I cannot see any involvement on VW part on [sic].'

The ticket inspector struck again in September, when Retail Acquisitions refinanced the £25 million 'Wonga' loan from Alex Dellal with £65 million from Grovepoint Capital, a private equity firm. On Friday 11 September, Hitchcock said he was 'very worried' that the £65 million had not appeared in BHS's main Barclays account, raising the risk that expenses might not be paid at the start of the week. Chappell casually replied that he had sent it to a Lloyds account instead. 'Any decisions of this nature I need to know about,' Hitchcock admonished. 'I cannot secure and control the cash flow of an £800 million retail business if these decisions are not discussed.'

The big showdown came in late November. On the eve of an away day in Dorset, Hitchcock and Topp discovered that Chappell and Parladorio had been drawing up a secret plan to asset-strip BHS by moving its profitable international and online businesses out of the group and into the direct ownership of Retail Acquisitions. BHS had eighty overseas franchise stores, mostly in the Middle East, which were earning £8 million a year on sales of £100 million. Chappell had already run up £350,000 of fees with Grant Thornton working on the restructuring, which was code-named Project Herald. Hitchcock and Topp voiced their opposition during the next day's lunch at 10 Castle Street, the private club. According to a BHS executive who was present, Chappell went 'absolutely mental', shouting, 'It's my fucking business! I can instruct you to do it as the number one shareholder! Your job is to run the business on our behalf.'

Project Herald was supported by all the members of Retail Acquisitions apart from Dominic Chandler, the Manleys barrister.

But Chappell's argument unravelled when he inadvertently referred to the plan as a 'lifeboat'. 'Yeah, we know what a lifeboat's for,' Topp shot back. 'That's how everyone will see it – that you're trying to extract something of value from the core business. It's not going to wash, Dominic.' Chappell backed down. There was a wine tasting, followed by dinner, but the mood was ruined. The dress code, 'Christmas party sparkles', suddenly seemed like a joke. The BHS executive said, 'That was the first time I thought that he might just fire everyone and say, well, we're going to do it anyway.'

The battle of 10 Castle Street opened up another front for Hitchcock. Chappell was not the only one sucking money out of BHS. His inept team had relied heavily on Grant Thornton for basic work such as compiling weekly cash-flow forecasts, and the accountancy firm had gleefully invoiced the stricken company for millions of pounds in fees. Hitchcock had already complained internally about Grant Thornton's 'quite frankly ludicrous' bills, suggesting that 'either they are taking the piss or we have lost control of the cost lever'. After the Project Herald fiasco, Hitchcock refused to pay Grant Thornton's fees for any services other than pensions advice. The finance director was forced to give in when Paul Martin of Grant Thornton threatened to stop work on pensions too. In fairness to the accountancy firm, it was simply carrying out work instructed by Retail Acquisitions and charging handsomely for doing so. Hitchcock complained to Chappell and Topp that Grant Thornton had made 'the guts of £3.5m' from BHS in less than a year. He said that Martin's stance was 'tantamount to blackmail'. 'I find it disgusting,' he emailed.

Chappell had raised an interesting point during the November lunch row. As clueless as he was, and as competent as Hitchcock and Topp were, he was the undisputed 90 per cent shareholder of BHS, and he held the whip hand. As Hitchcock tried to take control that winter, Chappell defiantly ramped up his spending. In September, he paid €320,000 (£236,000 at the time) for another yacht, a motorized Princess V62 gin palace called *Vista*, which he renamed *Maverick 6* and shipped to Miami in the care of his friend and retired

Formula One racing driver Eddie Irvine. Chappell and his wife, Rebecca, viewed a £3.5 million farmhouse with its own cricket pitch being sold by Savills and a £3.25 million modern arts-and-craft house marketed by Knight Frank – both in Dorset. He expressed an interest in a new Jaguar F-Pace luxury SUV and made an unsuccessful $2.75 million (£1.8 million at the time) bid for a Eurocopter EC-135P2+ helicopter that was being sold through a Texas-based aircraft broker, Global Jet Aviation.

Some of Chappell's financial moves were distinctly cannier. In September, he met a senior partner of the wealth management firm St James's Place. Chappell told the adviser that he had £10 million in cash, although he may have been exaggerating for bravado. He then asked how he might put £1 million into a trust as safekeeping for his two young children. The adviser wrote, 'I confirm that should you make as you say a disastrous business decision in the future that these funds will be ring fenced.' It was not clear whether Chappell went ahead.

On 13 December 2015, the Chappell family flew from London Heathrow to Nassau in the Bahamas for an early Christmas holiday. BHS's owner had tried to book the flights on its travel budget, but Topp had stopped him – to Chappell's annoyance. So he took his December salary early on the grounds of 'hardship'. The Chappells picked up their new boat from the Atlantis marina on Paradise Island and cruised south towards Exuma, an archipelago of cays and islands. The sun was beautifully warm; the sea was the dappled turquoise of a travel brochure. Chappell emailed a group of friends, 'Chaps, I am having to slum it in the Bahamas for the next three weeks. I know you will all feel my pain.' He sent Darren Topp a motivational message from the deck, saying, 'We bought into your team delivering, push them hard to believe. We must keep the momentum every day, I know retail is down the pan and it is hard work but please keep everyone on the same page.' He told another executive, 'All fantastic here thanks, totally relaxed and ready for the challenges for next year.'

Chappell sent his father pictures of the family playing with swimming pigs at Big Major Cay and posing next to a seaborne Father Christmas. It was Green's team who had codenamed the sale of BHS Project Rudolph, but Chappell must have felt as if the department store had at long last delivered his dream of becoming a tycoon. He had always felt entitled to such a lifestyle. He soaked it up, blissfully unaware of the hurricane heading his way.

14.

Turbulence

Brett Palos was thirteen when he and his sister moved into Philip Green's house in St John's Wood with their mother. Tina Green's son was different in temperament and looks from his future step-father. Calm and polite, Palos had sandy hair, a shy smile and a slim physique that gradually swelled to include a Mayfair paunch as he grew older. Despite the differences, he always looked up to Green. He was among the last to leave the party when Tom Jones and Earth, Wind & Fire played at PG50 in 2002, staggering around in a sparkly jacket with a couple of friends, holding up a number-ten sign purloined from one of the tables, joking, 'Out of ten, we give it ten.'

Green was reported to have footed the £1 million bill for perfor-mances from George Benson and Lionel Richie when Palos married his girlfriend, Magda Ramadan, in Marrakech in 2006. Three years later, Palos joined the board of Taveta Investments, Arcadia Group's holding company. 'This is a family business,' Green told the *Daily Mail*. 'Brett has a great relationship with my kids, so hopefully as life develops he is going to be their guide.'

Palos dabbled in deals of his own, buying and selling an office-supplies company called ISA Retail and the O2 shopping centre on Finchley Road in London. He went into residential property invest-ment with the corpulent trader Bruce Ritchie, one of Green's closest friends, and he made an unsuccessful takeover bid for the car dealer-ship Lookers with the octogenarian East End property wheeler-dealer Jack Petchey. But by 2015, when Palos was forty, he was still nowhere near Green's league. At the point of the BHS sale, he and his stepfather did a silly deal for a few million pounds that quickly boomeranged back at them.

On 6 March 2015, less than a week before Green sold BHS to Dominic Chappell for £1, he let a company co-run by Palos buy the freehold of BHS's well-located Ealing store for £6.9 million. Thackeray Estates, Palos's business, then sold the freehold on for £10 million three months later, pocketing a £3 million profit that would have belonged to BHS had the department store held on to the property a little longer. It was a fact that lay dormant in the Land Registry's records until I received a tip-off. No law had been broken, and in the grand scheme of Green's billions £3 million was a paltry sum, but it illustrated just how hard the family had shaken the piggy bank upside down before passing it on. According to a former insider, the small circle of people in Arcadia who knew about the transaction were very nervous of its hitting the press. One of Palos's colleagues at Thackeray Estates, Charles Thompson, told the commercial estate agent handling the £10 million resale to keep it secret. When she asked why, he wrote, 'I think you know why . . .'

When I put it to Green in October, he was almost plaintive. 'Why are you doing this?' he asked. 'We could be allies.' When that plea had no effect, he turned to scorn. 'People buy and sell buildings all day long,' he said. 'Do you think we would knowingly sell something for £7 million we could have sold for £10 million?' Green insisted the transaction had been carried out on an arm's-length basis and that it had been approved by Chappell, although Chappell later told Parliament he'd had no idea the buyer was Palos. Chappell claimed that when he challenged the billionaire after the story broke, Green told him, 'Well, that's show business.'

Green threatened to seek an injunction, but the facts were set out in black and white on Land Registry documents. The article, 'Quick BHS Profit for Green Stepson', caused the tycoon more trouble than I realized at the time. Green had assured the Pensions Regulator there had been no recent property transactions at BHS involving any members of his family. On the Friday before our publication, his company secretary, Adam Goldman, hurriedly had to contact the watchdog to correct the position. It cannot have pleased the already-suspicious regulator.

By now, the relationship between the billionaire and the *Sunday Times* had descended into a state of war. Green had bombarded Dominic O'Connell and Martin Ivens with complaints. He repeatedly tried to call Rebekah Brooks, News UK's chief executive, and Rupert Murdoch, its ultimate proprietor, to no avail. Rival journalists on other papers expressed amazement that I was being allowed to take on Green. One gave me a snippet of information that contributed to a front-page story on BHS. 'There's no way my editor will let me print it, so you may as well have it,' he said with a shrug. Green claimed the business community was 'mortified' by his treatment, although that didn't tally with the many emails of encouragement we were receiving. And however bad things had become, they were about to get a lot worse. The pension crisis Green had tried so hard to submerge was rising steadily to the surface.

Chappell had been using jargon like 'rightsizing' to describe his plans for BHS's two pension schemes ever since he bought the business. In our emergency interview in March 2015, he had said, 'It's been here for 20 years, it's been the wrong size for 20 years. It's got to be dealt with.' In July, Retail Acquisitions instructed Grant Thornton and Olswang to begin work on a new version of Green's Project Thor restructuring, using the codename Project Vera, but it went onto the back-burner while Chappell and Eddie Parladorio concentrated on their plan to asset-strip BHS's international and online businesses. As 2015 moved into 2016, the pension deficit became a more pressing concern. Any kind of restructuring would obviously require a big cheque from Green. There were two problems: Project Vera would be more expensive than Project Thor because of movements in gilt yields, and Green would not countenance paying anything until the Pensions Regulator abandoned its investigation into him.

Chris Martin, the chairman of BHS's pension trustees, was desperate to rescue the funds. On 21 January 2016, he had a phone conversation with Green. Martin recorded in his notes, 'SPG was clear that he thought a solution could be found but only if tPR agreed to discontinue their investigations as part of a settlement.' Martin asked 'SPG' whether he would be willing to join a round-table meeting with the regulator and the trustees to hammer out a peace agreement. He thought a £120 million payment from BHS's former owner might seal the deal. 'SPG indicated that he would not want to do so unless he knew that tPR will discontinue,' Martin wrote. 'SPG also noted that in his view, the £120 million would not have to be paid at once.'

Green was not as insouciant as he came across to Martin. Between late January and early February, he deluged the pensions minister, Baroness Altmann, with twenty-two text messages, some sent as early as 5.30 a.m. He seemed to be seeking her support for his tussle with the regulator. When Altmann's officials advised her that it would be inappropriate to intervene because of the watchdog's active investigation, Green texted, 'This is crazy we need a solution.' A few days later, he added, 'Ros I hear what you are saying but I am sorry to say you are behaving exactly like the regulator which is wholly unacaetable [sic]. Not your fault you are with totally incompeteanant [sic] people. I am happy to wait till wed night after which I will go where I have to go. This is not a threat but I have to look after our business.'

The stand-off between Green and the Pensions Regulator killed Project Vera, and with it any hope of making the two BHS funds more sustainable. On 3 February, the barrister Dominic Chandler sent an email around BHS's board members wondering whether they should tell the regulator that Green's attitude was 'a reason why Vera is no longer available'.

The company was already sliding towards a more radical solution. Chappell was planning to put it through a form of insolvency known as a company voluntary arrangement (CVA), which allows a business to rid itself of certain liabilities and renegotiate rents. Property costs were BHS's biggest single handicap. In Clydebank, it was tied into a rent of £440,000 a year when the local market rent was £240,000. In Monks Cross, York, it was paying £830,000 against a market rent of about £500,000. Whenever Darren Topp or his predecessor, Richard Price, had tried to reason with landlords under Green, they had run into the obstacle of their boss's conspicuous wealth. A former executive said, 'It was always difficult. You're sat in front of a landlord, going, "This store loses half a million pounds a year, we need the rent to come down." People would look at you as if to say, "Well, the business can't afford it but the bloke who owns this business has got a lot of money."' It had been apparent to Michael Hitchcock, the interim finance director, that BHS needed to go through a CVA as soon as he arrived, but Chappell had dallied – again, because of his fixation with the international and online businesses.

In January 2016, BHS engaged the accountancy firm KPMG to carry out a CVA under the codename Project Pipe. The planning was complicated by the growing tension between Retail Acquisitions and the management team. On 4 January, Hitchcock circulated a Christmas trading update showing that like-for-like sales had fallen by 2 per cent, leaving BHS £20 million behind budget. Later that month, Chappell emailed Parladorio, 'There is a lot of arse covering going on . . . Michael and Darren were at the helm, if we had that cash we would be good to June or even the end of the year!' He added angrily, 'We as RAL [Retail Acquisitions Limited] backed the BHS management in THERE [sic] turnaround plan and they are fucking miles off.'

In response to Topp's hiring of Hitchcock, Chappell appointed his own finance director, a rambling, ruddy-cheeked accountant called Aidan Treacy. The childish one-upmanship led to clashes and confusion. Hitchcock was interim finance director of BHS. Treacy became finance director of Retail Acquisitions, its parent company. They contradicted each other in emails and Treacy openly criticized Hitchcock for choosing KPMG to do the CVA when Grant Thornton had pre-existing knowledge of BHS. Despite the dysfunctional atmosphere, the process lurched forward. BHS had 164 stores. The intention was to keep seventy-seven as they were, cut the rents to market levels in forty-seven and close or substantially renegotiate rents for the other forty. BHS needed

75 per cent of all its creditors – not just landlords – to approve the restructuring.

Chappell had stayed in touch with Paul Sutton for the duration of his time at BHS. However, other than throwing him a few thousand pounds through a company called Capital Management, which received £730,000 from Retail Acquisitions, he had genuinely cut the fraudster out of the financial rewards of the deal. On 3 March, a day before the CVA was due to be announced, Sutton caught wind and leaked it to the press out of spite. The CVA blew the BHS story wide open. Until then, common interest had bound the protagonists together. In the heat of the media glare, the ties melted. The enmity between Green and Chappell caught fire. So did the mistrust between Retail Acquisitions and BHS. That day, a contact who was closely involved in the unfolding events called me with a tip that proved to be a turning point. For almost a year, insiders had been telling me that Green was under a Section 72 investigation by the Pensions Regulator. The billionaire had repeatedly blocked the story by denying it outright – even getting his company secretary, Adam Goldman, to ring my editor and explain why it would be impossible for the watchdog to make a claim on Arcadia.

The contact now told me that Green had made an £80 million settlement offer to the regulator, which had been rejected. He provided a specific detail that allowed me to confirm it with other sources: £40 million of the offer was in cash and the other £40 million was the charge Arcadia held over BHS's stock and the Cribbs Causeway store near Bristol. Green tried to deny it, but when he realized it had been confirmed elsewhere he tacitly acknowledged its truth. 'Just write that I'm keen to help find a solution,' he ordered. John Ralfe, a pensions expert, provided a punchy quote. 'This deal is coming back to bite Sir Philip Green,' he said. 'He was wrong to think that by selling BHS he was, with one bound, free of its huge pension problems.'

The story, 'Green Faces £80 Million BHS Pensions Bill', led the *Sunday Times* business section on 6 March 2016. It had an almost audible impact. For the first time, it revealed that Green was at loggerheads with the Pensions Regulator. More importantly for BHS's 20,000 pension savers, it reported that the funds were being dumped as part of the CVA. They were going into an assessment period for entry into the Pension Protection Fund, the industry-backed lifeboat. During that state of limbo, benefits for 13,000 members would be cut by at least 10 per cent to the PPF's basic levels. I awoke to a furious text message from Monaco. 'Morning why would i [sic] think you could change,' Green typed. 'I am unclear why you bother to phone, ask questions and then just write what you want.' The next day, Green rang to announce that he no longer wished to speak to me. It was like a teenage break-up. He followed it with a scrambled text message, 'Oliver to be a b4 [sic] person in life you have to apoligse [sic] when you are wrong clearly you dont [sic] see that . . . If you cant [sic] see that hey ho be lucky.'

Chappell and his cronies were mirthful. The fuse that had been lit with Chappell's dubious reputation a year earlier was burning down towards the powder keg of Green's pension liabilities, and for once Retail Acquisitions was not the main target. 'Would love to be a fly on the wall as young Phil tucks into his Cinnamon Grahams,' Eddie Parladorio chortled over email to Chappell. Green's excoriation was all the more welcome for them because, two days earlier, *The Guardian* had broken the crucial revelation that they had taken millions of pounds out of BHS via a loan at the point of the deal. It was the first hard evidence that Chappell's lavish lifestyle was being funded from the dying store chain's money. 'What spending spree?' Chappell protested in an email to BHS's PR adviser when *The Guardian* approached them for comment. 'Exactly – conspiracy theory,' the communications man replied.

Richard Caring also watched his former business partner's travails with satisfaction. Their friendship had long since soured into a state of resentful rivalry, to the extent that Caring would ask the crew on his superyacht to program the details of the Greens' *Lionheart* into its automatic identification system so they could steer away and avoid it. The rag trader-turned-restaurateur was cruising with a group of friends when the story emerged. To scare and amuse his guests, Caring instructed one of the boat's crew to mock up a version of the *Daily Mail*'s website with a spoof exposé of their holiday, which he printed out on A4 paper and distributed at breakfast. The headline exclaimed, 'Caring Parties on his 65 Metre Superyacht While BHS Burns'. The article said, 'Obviously, neither Philip Green nor Richard Caring have much concern for their staff's pension dilemma. Caring is currently throwing another "wild party" on his yacht, *Silver Angel*, in the Seychelles. Extravagance, wine, women and song are abundant on this "supposed" diving trip. Party guests Arun Nayar, the textiles tycoon; Mark Steinberg, the owner of Chelsea Harbour; and several other celebrities are amongst the "devil-may-care" crowd!' There was a quote from an imaginary BHS pension trustee, who said it was 'bloody disgusting how these people behave!!!'. The piece was illustrated with a photograph of Caring and his friends having fun in Mexican fancy dress, complete with stick-on moustaches.

Chappell organized a fine-wine tasting event for senior staff at Vintners Hall in the City to celebrate the 'important milestone' of the impending CVA. He had to withdraw the invitation almost immediately when Sarah Gillett, BHS's head of HR, pointed out that 500 redundancies had been announced that morning. 'The timing of this feels very inappropriate,' she said. Somehow, BHS muddled through to the crunch vote on 23 March 2016. It was held at the drab Novotel in Hammersmith, west London. I spoke to two typical creditors, Rakesh and Rita Verma, a genial couple in their late fifties who ran a business in Wembley making bean bags and cushions. 'We've been dealing with them for twelve years,' Rakesh said. 'I still believe it's a British brand and it can survive provided discipline is exercised on buying and costs.'

The CVA was passed with a thumping 95 per cent approval rate. BHS seemed to have given itself a fighting chance. Retail Acquisitions and Aidan Treacy sought success bonuses of £500,000 and £250,000 respectively, but they were vetoed by the BHS board. Chappell may have been irritated, but in any case he was not there to celebrate. Four days earlier, he had flown to the Bahamas with his family for another three-week holiday on board his yacht.

Until the CVA, most of Fleet Street had either ignored the BHS story or played along with Green's narrative. Now, other papers started to see the significance of the pension deficit. The *Financial Times* was the first. 'The Pensions Regulator needs to extract more than the £80 million he has reportedly offered so far,' wrote Jonathan Guthrie, the Lombard columnist. 'Otherwise, the weakness of the system created to protect promises regarding final salary pensions in the wake of the pensions scandal at Mirror Group will be starkly apparent.'

I was walking along Oxford Street – appropriately enough, past Topshop – when I was rung by a friend. 'You're not going to believe this,' he said with glee in his voice. He directed me to a specialist website for superyacht enthusiasts. The site had details and photographs of Project FB 262, a 295-ft boat being built by the Italian yard Benetti with a price tag of £100 million. Apparently, it was the biggest yacht Benetti had produced since *Nabila*, made for the late Saudi Arabian arms dealer Adnan Khashoggi in 1980. The soon-to-be-owner of the new *Lionheart* was none other than Sir Philip Green. Buying a new superyacht with its own gym and helipad at the outset of a pension crisis was guaranteed to be a PR disaster.

I called Green. 'Oh, please,' he groaned. 'Fuck off, OK? Fuck off. All right?'

It turned into our longest and most exhausting bout yet. I marvelled as Green ducked and weaved, skilfully moving from aggression and threats to righteous indignation and self-pity and then back to anger, all the while throwing out disorientating facts and numbers that made my head spin. I put it to him that it was an unfortunate time to take delivery of a superyacht, given the state of the BHS pension funds. 'And what's one thing got to do with the other?' Green demanded. 'First of all, I'm not, anyway. Where are they related?' Before I could answer, he interrupted, 'When did you last move your house?' I paused, bemused. I told him I didn't see the connection. 'Well, exactly!' Green shouted. 'So what somebody

does years ago – what the fuck's that got to do with the pension?'
'You can imagine how it'll look,' I said. 'It'll look like that because
that's how you want to paint it,' Green growled. 'Continue. This is
going to end up with the lawyers – you know that, don't you? But
go on. Carry on.'

Further probing revealed that he was denying the story on a
technicality. It was Tina who had ordered the boat. She had done so
four years earlier, hence the confusing reference to 'what somebody does years ago'. 'This is my family,' Green said. 'My wife
wants to do what she likes. Right? She hasn't robbed any banks.
And if by any chance she's got a boat to sell and she buys a new
boat, right, what's the big deal?' Then he lowered his voice and
sounded genuinely wounded. 'What is it that you want to achieve?'
the tycoon asked. 'That I'm a bad guy? It's very personal, isn't it. It's
all very personal.' I pointed out that Green's family and businesses
were inextricably linked, given Tina's ownership of Taveta Investments, Arcadia's holding company. He roared back into full blast.
'She can do what she likes!' he shouted. 'Is she putting anybody in
jeopardy if she wants to change her boat? Why don't you take a picture of my car? I've got a car – is that all right, or shall I go round on
a fucking bike?'

The conversation degenerated. It went like this:

OS: Your car probably didn't cost £100 million.
SPG: No – nor did a boat.
OS: How much did it cost?
SPG: I don't know.
OS: I don't believe that.
SPG: Sorry?
OS: You must know how much it cost.
SPG: I don't know. I'm not involved in it. I've never been there.
OS: Never been where?
SPG: The shipyard.
OS: You could still order it without going there.
SPG: Sorry?

OS: How can you know it's not accurate if you don't know how much the boat cost?

SPG: I didn't say I didn't know how much it cost.

OS: You just did.

SPG: I said it did not cost £100 million, is what I said.

OS: So how much did it cost?

SPG: It's none of your fucking business. How's that?

We ended on a war footing. 'It's not a threat – it's just I don't have a choice but to call the lawyers, 'cos I'm not going to put up with you,' Green said. 'I'm just telling you now: you'll get sued person-ally, and the *Sunday Times.*' Green took great pride in his ability to manipulate the media. It was a sign of how desperate he had become that he turned to Schillings, the most aggressive libel law firm in Britain. Schillings denied the story that Green had essentially already confirmed. 'Neither our client, nor anyone in his family has recently acquired or is about to acquire a yacht,' the law firm stated. Unfortunately for Green, his comments had been caught on tape. The article ran on 13 March 2016 under the headline, 'The £100 Mil-lion Boat Comes In – Just as BHS Pensions Need Bailing Out'. It included the first call for the tycoon to be stripped of his knighthood over the BHS pension scandal. Frank Field, the veteran Labour MP, said, 'This raises the question: is he a suitable person to bear that emblem? The government should employ every power it has to get him to pay up.'

A source inside Green's camp told me the thing he feared most was the *Daily Mail* picking up the story. He hated the *Mail* and its editor, Paul Dacre, who had the ability to pour petrol on a fire and turn it into a blazing inferno. At the end of March, exactly that hap-pened. The *Mail* plastered the story across two pages of its Saturday edition under the headline, 'A £100 Million Floating Gin Palace and the Pension Scandal That Could Scupper Sir Topshop'. The piece quoted a 'friend' of Green, who said it was 'all bullshit', that Field was 'behaving like a complete arsehole' and that he was 'not about to be strong-armed by a load of tosser MPs'. It was hubristic in the extreme. Green seemed to have provided a full jerry can of petrol himself.

While Green was flailing in the growing media heat and BHS's managers were concentrating on the CVA, Chappell was spiralling out of control, increasingly isolated from his Retail Acquisitions team. He had started 2016 in an upbeat mood, asking Eddie Irvine if he could leave his Princess V65 cruiser at the bottom of the ex-Formula One driver's garden in Miami, adding, 'If you want to use it no problem.' He spent $41,000 (£28,700 at the time) on a tender, made inquiries about a third yacht – a higher-spec Princess V85 – and added a Bentley Continental GT Speed and a Land Rover Defender to his car collection. He sent pictures of the Bentley to his wife, Rebecca. She replied, 'Tres chic mon Cher x.'

As the stress of the CVA process approached in March, Chappell went AWOL. He flew back and forth to Vancouver on a bizarre mission to open BHS stores in Canada, paying tens of thousands of dollars to a local consultant who happened to be an old friend. He made an even more fanciful £7 million takeover bid for the 116-year-old men's suits retailer Austin Reed, at a time when his advisers were warning that BHS did not have enough money to make contributions to its pension funds or pay its usual levy to the Pension Protection Fund. Chappell was becoming detached from reality, but he was still humoured by Grant Thornton, which put a team of six accountants onto the Austin Reed deal, and Olswang, whose lead lawyer, David Roberts, cheered, 'Roll forward RAL [Retail Acquisitions Limited]!'

Keith Smith, Retail Acquisitions' chairman and Chappell's uncle, must have had a better sense for how dangerously low BHS's fuel was running as it tried to clear the next mountain range. In February, he quietly suggested to Chappell that they resurrect Project Herald, the plan to fashion a parachute by taking direct ownership of BHS's profitable international and online businesses. Smith sent Chappell an email headed 'Shellco' – corporate slang for a shell company – setting out how they would use a new entity to buy the good parts of BHS, and then Retail Acquisitions itself. 'Properly handled,' Smith said, the process might also allow Retail Acquisitions to wipe out the millions of pounds of debt it owed to the faltering department store chain. Chappell took his uncle seriously enough to borrow a further £500,000 from Alex Dellal and spend $280,000 on Todex Corp, a shell company in Las Vegas, which he planned to rename RAL Global. But events moved too quickly.

Michael Hitchcock had resigned as temporary finance director on the eve of the CVA vote in protest at Retail Acquisitions' shambolic ownership. His antagonism with Aidan Treacy, his rival finance director, had come to a head in January, when Treacy approved a £90,000 BHS loan to Chappell while Hitchcock was away on a skiing holiday. Chappell, who had apparently needed the money to meet a personal tax bill, repaid it in ten days after the BHS board took legal advice. Hitchcock pressed on for another two months, but he finally lost patience during a board meeting on 21 March. Even with the rent cuts promised by the CVA, BHS needed £100 million of new funding to survive. Chappell's team was supposed to have arranged £60 million from Gordon Brothers, a tough American lender usually seen as a last resort for the destitute, £30 million from various property sales and £10 million from security deposits tied up in letters of credit.

Hitchcock realized the patchwork could not possibly come together. The terms being offered by Gordon Brothers were so strict that BHS would almost certainly breach them in weeks, allowing the US firm to take control. The property deals were also a mess. Retail Acquisitions had been supposed to sell BHS's Oxford Street flagship lease in 2015 to raise funds for the turnaround. Chappell had promised that it would bring in up to £90 million, but it was now about to be sold to Abu Dhabi's royal family for £55 million – well short of what BHS needed. Hitchcock apologized to Darren Topp and terminated his consultancy contract.

Topp made another alarming discovery. Chappell had sent more than £1 million of the proceeds of BHS's Oxford Street disposal and a separate sale of its Sunderland store straight to Retail Acquisitions' bank account. The amounts, £600,000 from Oxford Street and £440,000 from Sunderland, had been earmarked for VAT payments the cash-strapped store chain needed to make. Topp called an emergency board meeting on 5 April. Chappell admitted that he had instructed lawyers to divert the money without board permission. He agreed to return it after condemnation from his fellow directors, including Keith Smith, but Topp still threatened to resign. He emailed Chappell, 'Following our board meeting I have left the office as I need some time to go and consider my position. I would appreciate you allowing me that time.' Topp stepped back from the brink, but he made a discreet call to Green. Topp warned his former paymaster that the management team had lost confidence and was close to walking out. Green, who already knew about the latest crisis in BHS's finances, became desperate.

Paul Sutton lobbed another grenade into this combustible situation. It was the week of the Panama Papers, when a huge leak from the law firm Mossack Fonseca hit the press. Any headline involving Panama had special currency. Desperate for revenge on Chappell, the fraudster contacted me through an intermediary and provided details of Chappell's shareholding in Clarberry Investments, the Panamanian company they had established the previous year. Sutton also told me that Chappell had used £1.5 million of BHS's money, via Retail Acquisitions, to pay off the mortgage on his parents' house in Sunbury-on-Thames. A separate source called in with the story of Topp's emergency board meeting and the £1 million missing from the property sales. The emergence of the latter facts in particular sent panic through Chappell's team. Eddie Parladorio emailed the others, 'There must be a phone tap or DC's room is bugged or emails must be being hacked as I cannot imagine any board member going to Shah with such fresh news – this is a very close and very under cover leak!!!!'

The three-pronged scoop on 10 April 2016 was met with incredulity by creditors and landlords who had just voted for the rent cuts. BHS was in utter chaos. A few days later, Chappell and Parladorio almost came to blows in the Marylebone Road headquarters.

According to a BHS executive who witnessed it, the pair had a violent row about 'some fairly nasty people in London' who had threatened Parladorio's wife over money they believed Chappell owed them. Parladorio was said to have shouted at Chappell, 'My family's at risk!' The witness said, 'I thought he was going to break the table at one point. He whacked the table with his hand and then he flung the door open and smashed the side of the wall.'

Green was beside himself. Retail Acquisitions' tenure had been a year of uninterrupted bungling and scandal. The £100 million finance package Chappell had promised to deliver was in tatters. HMRC was threatening to issue a winding-up petition and there was a shortage of money to pay the coming month's wages. The tycoon decided it was time to cauterize the wound. He called in his outstanding £35 million debt and pushed BHS into administration.

15.

The Crash

At 8.21 a.m. on Friday 22 April 2016, Dominic Chappell sent me a text message saying, 'We are not going into admin.' Since the first *Sunday Times* exposé on his background more than a year earlier, the serial bankrupt had been forbidden from speaking to the press by his minders. As BHS hurtled towards a cliff, he lost discipline and opened up a back channel.

It was the end of a long, frantic week. The events that would lead to BHS's demise had been set in motion five days earlier. Sir Philip Green had planned to put the department store chain into administration by appointing Neville Kahn, his old ally at Deloitte. But Kahn had explained that Deloitte was conflicted because of its previous work on BHS's pension funds. For various reasons, so too were Grant Thornton, KPMG and PwC. Kahn recommended Phil Duffy, a managing director in the Manchester office of the restructuring firm Duff & Phelps. Duffy was a chipper character who had previously worked on the administrations of the furniture retailer MFI and the bookseller Borders. He had also been administrator to three small property companies in the Arcadia Group. At 4 p.m. on Monday, 18 April, Green made a terse call to Duffy and asked him to come to London the next day. He did not give a reason.

Duffy and one of his partners, Ben Wiles, arrived at Arcadia's headquarters on Berners Street at 10.30 a.m. Green explained the situation. At midday, the full BHS board arrived. According to a professional who was present, there were 'fireworks' between Green and Chappell as Chappell initially tried to resist the appointment of Duff & Phelps. Olswang and Weil, Gotshal & Manges, Retail Acquisitions' lawyers, advised Chappell that BHS was close to becoming insolvent. They told him there was no alternative. Chappell then tried to argue for the appointment of a smaller accountancy firm, David Rubin & Partners. He gave up when it was explained to him that David Rubin was nowhere near big enough to handle a job of BHS's scale. The administration was provisionally slated for the end of the week – Friday 22 April. Chappell hurriedly cancelled a weekend of clay pigeon shooting in the Cotswolds.

In a fit of pique after the Arcadia meeting, Chappell called for the dismissal of Darren Topp and the barrister Dominic Chandler, whom Retail Acquisitions perceived had defected to Topp's side. Chappell also demanded legal action against Michael Hitchcock for 'miss leading [sic] the board in relation to losses'. BHS's owner was persuaded to withdraw the proposals, but his attempts to dismiss Topp and Chandler indicated how quickly relations were descending into a state of outright hostility.

Topp quietly warned Green about Chappell, 'This guy is desperate for money. He wants to feather his nest.' Green contacted one of the most senior executives at Barclays, BHS's bank. He asked Barclays to flag any unusual transactions involving BHS's main account. The next day, Chappell transferred £1.5 million to BHS Sweden, a new shell company set up by his father's friend, Lennart Henningson. BHS had no stores in Sweden. When Topp was alerted to the transaction by his head of treasury, Harry Carver, his first instinct was to call the police. Instead, he rang Chappell, who knew about it straight away. Topp told him, 'That's theft.' Topp later recounted to Parliament, 'Now, if I take out all the expletives, [Chappell] basically said, "Do not kick off about this, Darren. I've had enough of you telling me what to do over the last few months. It's my business, I can do what I want. And if you kick off about it, I'm going to come down there and kill you." Then he threatened to kill me again. And I know it sounds silly, but apparently he says he was in the helicopter squad of the SAS. I know he's got a gun.'

The £1.5 million that Chappell moved had been set aside to pay the wages of shop staff, most of whom were on £7 an hour. Topp thought Chappell's behaviour was 'disgusting'. Chappell apparently told him, 'You've never done an administration before, Darren. You do not know what it's like. There'll be hell to pay and costs to pay, and I want to make sure I look after my home team.'

Green rang his contact at Barclays again and went 'absolutely mental', according to a BHS executive who witnessed Green's end of the conversation. Green shouted, 'Can you explain to me how the movement of £1.5 million to a company that isn't part of the group, in a country where we don't trade, is not an unusual transaction?' It must have been processed by a junior Barclays clerk who forgot about the instruction. Chappell was forced to send the money back to BHS, although he initially kept £50,000, claiming it was a fee for currency conversions. After pressure from Duff & Phelps, he eventually returned £43,000, keeping £7,000.

On Thursday, 21 April, at 11 a.m., the BHS board unanimously voted to appoint Duff & Phelps. Then Chappell pulled another surprise. He contacted a representative of Mike Ashley, the billionaire founder of Sports Direct, and tried to arrange an emergency sale. Ashley was a controversial suitor: he and Green had a complicated relationship. They had known each other since the mid-1990s, when Green was running Foothold, the chain of trainer shops that was part of Owen & Robinson. The overweight entrepreneurs had much in common. They loved gambling and were sometimes seen together at 50 St James's or Les Ambassadeurs on Park Lane. Green had tinkered with Tottenham Hotspur and Everton; Ashley bought Newcastle United. The tycoons' friendship was shot through with insecurity and rivalry. They often played games, keeping each other in the dark and fighting recreational proxy battles through obscure deals. Unlike Green, Ashley could come across as shy and socially awkward, but he was capable of behaviour that made Green look like a wallflower. On one occasion, he was alleged to have downed twelve pints of lager with vodka chasers in a drinking contest with one of his junior analysts, then vomited into a pub fireplace to applause from his senior team.

In his teens, Ashley had been a county squash coach – although nobody would have guessed it from the enormous beer gut he cultivated in adulthood. He gave up squash at sixteen and bought a sports equipment shop in Maidenhead, Berkshire, using £10,000 borrowed from his parents, who mortgaged their bungalow. Ashley's father, Keith, a production manager at Young's Seafood, did the books at weekends. His mother, Barbara, helped out in the shop. Ashley expanded Sports World with brutal efficiency, buying once-great brands such as Lonsdale and Slazenger and discounting them to lucrative oblivion. By 2007, it had more than 400 stores and sales of £1 billion. Ashley renamed the business Sports Direct. With Green's help, he floated it on the stock market for £2.2 billion, paying himself almost £1 billion in the process. 'I'm not being funny, but you struggle to spend the interest,' Ashley told the *Sunday Times* that year in his mild Estuary accent. Despite the change to his bank balance, he insisted his lifestyle had not changed. 'Some of our best nights out are impromptu – a few beers and then down the kebab shop,' he said. 'We still tell the same old stories, like the time I fell down the fire escape in the Maidenhead store and we still laugh and think it's funny.'

Like Amber Day two decades earlier, Sports Direct became a magnet for City opprobrium – although Ashley kept a majority shareholding, meaning he could not be removed. First, Sports Direct's share price crashed, then its independent chairman resigned over governance concerns. Among other things, it emerged that Ashley had settled a £750,000 legal bill using a round of spoof, the coin guessing game (and lost). A defiant Ashley told the *Sunday Times* he had 'balls of steel' and added, 'Some investors have been great and have been very supportive. But some of these City people act like cry babies. I'm not giving in.'

Ashley had first registered in Green's circle in 2007, when he attended PG55 in the Maldives. He made an impact by insulting Bob Wigley, the European chairman of Merrill Lynch, the investment bank that had carried out Sports Direct's initial public offering. Ashley later rang Wigley to apologize after a ticking off from Green. Having built Sports Direct from scratch, Ashley was by far the more talented retailer, but he was a less accomplished dealmaker than

Green and he was deferential towards the Topshop owner. He was also twelve years younger. Ashley referred to Green as the 'Big Emp'. Green called Ashley the 'Junior Emp' or 'Little Emp'. Ashley tended to listen quietly whenever Green vented his spleen over the phone.

Retail Acquisitions already had a connection with Sports Direct, having sold it BHS's stores in Southampton and Sunderland. Ashley had looked at buying House of Fraser, and he was known to be interested in adding a department store to his empire. In desperation, Chappell rang Justin Barnes, a hard-nosed trademark lawyer who acted as Ashley's fixer in deal situations. The Junior Emp, who delegated the work to Barnes, kept the talks secret from the Big Emp. The two sides hunkered down in Olswang's Holborn offices and worked for twenty-four hours non-stop between Thursday and Friday afternoon. Green sniffed a development. He grew suspicious when Chappell asked him for Ashley's personal mobile number at lunchtime on Friday. At 3 p.m. that day, Ashley finally called the Big Emp, laughing. 'You knew it was me, didn't you?' he said.

There are two entirely contradictory accounts of how Green reacted when he heard about the potential rescue. According to Chappell's evidence in Parliament, he 'went absolutely insane', 'screaming and shouting down the phone that he didn't want to get involved with Mike Ashley'. In contrast, Jonathan Hawker, BHS's PR adviser, described witnessing a second attempt by Ashley to buy the business a few days later, after it had gone into administration. 'I could hear Sir Philip Green on the administrator's mobile phone telling him loudly to sell the business to Sports Direct,' Hawker said in a written statement. 'Sir Philip was being very forceful and arguing his case so loudly I could hear much of what he said.'

Ashley's intervention meant the administration had to be delayed. However, Green formally demanded the repayment of his £35 million loan to BHS, giving Chappell an effective deadline of Monday, 25 April. On the Friday evening, *Retail Week* published a speculative story about the impending administration on its website. It contained inaccuracies, and it was taken down after a furious call from Green to the editor. Eddie Parladorio emailed Chappell and a few others, 'Who is the leaking pig???'

That weekend was dominated by frantic conference calls between Retail Acquisitions and Sports Direct. Chappell and his crew were eager to keep their gravy train rolling. They wanted a 49 per cent stake in BHS's international business, the cancellation of all Retail Acquisitions' debts to BHS and a promise that their consultancy contract would run for at least another six months. In return, they offered to sell BHS for £1. But Sports Direct wanted assurances from the Pensions Regulator and the Pension Protection Fund that it would have no liability for BHS's pension deficit. Retail Acquisitions' relations with the pension authorities were barely better than Green's. Their own advisers had described their first meeting with the regulator as a 'car crash'. Parladorio had bitterly complained about the regulator's 'witch hunt' over the money they had extracted from BHS. He had even mooted sending a legal threat to the PPF over sceptical comments made in the press by Malcolm Weir, its head of restructuring. On Saturday lunchtime, Chappell told his colleagues it was 'of utmost importance' that they secure support from the regulator and the PPF for the sale to Sports Direct, but the authorities were not minded to bend any rules to help Retail Acquisitions rush the deal through. Ashley's appetite waned over the weekend. At 8.03 p.m. on Sunday, 24 April, Chappell emailed the BHS management team, 'Gents, With deep hart [sic] I have just had confirmed that SDI [Sports Direct International] will not be coming up to the plate.'

He followed it with a longer note to senior staff. Under the subject line 'The final curtain', Chappell wrote, 'It is with a deep hart [sic] that I have to report, despite a massive effort from the team, we have been unable to secure a funder or a trade sale . . . I would like to say it has been a real pleasure working with all of you on the BHS project, one I will never forget, you all need to keep your heads high, you are [sic] done a great job and remember that it was always going to be very very hard to turn around. Bonne chance mon ami [sic]. DC.'

Paul Wareham, Chappell's best man and Retail Acquisitions' sometime project manager, replied, 'Gutted. No other words . . .' Eddie Parladorio wrote to Chappell, 'From me to you: well done for a massive effort all the way through. You have never given up and have worked tirelessly on what has been a tough gig from day one. We have had unexpected missiles heaped upon us from the beginning and we have had very little luck in any respect.'

Retail Acquisitions had invested nothing in BHS. It took more than £7 million during its year of ownership in salaries, bonuses and fees for arranging exorbitantly priced financing such as the 'Wonga' loan from Alex Dellal. Chappell personally banked £3 million – five times what the average BHS shop assistant would have made in their entire working life – not even counting the £1.5 million loan that was used to pay off the mortgage on his parents' house. Parladorio received £1.5 million. The cast of hangers-on, such as Lennart Henningson and Keith Smith, was paid generously. On top of that, Retail Acquisitions gave £2.4 million to Grant Thornton and Olswang in success bonuses, and BHS paid close to £5 million more to the firms for rolling advice.

Chappell claimed that he needed to travel to the US for an urgent eye operation. In fact, as BHS's 164 stores opened their doors on Monday morning to the announcement of administration, he boarded a 10.25 a.m. flight from Heathrow to the Bahamas under the name Captain Dominic Chappell. He was joined by his wife and Eddie Parladorio. It was Phil Duffy of Duff & Phelps who addressed the staff at BHS's head office half an hour later. He explained that the administrators would continue to run the company for at least a few months while they sought a buyer for some or all of the stores. A handwritten sign appeared in one of the lifts, 'Where are RAL [Retail Acquisitions Limited]? The thieving shits.'

BHS's collapse was the biggest high-street crisis since the failure of Woolworths eight years earlier. It sparked an unprecedented firestorm of public anger. Perhaps Green had hoped to copy Richard Branson, who escaped unscathed in 2007 when he sold Virgin

Megastores for £1 to its management team, who ran it under the Zavvi name until it went bust fifteen months later, albeit without a pension deficit. Maybe he thought he would be able to manage the press fallout, as he had with the administration of Allders, when hardly any newspapers had even dared to mention his name. But this story was devastatingly simple: Green and his partners, Richard Caring and Sir Tom Hunter, had extracted £423 million of dividends from BHS in the early 2000s. Green had taken tens of millions of pounds more in charges, starved the chain of investment and finally tossed its bones to Chappell and his ragtag consortium, who had gnawed off the last remaining scraps of meat. Eleven thousand staff faced losing their jobs and 20,000 pension-fund members were seeing their retirement plans thrown into jeopardy because of the £571 million hole in the schemes. Alastair Campbell, Tony Blair's former spin doctor, remarked that the whole thing had 'a whiff of the Robert Maxwells about it' (although, of course, Green was not accused of stealing from the BHS pension funds, as Maxwell had when he defrauded the Mirror Group).

The Guardian said BHS's death was a case of 'murder on the high street'. It advised, 'Prepare to dig deep, Sir Philip: forget Topshop, the yachts (a new 300-footer is on the way), the fashion academy and the knighthood. Your contribution to retailing will be remembered chiefly by the decency, or otherwise, of your behaviour towards BHS pensioners.'

I called Green that Monday morning. 'Do you think I'm really going to talk to you?' he said, his voice infused with a new venom. 'Fuck off. Is that easy? Fuck off. Do not phone my number. I've told your editor I don't want to talk to you.' Chappell rang from the Bahamas – although he told me he was in America. He sounded strangely relaxed. 'We're not the bogeyman in this one,' he said. 'You can portray it how you wish, but go into the business and ask anybody how hard my team have worked to turn this business around. They've worked night and day on this for over a year and I doubt you can find one wrong word said about anything that we've done in the business.' Chappell defended Retail Acquisitions' use of

Alex Dellal and the 'Wonga' loan. 'It's very easy to be criticized about raising expensive money, but listen – when it's the only girl in town, you've got to dance with her,' he said.

As well as undergoing his alleged eye operation, Chappell claimed to be travelling in search of funds to buy back parts of BHS. 'Who's backing him – the Bank of Toytown?' Green scoffed. It said a lot about Chappell's falling star that even Paul Sutton now rang me to distance himself from his former protégé. The fraudster described Retail Acquisitions' dealings with BHS as 'mind bending'. 'It's absolutely mad,' he said. 'The day I signed that thing not to be involved, they shafted me completely. I got completely rumped. The minute they got in there, they cut me off.' He added, 'On Sunday, I appreciate you're doing an article and whatever, but try not to throw me under a bus. I've had enough of these people trying to damage me.'

Duff & Phelps barred Retail Acquisitions from BHS's headquarters. Five tumultuous days after the administration began, a group of head-office staff gathered at the Union bar in Marylebone to let off steam. There were tears amid the dogged optimism. 'People are carrying on,' one woman said. 'The business is up for sale. It's still credible. A lot of us have got a lot of faith in the business.' She was damning about Chappell and his farewell message. 'When he called it a project, that was a real insult,' she said. 'We had our doubts from the start in terms of his business acumen. He just wanted to make a quick buck for himself.'

Chappell's name had already turned to ash, but Green's reputation was burning with a fierce flame. For years, the tycoon had controlled the press with the carrot of leaks about other people's deals and the stick of his ferocious temper. Over time, he had gradually drifted away from the centre of the business action, coming across less and less information to trade, but his temper had got worse. It was a weaker negotiating position, but he had failed to notice. *The Times* described the surge of media outrage as 'payback time for a man never far from an F-word'. Green offered Dominic O'Connell, my editor, a dossier on Chappell's wrongdoing. 'Just take me off the menu for Sunday,' he pleaded. O'Connell refused his deal.

The cultural ground beneath Green's feet had also shifted. Before the financial crisis, the tabloids had seen his gold Monopoly set and Gulfstream private jet as the well-deserved trappings of success. In the straitened post-crisis reality, taking delivery of a £100 million superboat would have been risky even without a pension scandal in the foreground. Added to the BHS situation, it was a potent symbol of excess. 'Crisis? Yacht crisis?' mocked *The Sun*. *The Independent* called him 'a grotesque poster boy for celeb age ultra-exhibitionism'. Even Green's most loyal supporters in the press turned on him. The *Daily Mail*'s veteran City editor Alex Brummer, one of his close journalistic contacts, asked, 'Can the man who milked the millions from BHS really be allowed to keep his knighthood?' Brummer rapidly revised his view of the billionaire, writing, 'Green's career is littered with the bodies of those who got in his way as well as those he seemingly befriended only to dump mercilessly later on.'

Green, who had donated £100,000 to the *Mail*'s relief fund for victims of the Boxing Day tsunami in south-east Asia twelve years earlier at Brummer's request, barked at the City editor, 'How can you do this? I thought I could count on you as an old friend.' Brummer replied, 'I never went to any of your parties or went on your yacht, Philip. Those people who did – *they're* your friends.' Green's anger increased when Brummer wrote a front-page editorial for the *Jewish Chronicle* declaring that the tycoon's behaviour had 'cast a broader pall over the reputation of the ethics of Jews in business'. Green called Brummer and ranted, 'You're meant to be a leader of the community! Next time you go to synagogue, pray a bit harder.'

As the Pensions Regulator finally confirmed that it was investigating Green and Chappell, the media frenzy heated up Westminster. Mark Field, Tory MP for Cities of London and Westminster, described BHS's collapse as 'a cautionary tale about how the rules of the game can be manipulated by those who are happy to pocket cash in the good and bad times'. Frank Field (no relation), the Labour chairman of the Work and Pensions Select Committee, announced that Green would be called to give evidence in Parliament. Lord Myners, Green's old foe from Marks & Spencer (who had been enno-bled by Gordon Brown eight years earlier), tabled eleven questions in the House of Lords, urging the government to look into the scan-dal. Green rang Myners and demanded, 'Why are you asking all these fucking questions? Just come round for a cup of tea and a chat.' Myners told him that was not how parliamentary questions worked. 'If you carry on, I'm going to punch you on the fucking nose,' Green warned him. 'Philip, you're getting close to contempt of Parliament,' Myners said – to which the tycoon growled, 'I don't know about Parliament, but I've got contempt for you, you cunt.'

Green had not used a PR adviser since his second failed takeover bid for M&S. He preferred to handle calls himself, believing a burst of invective delivered through a battered Nokia was more effective. For the first time, in the aftermath of BHS's failure, he found himself unable to handle the sheer volume of inbound calls. The outpouring of political anger was also an entirely new phenom-enon for Green. In need of support, he hired Neil Bennett, the PR man he had brought in to help the disgraced HBOS banker Peter Cummings four years earlier.

Bennett, a gangly running enthusiast, had spent eighteen years in journalism before going into PR in 2002 – latterly as City editor of the *Sunday Telegraph*, where he broke landmark stories including Rupert Murdoch's attempt to take over Manchester United. He had first met Green on a trip to Worcester races in the late 1980s with the rag trader Irvine Sellar, who was celebrating the stock-market listing of his property company, Ford Sellar Morris. Bennett, then a young journalist on the *Investors Chronicle*, was amused by the gre-garious rag trader who reeled off one-liners and threw money at the horses. Years later, at the *Sunday Telegraph*, he was among the admirers of Green's supposed BHS turnaround. At Christmas 2000, after Green acquired the business, Bennett invited him and a few other entrepreneurs to play Monopoly at the London Capital Club in the City. Green went to jail more often than any of the other players, declaring that it was 'a good place to be'. But he coolly took huge risks early in the game and collected rent 'like a mugger at a cashpoint'. He emerged the clear winner, hoarding 'an obscene stack of notes'.

Bennett had also seen the darker side of Green. In 1997, Helene, a clothing supplier listed on the London stock market, went bust with debts of £29 million. There had been a number of odd-looking transactions in the year before its demise. Helene had announced its intention to purchase Dyckhoff, a struggling German retail operation that was being run by Green's associate Harold Tillman. Then a mysterious offshore company called Madrigal International bought Helene's £14.5 million of bank debt, and the Dyckhoff talks failed. Michael Harris, Helene's chief executive, was investigated by the Department of Trade and Industry, and in 2001 he was barred from acting as a company director for thirteen years. A judge ruled that he had 'systematically looted' Helene, running up credit-card bills of £594,500 and spending £586,900 on travel expenses through a subsidiary. Green was linked to Harris. The DTI investigators obtained telephone records showing a flurry of calls between Helene's offices and Green's numbers in spring 1997, although Green argued that they constituted no evidence of any business dealings. The tycoon said he was simply friendly with Harris.

According to a journalist who was involved, when the *Sunday Telegraph* tried to dig into Helene's collapse, Green called the reporter who was working on the story, Richard Rivlin, and warned him darkly, 'We know where you live. We're going to come after you.' Bennett, who was Rivlin's editor, 'acted impeccably'. He took the remarks seriously enough to call the City of London police, who visited the newspaper's offices. Incredibly, the police told Rivlin and Bennett to 'leave Philip alone', and after taking a statement from Rivlin they went away. Two decades later, the former *Sunday Telegraph* City editor was perfectly happy to become Green's spokesman. There was consternation among some of Bennett's colleagues at the PR firm Maitland. One said that Green showed off in their first meeting, taking a call from Tony Blair and making it clear that he knew best how to handle the media. But the billionaire offered

Maitland a £20,000-a-week retainer. (Bennett claimed the rate dropped sharply after the first few intensive months, making it worth far less than the full £1 million a year.)

Bennett's first job was to engage with the Labour MP Frank Field, joint chairman of the select committee that was due to question Green. Field told the press he would recommend stripping the tycoon of his knighthood unless he repaid the £571 million BHS pension deficit in full. Bennett issued an expletive-free statement that was more finessed than Green's usual off-the-cuff responses. 'Clearly he has made his decision as to what he feels the punishment should be without even hearing any evidence from anybody,' it said. 'I think Mr Field needs to stand down from the inquiry immediately as he is clearly prejudiced.' Field stuck two fingers up at Green. The next day, he appointed two special advisers – Lord Myners, the former M&S chairman whom Green had offered 'a proper fucking kick in the head' after his second takeover bid, and Sir David Norgrove, as the former head of the M&S pension trustees was now titled, whom Green had accused of spouting 'pious nonsense'. Field told *The Guardian*, 'Sir Philip is a master of bullying but he will find that parliament isn't for being bullied.' Myners doubled down a month later, telling the BBC that selling BHS to Chappell had been 'like giving the keys of your car to a five-year-old'.

Field was an unusual Labour MP. A devout Christian and an admirer of Margaret Thatcher, he was once described in the *New Statesman* as 'a cross between a monk and a Tory'. He had forged a career as an odd but principled backbencher, opposing what he saw as the generosity of the benefits system and the iniquities of mass immigration from his seat in Birkenhead, one of the poorest parts of Britain. Field had flirted with a cabinet position only once, when Tony Blair appointed him to 'think the unthinkable' on welfare reform in 1997 – then sacked him for doing just that a year later. Aged seventy-four, Field was now free from political ambition. He commanded cross-party respect for his independent thinking and moral rectitude. Stooped and tall, with sallow skin and a priestly manner, he had an air of serene authority.

Field's Pensions Select Committee inquiry into BHS was merged with a parallel probe by the business committee, chaired by Iain Wright, the Labour MP for Hartlepool. Wright, forty-four, was very different in character and temperament. A floppy-haired, boyish family man who had been born and raised in the area he represented, he had an excellent commercial nose, having worked for the accountancy firm Deloitte before going into politics. He was a more buttoned-down and conventional politician than Field, and at first he was concerned by some of the unscripted statements his older colleague was giving out to journalists. But Wright's attitude towards Green hardened when he saw the way the tycoon tried to silence Field.

As the inquiry opened on 9 May, a painting of Green appeared in the window of BHS's store in Southend-on-Sea. 'Phillip [sic] Green,' it said, with the 'Sir' crossed out in red pen. 'Where's my pension?' It was representative of the feeling coursing through BHS's shops, which gave the parliamentary hearings an unusual emotional charge. They took place in Portcullis House, a modern building opposite the Houses of Commons. Witnesses were asked to sit before a horseshoe of ten MPs, led by Field and Wright. Alan Rubenstein, a flinty Scottish banker who ran the Pension Protection Fund, was the first to give evidence. He explained how alarm bells had rung in 2012 when Green was found to have exploited a widely used loophole to lower BHS's levy payments to the PPF insurance scheme. He said that BHS had put up a property subsidiary as a guarantee for its pension deficit, knowing that the PPF allowed companies backed by guarantees to pay lower premiums. But the subsidiary, Davenbush, had turned out to be 'pretty much' worthless. Green had withdrawn the guarantee after being challenged by the PPF, and the lifeboat had passed the information to the Pensions Regulator.

Rubenstein was followed by Lesley Titcomb, the regulator's chief executive. She put on a shaky and unconvincing performance. Richard Fuller, a Tory MP, pointed out that it had taken Titcomb's team seventeen months to obtain the infamous 2012 recovery plan for BHS's pension funds, which stretched for twenty-three years owing to Green's refusal to pay more than £10 million a year. Even then, Fuller said, the watchdog had not deemed the BHS funds worthy of 'proactive' engagement. Titcomb leaned back in her seat as he delivered the criticism, bristling like the mother of an unpopular child at parents' evening. 'You're not much of a regulator, are you?' Fuller prodded her. 'Well, I don't agree with that statement,' Titcomb replied, leaning forward and clasping her hands. Fuller then asked when the regulator had found out about Green's £1 sale to Retail Acquisitions. 'We were not, that I'm aware, advised in advance,' Titcomb told the surprised MPs. 'We learned about the deal from the newspapers.'

Green scoffed as he watched. He called Dominic O'Connell, the *Sunday Times'* business editor, and complained about the nonsense 'that fat bird' was talking. Two days later, Arcadia sent a letter to the select committee. It said, 'The evidence of Ms Titcomb has been widely reported in the press, but it is incorrect.' Arcadia said it had told the regulator about the sale on 6 February 2015. The truth turned out to be somewhere in between. As Titcomb then clarified, the BHS trustees had mentioned a buyer called Swiss Rock in February, but the watchdog heard nothing about Retail Acquisitions specifically until the deal hit the press.

The suffering of BHS's 11,000 staff continued. London landmarks such as Marble Arch were lit up with the slogan #SaveBHS on a Union Jack background. The administrators desperately tried to find a buyer, sounding out suitors including John Hargreaves, the Monaco-based founder of Matalan, and Cafer Mahiroglu, the Turkish retailer. Meanwhile, the hearings intensified in the sticky heat of late May and June as the MPs moved towards Green's inner circle. The protagonists fought like rats in a sack to point the finger of blame at each other. Anthony Gutman, the Goldman Sachs banker who had helped Arcadia vet Chappell, tried to play down Goldman's involvement, saying it had been offered a formal advisory role but had declined 'for commercial reasons' because the deal was 'too small'. Then he elegantly skewered Green. 'We indicated to them that clearly the potential buyer did not have retail experience,' he said. 'We indicated that the proposal was highly preliminary and lacking in detail. We also indicated that the bidder had a history of bankruptcy.' Gutman was sitting alongside Owen Clay, Green's lawyer at Linklaters, and Steve Denison, Arcadia's auditor at PwC. Amanda Solloway, a Tory MP, asked them, 'I am intrigued about what, given [Retail Acquisitions'] lack of experience and the fact that it was paying £1, made it the preferred buyer?' After a pause, she asked, 'Anybody?' There was stony silence from the three men. Later that evening, Gutman and Neil Bennett, Green's PR man, were seen mingling at the opening night of the Chelsea Flower Show, one of the most prestigious networking events in the City's calendar.

Next came four of Green's closest lieutenants. Lord Grabiner, a furrier's son from Hackney who rose to become one of Britain's top commercial barristers, was reduced to desperate semantics as he tried to justify his role as Taveta Investments' £125,000-a-year chairman. Green was always said to have enjoyed treating Lord Grabiner as an ornament, and the select committee picked apart the fact that he had not even been invited to the key board meeting on the evening of 10 March 2015 when the £1 sale to Chappell was finalized. 'Do you feel aggrieved by that?' Iain Wright needled him. 'Because I'm chair of the biz select committee. If there was a meeting of the select committee and I wasn't invited, I'd be really angry.' Lord Grabiner stammered, 'But – but – but – the point is that we had appointed this subgroup to investigate the possibility of disposing of BHS.' Scowling, the QC admitted he had not been properly briefed on Green's deal with Chappell until five days after it happened, and that he had found out about Chappell's bankruptcies only when they were reported in the press.

To his left was his cousin, Ian Grabiner, Arcadia's chief executive; Paul Budge, the finance director; Gillian Hague, the group's financial controller; and Chris Harris, its property director. Harris made a comment that quickly came back to bite him when details of Chappell's complete lack of cash entered the public domain. 'He had managed to put £35 million in a bank within about three days – I think it was something like that – which showed credibility,' Harris said. 'He injected £10 million into the business at the time of the sale. So there were many things – a package of things – that made us comfortable that RAL [Retail Acquisitions Limited] was a credible buyer.' In fact, the £35 million in Olswang's escrow account had come from Alex Dellal, and the £5 million, not £10 million, of 'equity' Chappell had injected had been a loan – also from Dellal.

Field and Wright summoned the pension trustees past and present, including Dr Margaret Downes, who gave a nuanced picture of relations with Green in her era. She cut an elegant figure in chunky tortoiseshell glasses and a navy jacket. Downes prompted laughter when she described Green as 'different to most'. She recalled her single face-to-face meeting with the billionaire, and how he had 'categorically' refused to pay more than £10 million a year into the pension deficit. But she added, contradictorily, 'I do believe that he had at heart a caring approach towards the 22,000-odd investment members . . . He appeared to me to be aware that he had so many members and especially that a number of them were lower-paid.'

Grant Thornton and Olswang hid behind client confidentiality, which Retail Acquisitions refused to waive, and the partners they sent to give evidence were not the ones who had been directly involved with BHS. Paul Martin, the Grant Thornton adviser who had described the deal's closing meeting with Green as 'legendary', and David Roberts, the Olswang lawyer who was said to have been 'tingling' with excitement at the prospect of working with Chappell, were nowhere to be seen. Frank Field described the firms' conduct as an 'insult' to Parliament and the nation. 'Why should we talk to the monkey when we can have the organ grinder?' he asked. 'That Philip Green is coming but these bastards aren't coming is outrageous.' In the next session, Robin Saunders, the former WestLB banker, answered hardball questions on BHS's past. She said the magic behind Green's improvement in profitability in the early years had been cost-cutting. 'The joke was that everyone would have to use their pencils down to the nub before they could be thrown out,' she said.

On 2 June, Duff & Phelps announced that all 164 of BHS's shops would close. Rescue talks had failed with the last remaining bidder, a Portuguese consortium fronted by Greg Tufnell, brother of the former England cricketer Phil Tufnell. Heartbroken store staff put away signs they had prepared saying 'Thankyou for saving BHS'. Alex Brummer, Green's former friend on the *Daily Mail*, wrote, 'Sir Philip Green plucked the carcass of BHS and the vultures have been picking at what was left ever since.' Chappell, who had already branded Darren Topp a 'jumped up store manager' in a newspaper interview, texted his former chief executive, 'Well done. I hope you and Michael are happy that you got the out come [sic] you wanted. You fucking prick.' A BHS spokesman described it as a 'new low' for the 'fantasist'.

A few days later, Topp and Michael Hitchcock electrified the inquiry with their evidence. Topp, who had tried so hard to rein in Retail Acquisitions' excesses, said that Chappell had 'literally had his fingers in the till'. He told the story of how Chappell had threatened to kill him over the £1.5 million he siphoned off to Sweden. Hitchcock, who had valiantly tried to support Topp as his interim finance director, also condemned Chappell. 'Like many others throughout this process, I think I was duped,' he said. 'I think the technical term is a mythomaniac. The layperson's term is that he was a premier league liar and a Sunday pub league retailer, at best.'

Topp and Hitchcock were followed by Stephen Bourne and Mark Tasker, the professionals who had advised Retail Acquisitions in the run-up to the deal; Eddie Parladorio, Chappell's right-hand man; and Aidan Treacy, the finance director brought in by Retail Acquisitions to rival Hitchcock. Bourne and Tasker answered questions in a straightforward manner, Bourne explaining how Green had 'effectively' provided financial 'assistance in the transaction'. Parladorio kept his head down, allowing the others to do the talking. The way he referred to his close friend as 'Mr Chappell' made it sound as if they barely knew each other.

As they finished giving evidence, a porcine, sun-tanned figure in an expensive-looking suit bundled into Portcullis House. Dominic Chappell sat down in front of the select committee, somehow managing to look furtive and indignant at the same time. Running a hand through his thick brown hair, he blamed Green ('If Philip had assisted us, we could have saved BHS'), the Pensions Regulator ('We were absolutely held to ransom'), Darren Topp ('He took it upon himself to start trying to wriggle his way into the ownership structure of the business') and Michael Hitchcock ('He is a man of many words and very little delivery'). At times, Chappell sounded almost convincing in his deep public-school tones. But he grew testy when Jeremy Quin, a Conservative MP, asked about the £1.5 million loan from Retail Acquisitions that paid off his parents' mortgage. '[BHS] was a company that was losing millions of pounds a month,' Chappell protested. To gasps from the audience, he added, 'What difference would that have made in the grand scheme of the thing? This is a sideshow in what you're discussing.'

By coincidence, Green's frenemy Mike Ashley had appeared in Parliament a day earlier to answer questions about the allegedly 'Victorian' working conditions at Sports Direct's warehouse complex in Shirebrook, Derbyshire. At the end of the session, Iain Wright asked Ashley if he had really wanted to buy BHS. 'I think it's a "no comment",' Ashley's PR man interjected. But the childish billionaire overruled him. 'I cannot resist it,' Ashley blurted out. 'One hundred per cent, I wanted to buy BHS. Now I am going to get told off by everybody.'

On 30 June 2016, the queueing started early outside the Wilson Room in Portcullis House. At 9 a.m., journalists, lawyers and PR advisers filed in past a portrait of the former Labour chancellor Denis Healey, filling every available seat. The air buzzed with anticipation. At 9.17 a.m., the committee room doors swung open and Sir Philip Green lurched in like an old bull into a ring, his face twisted with contempt for the politicians seated in front of him. He had just had a ninth stent fitted into his coronary arteries, and he looked short of breath. Green had been coerced into coming with threats that his wife would be summoned from Monaco otherwise. In the days before the hearing, there had been intense speculation that he would use the stage to announce a blockbuster payment to BHS's pensioners. Frank Field had even told the *Financial Times* that he and his colleagues would 'just laugh' at Green if he put less than £600 million on the table. Field and the pensioners were in for a rude surprise.

His eyes flicking from side to side, Green started off with a statement that was half apology, half excuse. 'Nothing is more sad than how this has ended,' he said. 'I hope during the morning you will hear that there is certainly no intent at all on my part for anything to be like this. It didn't need to be like this. I just want to apologize to all the BHS people who have been involved.' Then he slipped seamlessly into his trademark mode of menacing banter.

Half an hour in, Green broke off from a discussion about his management methods to snap at the stunned Tory MP Richard Fuller, who had been sitting quietly, 'You just want to stare at me? It's just uncomfortable, that's all.' Later, when Fuller suggested that Green should have modified BHS's business model to protect it from online rivals, the billionaire shot back, 'Without wishing to be rude, maybe in your next career you should try retail.' Karen Buck, a polite Labour MP, pressed Green to remember whether the BHS trustees had asked for more than £10 million a year in pension contributions. Claiming that he had no idea, he said, 'You must have been a mind reader in your previous life. Were you?' Richard Graham, an astute, silver-haired Conservative, pursued Green over a commitment he was said to have made to the then pensions minister Steve Webb. 'Sir, which bit of "don't remember" is difficult for you to listen to?' Green asked. He then advised Jeremy Quin, a podgy shires Tory, 'Put your glasses back on – you look better with your glasses on.'

Fuller challenged Green over his behaviour. 'You have complained about Mr Quin putting his glasses on or not,' he said. 'Oh, I didn't complain,' Green groaned. 'I was having a joke with him. Lighten up.' Fuller continued, 'I just wonder, is that your usual pattern of behaviour, particularly with your directors?' Green chose not to answer. 'Shall we carry on?' he sniffed. The tomfoolery continued. When Iain Wright asked Green what had stopped Mike Ashley's Sports Direct rescue of BHS, Green pulled out his chequebook and brandished it. 'One of these,' he said.

The tycoon said he had not 'brought twenty people here to share the blame with me' – although the front row was packed with his supporters, including Neil Bennett and Owen Clay. Green emphasized, 'It's not my style to blame anybody else.' Then he sprayed blame around liberally. He suggested that Dr Margaret Downes, the pension trustees and their advisers had made 'some stupid, stupid, idiotic mistakes'. He said he 'one million per cent' would not have sold BHS to Chappell without Goldman Sachs' seal of approval. He even blamed me – 'one of our lovely journalists in the room' – for damaging Chappell's chances of restoring BHS's credit insurance by 'beating him around the head every Sunday'. One of the most telling moments came when Green protested, 'I can't be buyer and seller [at the same time], can I?' 'Can't you?' asked Iain Wright, pointedly. Arguably, through his direct and indirect financing of Chappell's acquisition, that was exactly what he had been.

There were two intervals. Green's advisers made him eat to keep his blood sugar levels up. According to one of Bennett's former colleagues, the billionaire also made two calls – one to Tina Green and one to Prince Albert of Monaco, who was following the proceedings, anxious about the reputational impact on the principality. Towards the end of his marathon six-hour grilling, when the air in the committee room was heavy with fatigue, Green smiled teasingly at his interrogators. 'I wrote something down on my pad, because I thought I might forget it,' the king of the high street said, clearly relishing this late moment of theatre. 'Whether it's right or wrong to say it – I thought about "Should I? Should I not?" – I'm going to. Envy and jealousy, my doctor told me, are two incurable diseases. I have done nothing wrong.'

Green larked about and haggled right until the final whistle. As the clock ticked towards 3 p.m., Iain Wright declared that he wanted to wrap up the session in the next thirty seconds. 'Forty-five – come on, Iain,' Green implored him, to laughter from the audience. 'Let's do one deal.'

By Green's standards, the expletive-free performance had been a success. In the eyes of ordinary people watching on TV, it was comically terrible. An acquaintance said that Green was shocked by the next day's coverage. Quentin Letts, the *Daily Mail*'s sketch writer, described it as 'six hours of nasal niggle'. He wrote, 'Here, in this bloated, truculent billionaire, hands caramel from the sundeck of his superyacht, sat the caricature of a capitalist system which . . . allows tycoons great freedoms.'

There were two further sessions as a coda to the main event. In the first, a dead-eyed and unsmiling Alex Dellal gave crisp but unexpansive answers about the money he had made from Retail Acquisitions (Green's estimate was a staggering £16 million). Dellal was followed by a red-faced and nervous Paul Sutton, who tried and failed to have two of his victims removed from the audience. Sutton claimed, 'I maintain to this very day that the way we were doing it, if it hadn't been stopped, [BHS] would be part of a much larger company now on the stock exchange. It wouldn't be in the terrible place it's in right now.' Last came Neville Kahn, Green's adviser at Deloitte. Kahn put on a skilful performance, playing down his involvement in the sale of BHS and insisting that he was not part of Green's inner circle. Chappell, who was watching the live stream, texted me angrily, 'Neville was up to his neck with this whole deal.'

In the second coda session, one of Europe's most powerful investment bankers was humbled. Looking surly and uncomfortable, Mike Sherwood of Goldman Sachs described how the bank had helped Green for free because it was hoping for a highly paid role in an eventual sale or float of Topshop. 'It is obvious to everybody there is a very significant asset that Sir Philip Green owns and at some point he may decide to do something with it,' Sherwood blundered. 'That was the transaction that we would like to hang around the hoop for.'

The second session ended with a recall of Paul Budge and Chris Harris, two of Green's lieutenants, who were joined by Brett Palos, the billionaire's stepson. Frustrated with their evidence, which he perceived to be evasive, Frank Field finally exploded. 'A huge amount of money has gone out of these companies, gone to one family,' he said. 'Literally, Mr Budge, we have heard evidence that if it was in a novel, you would get the novel thrown back at you by the publisher because it was unrealizable ... It is preposterous, what has been presented to us as joint committees, and we are left with 11,000 people's jobs being destroyed, despite all the protestations that they are the most important people in the world to Sir Philip.' Field concluded his rant, 'We have had nothing but people coming here, trying to disguise what has really gone on. That is the truth of it, is it not? You are past masters at this.' Harris protested that Field's comments were 'disrespectful'. It was a bitter ending.

The select committee's report a month later was excoriating. It condemned Green for the 'systematic plunder' of BHS, accusing him of 'fantastically enriching himself and his family, leaving the company and its pension fund weakened to the point of the inevitable collapse of both'. It said he had rushed through the sale to Chappell, an 'inept and self-serving' buyer who was 'manifestly unsuitable' to be the director of a company. The report described Retail Acquisitions' thirteen-month ownership as 'shambolic' and said that Chappell and his cronies had 'used BHS for their personal gain as it crumbled around them'. Lord Grabiner was branded 'the apogee of weak corporate governance'. Goldman Sachs was criticized for having exercised 'authority without accountability'. Grant Thornton and Olswang were said to have been 'content to take generous fees' for providing Chappell with 'an expensive badge of legitimacy'. The report, which Iain Wright described as 'my Sgt Pepper' – the Beatles' masterpiece – concluded, 'Sir Philip Green, Dominic Chappell and their respective directors, advisers and hangers-on are all culpable. The tragedy is that those who have lost out are the ordinary employees and pensioners. This is the unacceptable face of capitalism.'

It was an unprecedentedly damning verdict from a select committee, and it drew support from voices that were not typically critical of free-market capitalism. The *Daily Mail* ran the front-page headline, 'The Shaming of Sir Shifty'. Theresa May, who had become the second female Conservative prime minister less than a fortnight earlier following the Brexit earthquake, said the BHS scandal reinforced the need to tackle 'corporate irresponsibility'. The Institute of Directors singled out Lord Grabiner, describing the lack of oversight during the sale of BHS as 'staggering'. Chappell seemed to shake it all off like water from a duck's back. He continued to take my calls, breezily explaining that he had voted for Brexit in protest against the Westminster elite that had just torn apart his ownership of BHS.

Green continued to fight back aggressively against the *Sunday Times'* coverage as the gory details of his arrangements with Chappell dripped out. When I picked up the story of the £10 million gifted to Retail Acquisitions in June 2015 – compensation for the cancelled Marylebone House deal – Green said, 'It's like a blind darts player throwing darts at me. I can't be bothered with it, OK? You know the rules. You print it and get it wrong, you get sued.' He added, 'You're a dishonest bloke and you just want to fuck me. OK? And that's all you've done all along. Right? . . . Maybe you'll be in the next cell to [Chappell] in the end.' The conversation ended with Green saying, 'Have we done anything illegal? Write what the fuck you like.'

I had always had a good relationship with Neil Bennett, his PR man, but it disintegrated over the course of that summer. Seemingly in hock to his powerful client, Bennett refused to answer calls or emails from the *Sunday Times*. In August, after I perceived that Bennett had lied about a story on one of the rare occasions when he had responded, I wrote a serrated diary piece juxtaposing the PR man's £20,000-a-week retainer, and the holiday home he had just bought in Bordeaux, with the fortunes of BHS's staff. Bennett emailed one of my colleagues wishing me a 'slow and exquisitely painful death'. Then he sent me an emotional email about Green.

It said, 'He's made a series of bad business mistakes, which he's admitted. But he's not the two-dimensional villain you see him as. I see him very differently. He's someone who's beaten the odds time and again – failed at school, lost his father when young, suffered multiple business setbacks and almost died from a massive heart attack in 1995. He always comes back and he will this time. Will he use me and discard me? Maybe – as you say I've been completely useless in defending him against you and your competitors. But it's worth noticing that his closest staff and advisers have been around him for years. Why? In the words of Sean, his security guard, "He's more than a father to me."'

In fairness, Bennett was under huge pressure from Green. The billionaire rang his PR adviser on an almost hourly basis to rage about the relentless coverage. Tina and their son, Brandon, took over at weekends, haranguing Bennett via email about his failure to douse the flames. A close friend said that Tina was 'hysterical' during those months. Like her husband, she had always believed that Britain was too small-minded to give the Greens the recognition they deserved. In 2005, she told an interviewer, 'I think, unfortunately, in this country there's a lot of jealousy. No one likes a winner, they just want the bad news. I just find it very sad.' Tina liked to see herself as the godmother of Monaco's social scene, and she was known to admonish those who forgot to address her as Lady Green. Now she found herself splashed across the tabloids as Lady Shifty. The *Daily Mail* mocked her for cancelling a 'yacht-warming party' planned to coincide with the Monaco Grand Prix because of her husband's forthcoming parliamentary appearance, and paparazzi snapped her the moment she went to inspect the new *Lionheart* at a harbour in Malta with her dog ('Another Tough Day in Paradise for Lady Shifty' was the *Mail*'s take). There was even speculation that Tina might be stripped of her Monaco residency by the ruling Grimaldi family as part of an effort to dispel the Somerset Maugham view of the tax-free principality as 'a sunny place for shady people'.

As much as attacks on Tina hurt him, Chloe was Sir Philip

Green's Achilles heel. He had been the first to give his daughter a bottle when she was born in London's exclusive Portland Hospital, and she had been the only one who could displace Cassius, his cat, as the object of his affections. Chloe described herself as a daddy's girl. Green admitted that she could wrap him around her little finger. At the outset of the crisis, the *Daily Mirror* criticized Chloe for partying at the Coachella festival in California and the Chiltern Firehouse restaurant in London. As BHS's 164 stores closed and the administrators sold off everything – including clothes rails, fridges from staff rooms and mannequins – the *Mail* ran pictures of Chloe 'pouting alongside models and millionaires' in St-Tropez with a pink Chanel bag, which cost £2,000 – 'the same sum [as] the redundancy packages BHS workers were given'.

Anger was surging through BHS's 11,000 staff. Lin Macmillan, who had been a manager at BHS's stores in Aberdeen and Lincoln in the 1980s, called the situation 'morally repugnant'. She started a campaign titled 'Sell the yachts, pay the pensions'. A group at the South Shields store posted a picture of themselves holding a sign saying 'Fuck Phil Green'. Robert Stroud, a shop worker who had been about to celebrate his twentieth anniversary at the branch in Worthing, told his local paper, 'I feel like I have been chucked out on the scrapheap.'

Green had promised to 'sort' the BHS pension hole in his parliamentary appearance, but no deal materialized. As he and Tina set sail from Malta for their first summer cruise aboard *Lionheart*, sunbathers stuck up two fingers and bared their backsides. Reporters chased the yacht around the Greek islands. Green was too overweight to go jogging, but his doctor advised him to take a morning walk wherever possible. In mid-August, Sky News caught him as he was about to board a tender back to *Lionheart* after one of his strolls. 'I'm going to call the police if you don't go away,' Green growled at Sky's reporter, David Bowen. 'Which bit are you not understanding? Go away!' Richard Caring watched the clip of his former business partner's humiliation on repeat from the comfort of his superyacht, laughing hysterically with a few friends, revelling in schadenfreude. Three weeks later, Simon Brodkin, a comedian known as Lee Nelson, managed to sail up to *Lionheart* on a dinghy and attach a banner renaming the 300-ft ship 'BHS Destroyer'. The Greens had once commanded fear and respect. Over the course of five months they had become the punchline to a national joke.

Jeff Randall watched his old friend's reputational self-immolation with despair. Randall had enjoyed a long and successful career as a journalist, culminating in six and a half years as Sky News's chief business inquisitor. Having retired in March 2014 and taken a non-executive job with the engineering company Babcock, he was keen not to involve himself in the row publicly. But from the start, behind the scenes Randall had urged Green to defuse the pension crisis by depositing a big sum into an escrow account pending the resolution of his dispute with the regulator. One day, Liam Halligan, a friend of Randall's at the *Daily Telegraph*, texted to ask if he would speak to Frank Field. Randall had known Field since the late 1980s, when Andrew Neil, editor of the *Sunday Times*, commissioned him to write a column as 'the intelligent voice of the left'. (Field was unfashionably centrist and had twice survived deselection by the hard-left group Militant, joking that his patron saint was Lazarus.) Field had helped Randall with a documentary on pensions in 2007, and the two respected each other. Randall agreed to try to bridge the gulf between Green and his fiercest critic.

Randall thought Green would have to offer about £350 million to solve the BHS crisis. He advised his friend to settle early and present himself as a hero, rather than be dragged to the inevitable solution by a baying mob months later. Field initially said he would be prepared to bless an offer of £400 million as 'the gold standard of pension rescues'. Randall considered hosting a peace summit for the tycoon and the Labour MP at his home in Essex, but the negotiations never got that far. Green refused to budge above £280 million, and he blew up every time Field made a comment in the press. 'You can tell your mate Frank Field to fuck off,' he shouted to Randall down the phone. Randall's heart sank as Field demanded £600 million on the eve of Green's select-committee appearance – then Green put on his brash performance, which Randall told friends was 'suicidal'. Any hope of a rapprochement died when Field described Green as 'much worse' than Robert Maxwell in a radio interview. Green threatened to sue. Field told *The Times*, 'I thought he would actually do the decent thing. I misread him totally.'

Randall thought Field's rhetoric was unhelpful, but he was more frustrated by Green's refusal to listen. He was heard to say that it was 'like watching a child put its hand in the fire'. The sharp judgement of the cheeky trader he had first met in the late 1980s seemed to have been warped by decades of power and money. A coolness descended over their friendship.

Green had apparently been surrounded by 'yes' men for so long that he had lost all perspective. He had grown used to bending bankers, business partners, newspapers and prime ministers to his will. In the aftermath of BHS, he refused to accept that reality itself would not bend. Green commissioned a seventy-nine-page legal opinion from four barristers, including the renowned Lord Pannick, dismissing the select committee's process as 'unfair'. He gave an interview to ITV's Robert Peston, saying he was 'very, very, very sorry', before complaining, 'This has been a horrible, horrible, horrible period.' The qualified display of contrition was not enough to stop MPs voting two days later, on 20 October, to take away his knighthood. It was less a parliamentary debate, more a free-for-all. David Winnick, a Labour MP, decried him as 'a billionaire spiv who has shamed British capitalism'. Iain Wright, the Labour co-chair of the BHS committee, came out with a quote that made even Green's critics wince. 'He took the rings from BHS's fingers,' Wright said. 'He beat it black and blue. He starved it of food and water and put it on life support. And then he wanted credit for keeping it alive.'

16.

The Aftermath

On a chilly, overcast afternoon in January 2017, I went to see three of the former South Shields BHS staff members who had held up the defiant sign when their shop closed telling Sir Philip Green where to go. Over sandwiches and soup in a café overlooking the Tyne, Jean Costello, Tracey Headley and Liz Lloyd – bright, chatty women in their fifties – reminisced about the sense of community that grew up around their store. Headley and Lloyd had known each other since junior school. They met Costello, who described herself as 'the gobby one', on the first training day when the shop opened in October 2005. 'We've been through personal tragedies, we've been through nice life events and we've always been there for each other,' Costello said. 'I lost my son, tragically, and they were so supportive.'

The three friends described the department store as a kind of community centre. 'There were people who didn't come in to buy – they came in to see us for a chat,' Lloyd said. 'They'd bring photos of their holiday and that.' They laughed at stories about smuggling in saveloys to eat and wearing beach clothes on a particularly hot summer's day in protest at the lack of air conditioning. The tone turned sadder as they remembered the last few days in July 2016. 'We stood at all the windows with the mannequins and customers were going past and taking photographs,' Headley said. 'One old couple – they weren't even from Shields, they were on a day trip – took photographs and went to get them developed from their phones. I don't even know how they found us, but they came to the pub and gave them to us.'

Costello said, 'Philip Green doesn't realize the human side of what he's done. It's not just about the business, it's about everything that's gone, that we've been used to for eleven years. It's hard to change your life around.' Two angry questions were on all of their lips: when was Green going to settle the pension deficit? And why was it taking so long?

There was undoubtedly an element of truth to the complaints Green voiced about the maze he had to find his way through. Pension funding is complicated and changeable, and the regulator could be a bureaucratic, cumbersome negotiating partner. In his parliamentary grilling, Green had said, 'The regulator has never found my number in three years . . . They've been looking at the scheme since '13. Do you think it is reasonable that [Lesley Titcomb, its boss] shouldn't have telephoned us, emailed us or had any contact in three years?'

But Green's desire to pay the lowest possible price and his lack of empathy for the BHS pensioners dominated the headlines. His loathing for the establishment was also a strong subplot. A friend thought Green became distracted by the Punch and Judy show with Frank Field to such an extent that he forgot the Pensions Regulator was actually the arbiter of any deal. 'He was the dog who lost sight of the rabbit,' the friend said. In November 2016, the frustrated watchdog launched legal action against Green and Dominic Chappell, sending them 325-page 'warning notices' setting out its case. In February 2017, a month after Jean Costello and her friends demanded to know what was stopping him, Green and the regulator finally announced a resolution. Green agreed to pay up to £363 million to save the BHS schemes from entering the Pension Protection Fund. The rescue deal, codenamed Project Atlantic, offered BHS's 20,000 pension-fund members 88 per cent of their original benefits, versus the 75 per cent they would have received in the PPF. The big winners were ten former senior managers – Green's old lieutenants – who would have seen their generous pensions capped at £33,700 a year by the PPF. They were now guaranteed almost full payouts of up to £100,000 a year.

This was nine months after the start of the crisis. As Jeff Randall had warned, the huge settlement came far too late to save Green's charred reputation. The regulator's legal case had never been proven, but the public perceived that he had been dragged to the negotiating table kicking and screaming, and signed the cheque with a gun held to his head. The *Daily Mail* 'pardoned' Green and revoked the Sir Shifty title, saying he had 'belatedly' done the decent thing. The *Sunday Times* asked, 'What Next, Sir Philip?* (*Yes, He Keeps the Knighthood)'. But former BHS workers were unimpressed, and Frank Field said, 'Anybody who can't walk down the street in their own country without bodyguards . . . you have to question whether they ought to have a knighthood.'

Even in death, BHS was the subject of unseemly squabbling. Chappell accused the administrators at Duff & Phelps of acting as Green's 'ponies', saying, 'They do exactly what Philip tells them to do.' Duff & Phelps brought in Hilco, the restructuring firm that had been Green's 'jockey' on the break-up of Allders, to liquidate BHS. Phil Duffy of Duff & Phelps insisted there was no improper relationship with Green, and Hilco's Paul McGowan said that his firm had won the work in a competitive tender. But the Pension Protection Fund, BHS's biggest creditor, pushed for the appointment of a second administrator who would be independent of Green. FRP Advisory, brought in at the PPF's urging, fought a tug-of-war with Green over the £35 million charge he still held against BHS's assets. Despite the endless column inches written about his greed, the billionaire was still keen to recoup the money. The PPF believed his charge was invalid, and it wanted the £35 million to be distributed evenly among all BHS's creditors. Green eventually backed down in the face of a legal action started by FRP.

The characters who had contributed to his downfall scattered after the BHS scandal. Chappell retreated to his Grade I-listed manor house in Dorset. He refused to return the £3 million he had received from Retail Acquisitions' £7 million haul, telling BBC's *Newsnight* it was a 'drip in the ocean compared to the money that had been needed to turn around BHS'. In spite of the huge profit he had made, Chappell still seemed to have financial problems. Two months before BHS collapsed, he asked Alex Dellal for a short-term personal loan of £150,000 to meet a tax bill. At the time of his select-committee appearance in June 2016, £75,000 was outstanding, and Dellal had served a formal demand. Iain Wright asked Chappell, 'Are you going bankrupt again?' 'No I'm not, no,' he said with an awkward smile that turned into a grimace.

Neighbours occasionally saw Chappell pulling up in his new Bentley outside 10 Castle Street, the private members' club in Cranbourne. But a stream of embarrassing stories poured out in the wake of BHS's failure. Chappell was reported to have evicted his brother, Damon, from his parents' home in Marbella after persuading them to transfer ownership to him (he said Damon had struggled to pay the service charge and that he had helped his brother move to a cheaper property). He was banned from driving for six months for speeding, having pleaded unsuccessfully with magistrates that he would be unable to take the train because he suffered 'abuse' from fellow passengers. Steve Rodger, Chappell's former business partner in Cadiz, threatened to file a 'denuncia' – a legal complaint – over the €368,000 of allegedly unauthorized payments he had taken from the oil depot. Chappell was arrested and released by HM Revenue & Customs over more than £500,000 of unpaid taxes on his BHS gains – less than a month after he was spotted viewing a £1 million Grade II-listed Georgian townhouse in Blandford Forum, which he said would be for his parents. (In the end, he didn't go ahead with the purchase.) At the time of writing, Chappell had been found guilty on three charges of failing to hand over information to the Pensions Regulator. The judge overseeing the case described some of the former owner's evidence as 'incomprehensible' and 'not credible'. He was fined £87,000, but told the court he had no money. Chappell said he had a monthly income of up to £3,000 from a job working as a consultant to a small cosmetics company, but that his outgoings reached almost £9,000 for rent on his mansion, a finance agreement on a Range Rover and school fees for his two children. He said, 'I'm an entrepreneur. It's the nature of the business. There are boom times and slack times.' The watchdog was continuing to pursue Retail Acquisitions for up to £10 million over the BHS pension deficit. BHS's administrators, having put Retail Acquisitions into liquidation after a lengthy battle, were trying to recover the £1.5 million loan that paid off Chappell's parents' mortgage – although he had switched the security from the property in Sunbury-on-Thames to a plot of land in Portugal. Shortly before publication, the Insolvency Service announced that it would seek to ban Chappell and three others – including his father, Joe – from acting as directors for up to fifteen years. Green was not among those targeted. Chappell said in a texted statement that he was 'extremely angry' at the process and considered it an 'outrage' that 'Phillip [sic] Green has managed to slip his way through the net'.

Eddie Parladorio resigned from Retail Acquisitions a month after BHS went into administration. He kept the £1.5 million he had banked and set up a new legal practice, Hanover Bond. One of his first clients was Nicola Tarrant, girlfriend of the convicted fraudster Paul Sutton. Tarrant fought – unsuccessfully – to stop Sutton's creditors taking over B52 Investments. Sutton told me that he was 'really fed up with the way the whole thing's gone'. He and Tarrant vanished, although victims of the B52 Investments scam reported having seen them in Windsor and Belgravia.

Stephen Bourne and Mark Tasker gave back their shares in Retail Acquisitions following the scandal. The professionals, who had been handed 2.5 per cent each in December 2014 as an inducement to join Chappell's board, wrote to Parladorio's old law firm, Manleys, in May 2016, 'Given the recent widespread reports of alleged wrongdoing at the company in relationship to its ownership of BHS in the period after we resigned as directors, we wish to sever all remaining involvement.' Bourne carried on working as a corporate adviser. Tasker continued to run the commercial department at Bates Wells Braithwaite. Paul Martin remained at Grant Thornton. David Roberts, who stayed at Olswang, received a fiery letter from Linklaters on behalf of Green, accusing him of helping Retail Acquisitions break covenants by taking money out of BHS to pay fees. In any case, Olswang merged with the law firms CMS

Cameron McKenna and Nabarro in May 2017 and the Olswang name disappeared.

Darren Topp and Michael Hitchcock, perhaps gluttons for punishment, both moved to L. K. Bennett, the struggling women's fashion brand favoured by the Duchess of Cambridge. Topp joked that it was the first job his wife had actually wanted him to take. He and Hitchcock had bonded through the tribulations of the Retail Acquisitions days, and they were firm friends, although Hitchcock stood down in November 2017, having only ever planned to do the job as an interim assignment. Topp resigned as chief executive five months later.

The publicity over Green's looting of BHS was embarrassing for Richard Caring, given his secret roles as both shareholder and supplier in the early days. Green had drifted apart from his old business partner after 2006, when Caring sold his shares in BHS and started buying trophy assets such as Annabel's nightclub in Mayfair. Caring had tried to shake off his past as a grubby rag trader, spending more time in Los Angeles on Soho House business. His wealth was estimated at £700 million by the Sunday Times Rich List, but he let it be known that he was worth far more. Soho House insiders laughed about an incident that became famous internally as 'the billionaire dick-off', when Caring shouted at Ron Burkle, the majority shareholder, during a dispute, 'Ron, I'm a billionaire too, you know!'

Caring refused to appear before the BHS select committee, but he was forced to dispatch two letters from his rarefied bubble confirming that he had held a secret 22 per cent stake in BHS through two offshore funds, which received £93 million in dividends. Caring wrote, 'Given that I was a supplier to most of the brands in the high street, the belief was that it would be better if it was not public knowledge that I was both a supplier and shareholder to a retail competitor.'

The attention was particularly unwelcome because Caring had just left his wife of forty-five years, Jackie, for a Brazilian model half his age, Patricia Mondinni. He had moved out of the Palace of

Versailles in Hampstead and into a ten-bedroom house in St John's Wood with Mondinni and their toddler son (they had a daughter the following year). The split upset many of Caring's older friends, who liked Jackie and complained that he no longer wanted to socialize with people over forty. It even caused problems with some of the crew on his yacht, *Silver Angel*, who apparently bridled at the peremptory way their new mistress handed out orders. In one anecdote, on a trip to the Maldives during an outbreak of the Zika virus, Mondinni asked the crew to stand around the edge of the boat with fly swatters to fend off any mosquitos that might come their way. The captain persuaded her that it would be impractical.

The more minor lieutenants who had helped Green build his empire went to ground. Paul Coackley, who had retired after his long career at the billionaire's side, declined to speak about the decade or so he had spent liaising with BHS's pension trustees. I tried to have a conversation with Coackley's former sidekick, John Readman, Green's old property director, who had also retired – perhaps to spend more time on his yacht, *Marmalade of Manchester*. 'That's not going to happen,' Readman said, before hanging up.

The individual who suffered the most was Mike Sherwood, Green's one-time confidant at Goldman Sachs. As recently as October 2015, Sherwood and Anthony Gutman, his right-hand man, had been instructed by Green to start planning a stock-market listing or sale of Topshop – the big deal for which they had been 'hanging around the hoop'. The plan died as the BHS scandal exploded and Topshop's sales slipped into reverse. Goldman was shown to have made, sent or held ninety-five calls, emails and meetings involving the sale of BHS. As the fire raged, 'Woody' was caricatured as Green's Mini-Me in the *Sunday Times*, complete with an Austin Powers graphic. He resigned as Goldman's joint European head in November 2016, five months after his parliamentary grilling. Sherwood insisted that his decision to leave was unrelated to BHS. Some Goldman insiders thought it was the final straw for the bank's New York management after a series of misjudgements, including the hostile Marks & Spencer bid in 2004, a controversial arrangement to help Greece massage its finances for entry into the Eurozone and work for the Gaddafi-era Libyan Investment Authority, which resulted in an embarrassing $1.2 billion court case alleging that Goldman bankers had paid for private jets and prostitutes (Goldman successfully defended the case).

Sherwood described BHS as a 'blip' in his thirty-year career. He said he was 'ready to live [his] life at a different pace for a little while'. But observers were struck by the way Green had thrown Goldman under the bus during his hearing. Green had gone as far as to read out the ingratiating email from Gutman, Sherwood's trusted deputy, congratulating Chappell on his acquisition. A property financier who admired Sherwood said of his treatment, 'There was nobody Philip Green wouldn't fuck to get this deal done.'

17.

Trouble in Arcadia

O wad some Power the giftie gie us
To see oursels as ithers see us!
It wad frae mony a blunder free us,
An' foolish notion:
What airs in dress an' gait wad lea'e us,
An' ev'n devotion!

*Robert Burns, 'To a Louse, on Seeing One on a
Lady's Bonnet, at Church', 1786*

Sir Philip Green's sixty-fifth birthday party was not branded PG65, nor was it held in Cyprus, the Maldives or Mexico. Instead, eighty friends gathered in China Tang, the Chinese restaurant in the basement of the Dorchester hotel, on a Wednesday evening in March 2017. Leonardo DiCaprio and Kate Hudson were conspicuously absent. The crowd included Tess Daly and her husband, Vernon Kay; the singer Alesha Dixon and her boyfriend, Azuka Ononye; and the ex-footballer Jamie Redknapp and his then wife, Louise. Business guests included the property investors Bruce Ritchie and Robert Tchenguiz, both of whom were present – along with Green and his son – at the scandal-hit Presidents Club dinner a year later, when hostesses were alleged to have been groped and propositioned by some of the businessmen. Kate Moss made a late appearance.

According to someone who attended, Chloe, Brandon and Tina made emotional speeches. Green, who had settled with the Pensions Regulator a fortnight earlier, joked that handing over a chunk of his fortune had been 'cheaper than getting divorced'. By Green's standards, it was a low-key affair. 'It was appropriate for what had happened,' the guest said.

It was some nine months since Green and I had spoken. In our last conversation, deep in the crisis following BHS's administration, he had said, 'I'm not dealing with you, because you seem to twist [and] turn everything, and that's all you've done all along.' The day after his pension settlement, I decided to give him another try. 'You've got to stop being an arsehole, then maybe I might talk to you,' he grunted. 'I'm not dealing with the *Sunday Times*. You've been a bunch of arseholes and I've got no reason to want to deal with you.'

A few minutes later he rang back, suddenly flickering towards a more conciliatory tone. 'All you've got to do now, if you want to draw a line under it, is be a big boy, do what I said – and who knows, maybe we draw a line and we start afresh,' he said. 'If you want to keep attacking then fine – I don't give a fuck, to be honest. So you decide . . . For over twenty years, I had a great relationship with the *Sunday Times*. You've done your best in the last year, as you know, to trash it.' I remarked that he sounded more upbeat than he had during our last meeting. 'I'm not upbeat, I'm not downbeat,' Green sniffed. 'I'm just bored.'

There was silence for another six months. On a Friday at the end of September 2017, I had breakfast with Neil Bennett to ask whether his client might cooperate for this book. 'With Philip, you never know,' Bennett said. That afternoon, a withheld number popped up on my mobile. It was an unmistakeable voice. 'Hopefully you've got insurance for the book,' it rasped. The conversation that followed was not unfriendly, although as usual there was an edge to Green's humour. He asked why I hadn't moved to the *Daily Mail*. 'You and Paul Dacre deserve each other,' the billionaire said. He continued, 'Your idea of straight is going around eight bends. What are you laughing about? Eight bends is probably me being limited. It's probably fifty-eight fucking bends, but anyway, never mind . . . I'm a very straightforward bloke. You're very tricky.'

Green complained that Chappell had 'been allowed to get away with murder' by the media, 'just taking the piss out of everybody'. 'Do you think we'd have done business if we'd known he was a scumbag?' he asked. He said that Frank Field was a 'nasty, nasty, nasty, nasty, nasty, twisted individual who's got some personal vendetta'. He moved on to Geoff Cruickshank, the Pensions Regulator's head of intelligence – 'this complete – excuse me – cunt'. Green said he had made his £363 million offer months before it was announced, even before the warning notices were issued the previous November. 'They were dishonest people,' he said. 'Because of Mr Field writing probably north of twenty or twenty-five letters to them, and therefore them being subjected to political pressure and not wanting to be called back to Parliament, they issued the warning notices . . . [But] I took a decision not to go to war with the regulator, on the basis we were trying to settle it. And I thought if we went publicly to war, that would be the end of the movie.'

He had nonetheless enjoyed winding up his tormentors. He described a meeting with ten people at Deloitte's offices where Cruickshank had barely spoken for two hours. Green said he had asked the enforcer, 'Mr Cruickshank, do you play poker? No? That's a shame, because if you look around the table and you can't spot the schmuck, it's you.' He then instructed the 'bird making the notes' to spell schmuck correctly. 'You're going to put this in your book,' Green told me.

The man who was once fêted for turning BHS into a £1 billion business expounded the virtues of the rescue deal he had eventually struck with the regulator. 'If you look at the pensioners and you look at the pecking order, if you go to the top of the tree, there was a guy who was getting ninety thousand quid a year – that was his pension,' he said. 'When all the shit hit the fan, I think he got cut down to thirty thousand. So I called him up, and I said look, I'm sorry, if I got you back to seventy thousand, where would you be? He said I'd be over the moon. You know where I put him back to? He got 80 per cent of the future benefits instead of 100 per cent, but he went back to ninety thousand quid a year. So if Frank Field had 1 per cent decency, instead of wanting to go and always beat me up . . . I think I behaved very well with all these people.'

As I listened, Green exclaimed, 'This is one of our rare sensible conversations, Oliver! There's a lot of jealous, twisted, anti-Semitic, la la la people out there. Right? And there aren't many people that actually turn up with a cheque and write it.' We ended with Green running through his track record: how he had never been in litigation, never refused to pay a supplier, never 'fucked people over'. He seemed to have forgotten his libel case against the *Sunday Times* in 2000 and the legions of BHS suppliers who left after his takeover of the business later that year. Perhaps people have been too scared to complain, I suggested.

'What are they scared of?' Green asked. 'Are they scared because black is black and white is white?' They're probably more scared of your boys in south London, I said, thinking of Leslie Warman and the Amber Day incident in 1992. 'Oliver,' Green tutted. 'Let's leave on an amusing note. If I had any boys in south London, they'd have been round to see you long before now.'

Our ceasefire lasted barely twenty-four hours. That Sunday, I wrote a story about Chris Harris, Green's property director, leaving for a job at John Lewis. I noted that Harris was well regarded in the industry, but I had the temerity to mention his involvement in the BHS saga. I awoke to a text, 'Shame i thought we had made a step forward.' I called Green. 'You've earnt a living off writing about fucking BHS,' he roared. 'Now you want to go and write some stupid fucking book!' The prospect of an interview receded yet further a week later, when Green heard that I was asking around about the loan shark Tony Schneider. 'You really are a sick fucker,' he said, by way of an opening gambit. 'I thought you told me you were going to try and write an intelligent book. I'm not sure you could spell the word intelligent, but never mind. What is it you want to achieve? Nobody's going to buy your fucking book.' I emailed a series of questions to Green before publication, but he declined to reply.

Harris was the latest in a long line of Green lieutenants to leave in the wake of the BHS scandal, although in fairness they all probably had slightly different reasons for moving on. Adam Goldman, the company secretary who had given Chappell his non-disclosure agreement and handled many of Green's responses to Parliament, resigned at Christmas 2016. Lord Grabiner, who had been accused by the select committee of giving Green 'a veneer of establishment credibility', stood down as chairman in July 2017. He was replaced by Baroness Brady, vice-chairman of West Ham United, who started her career working as an assistant to the pornographer David Sullivan. Wesley Taylor, Burton's brand director, walked out in February 2017 after what insiders said was a furious row with Green. Taylor, who is black, then alleged that Green had used racially abusive language on several occasions in the past, and threatened to take him to an employment tribunal. Green denied having made any racist remarks. The two sides settled out of court, and Taylor signed a non-disclosure agreement that barred him from ever speaking about the alleged incidents again. Yasmin Yusuf, the creative director of Miss Selfridge, and Craig McGregor, Topshop's retail director, left the same month. Mary Homer, who had run Topshop since Jane Shepherdson's bitter departure in 2006, went to The White Company a month later. As her replacement, Green hired Paul Price, the merchandising director of Burberry. Insiders immediately speculated on how long the relationship would last when Price's boyfriend, a flamboyant reality TV personality called Fletcher Cowan, posted a cartoon on his Instagram feed of Green shouting 'You're hired' next to a chart of falling sales and profits.

Topshop is on shaky ground. The company's implosion is a development that could pose a far greater threat to Green's empire than BHS. In January 2017, a well-placed source gave me detailed figures for Arcadia Group's performance over Christmas 2016. They showed that Topshop, the engine that had kept Arcadia's weaker brands running for years, was faltering badly. Its like-for-like sales had fallen by 10.9 per cent over the peak season, compared with 6.5 per cent for Arcadia overall. Wholesale orders for Topshop's Ivy Park athleisure collaboration with Beyoncé had come in lower than expected and Topshop's much-hyped American stores were bleeding sales and profits. Anecdotal reports suggested that Topshop's trading at Christmas 2017 was worse. According to property agents, its sales were down by as much as 20 per cent in some shopping centres. In his inimitable patter, Green told friendly journalists that trading was 'shit'.

Green has never understood the power of the internet. Out of greed or pride, he refused to sell Topshop's clothes through Asos. He missed several chances to take over the online platform for a song in its early years. According to a senior Asos insider, he was always too cute, trying to offer cheeky deals such as giving it the right to sell Topshop's fashions in exchange for a 29 per cent stake. The opportunity passed for good as Bestseller, a Danish fashion group run by the billionaire Anders Holch Povlsen, built a 29 per cent blocking stake between 2010 and 2017. As well as dismissing the opportunities Asos could bring Topshop, Green was unable to comprehend why his staff would want to leave for the fashion site. At a *Retail Week* industry event in the late 2000s, the tycoon plonked himself down at the table where Nick Robertson, Asos's founder, was drinking with some of his senior employees. Green reportedly pulled out a wad of cash and waved it at them. 'Right, who wants to come and work for me?' he asked. One of the Asos people cleared his throat. 'Philip, we used to work for you,' he said.

The rise of web retailers like Asos and Boohoo.com is part of the story, but Topshop's alarming decline also speaks to the way Green runs his businesses. Rather than investing for the long term, he digs out mountains of cash, which he ferries back to Monaco. In the same way that BHS was hollowed out by the £423 million of dividends he and his partners took in the early years, the record-breaking £1.3 billion dividend for which Green was so lauded in 2006 did untold damage to Arcadia. It diverted resources from the group and loaded it with expensive interest charges just when the retail market was changing. Topshop's flagship on Oxford Street is still a world-class store, but many of its other shops look tired, and the business has been starved of investment for its digital platform, IT systems and warehousing. An online expert who left in frustration after a year said, 'Anywhere you can imagine where there was a need for money – an ad campaign or whatever – it was all "I'll sort that", and then it was always slashed down. We always took the shit option.' On a more old-fashioned note, a shoe supplier said that deliveries often had to be delayed by up to two months at the start of autumn because Topshop's two outdated distribution centres in Milton Keynes were unable to cope with the seasonal rush of stock. Topshop's health is of critical importance to the 22,000 staff and 11,000 pension savers at Arcadia, whose two funds had a total buyout deficit of almost £1 billion at March 2016 – nearly double the size of BHS's shortfall. The picture is eerily familiar.

The implications stretch across the Atlantic. Green may already have taken handsome profits from Arcadia, but Topshop has been a disastrous investment for Leonard Green & Partners, the American private equity firm that paid £350 million for a 25 per cent shareholding in 2012. LGP has written down the value of its stake, but Jon Sokoloff, its joint managing partner, was so besotted with Green that he negotiated very few rights at the time of the deal. Green promised to shield LGP from responsibility for Arcadia's pension deficit, and both sides reserved the right to call for a sale or stock-market listing of the business after five years. Realizing that he will be unable to leave his empire in the hands of his daughter, Chloe, who is currently dating the 'hot felon' Jeremy Meeks, or his son, Brandon, who has faded into the background, Green has consulted bankers about trying to separate Topshop from Arcadia and market it to Chinese suitors. In early February 2016, in the ominous period before the BHS scandal burst into the open, Green had dinner with Ian Stuart, his senior contact at HSBC, and one of Stuart's colleagues, David Barraclough. The meeting was supposed to have been about the succession conundrum at Arcadia, which had been on the bankers' minds for some time. Little more than two months earlier, in late November 2015, Barraclough had emailed the following to a group of colleagues, including Stuart: 'PG will [soon] be 65 and there are no signs his two children have the slightest ability to move into the business . . . Whilst PG has substantial wealth outside of Arcadia, this equity holding remains his single largest investment. It's a very complex group, close on 2,500 stores in the UK and with no family in the business should PG not be able to properly function. This is a significant financial risk for him. I fully accept dealing with him won't be easy, but he is not getting any younger, he is not immortal and the day is approaching when he has to address succession issues.'

Stuart and Barraclough expected to find Green on typically ebullient form when they gathered for dinner in February 2016, but he seemed distracted and worried. After a few minutes, he blurted out his problems with the Pensions Regulator and told the bankers he wanted to sell up. He offered to meet any prospective Chinese buyer the HSBC men could find, accepting that he would probably have to retain Arcadia's pension funds and offset any proceeds from the Topshop sale against the deficit. Once the most fearsome predator in the retail jungle, Green seemed to have realized that he was encircled and hopelessly outmuscled by stronger rivals like Asos, H&M, Inditex and Primark.

After the dinner, Barraclough sent a briefing note about Green's secret plan to retire from the high street to a group of colleagues, including Philip Noblet, HSBC's joint head of investment banking. It said, 'As emotions were running high, PG's thinking was the need to sell, and having heard my comments . . . [he] sought our assistance and offered to meet any Chinese prospective partner we consider appropriate. After further discussion, PG agreed to source a sale solution. The strategy should be to sell Topshop/Topman separate to the rest of the Arcadia portfolio of lesser brands . . . Whilst the Topshop/Topman sale should be straightforward, he accepts residual Arcadia will be a tougher task and may need to be sold by way of individual brands over a protracted period . . . Mike Sherwood at Goldman's will probably be involved too but PG acknowledges we are best placed to bring an Asia solution.'

A month later, Andrew Judge, another senior HSBC banker, wrote an email to a group of colleagues summarizing the strange puzzle in which Green was trapped. He speculated about putting the whole of Arcadia through an insolvency process, but concluded that would be 'too risky with a £2.5 billion asset [Topshop] being thrown in the air'. 'Stepping back, we have to legally separate Topshop from the leases of all the other brands,' Judge said. 'We will never separate the pension fund – depending upon its position that must be assumed by the buyer – private equity are likely out on that basis – making a standard retail auction (with PE as the underwriters) v difficult. Green needs to stay in for more years . . .'

Barraclough brought up another obstacle to a normal auction. 'I can't see PG adopting a sale process,' he predicted. 'Whatever he decides to do it will be with a very small circle of insiders and . . . the market will only know when the deal is done.'

In February 2018, the *Sunday Times* broke the news that Green was trying to sell all or part of Arcadia to Shandong Ruyi, a Chinese textiles giant that had been on a buying spree for Western brands such as Sandro and Maje. The article said Green was 'thought to have been seeking a buyer for some time' and that he had 'been discussing separating Topshop from Arcadia with bankers from HSBC since at least 2016', as per the meeting with Stuart and Barraclough. It prompted an immediate reaction from Green's parliamentary foe, Frank Field, who wrote to Green urging him to clear any sale in advance with the Pensions Regulator. Field's intervention showed how Green's every move would be subjected to intense political scrutiny after the BHS scandal.

Green was silent for more than twenty-four hours after publication. Then he issued a furious denial through the PR firm Maitland. The tycoon described the article as 'malicious rumour-mongering'. He said the suggestion that he was planning to sell up was 'totally false'. 'We regard this article as further evidence of the journalist Oliver Shah's personal vendetta against Sir Philip and the companies,' the announcement said. 'This is disgusting and his being allowed to use the front page of a prominent Sunday newspaper by his editors for a totally false story and his own personal vanity project [this book] is wholly unacceptable.'

Green followed the statement with a call to my line manager, demanding my sacking. I spoke to him a few days later. 'The story was one million per cent wrong,' Green said. 'Twenty million per cent wrong . . . Let's go to Harley Street tomorrow morning and do a lie detector test, shall we?' He said he had never heard of 'Ring Dong Ding', adding, 'There's no Chinese plot, there's no nothing, we don't know who the fuck they are. Like I told you, somebody maybe bought you a puppy because it's the year of the dog, and you got confused.' When I asked why he was responding so aggressively, he said, 'That's show business.' However, senior Arcadia insiders and sources close to the company confirmed that Green had been in early-stage talks with Shandong Ruyi via an intermediary. One said he was amazed to read the denial statement, adding, 'He's making elementary mistakes, and that's his emotion being allowed to run without talking to a fucking lawyer.'

Green's statement had said it was 'totally untrue' that he had held any discussions with HSBC about any kind of sale. Ian Stuart, who was now UK chief executive of HSBC, provided Green with a personal statement. It said, 'There has been NO dialogue with myself or (to my knowledge – I have checked) HSBC in respect of any sale of any part of the Arcadia Group.' The tycoon and the banker must have been embarrassed when their fulsome denials were splashed across the front page of the *Sunday Times* the following weekend, juxtaposed with details from Stuart and Barraclough's dinner with Green in February 2016.

Topshop, the one-time jewel in Green's crown, would be unlikely to fetch an attractive price now, given its deep-rooted problems – and other loss-making Arcadia brands such as Evans and Wallis would almost certainly have to be put into administration. Green appears reluctant to confront the new reality. At LGP's instigation, Ian Grabiner, Arcadia's chief executive, hired the consultancy firm McKinsey to review how Topshop might be able to compete better online. Green, who famously detests consultants, was said to have erupted fifteen minutes into the final presentation and stormed out of the room, leaving a McKinsey partner close to tears. He came back two hours later and shouted, 'What the fuck are you all still doing here?'

Green's belligerent exterior is a protective shell, grown at a young age in response to his mother's harshness. It conceals a soft underbelly. An old family friend suggested that Green's 'characteristic of barking at everybody' was reminiscent of the boxer Muhammad Ali, 'who started off as a really lovely guy and then found it actually paid to be thought of as Mr Nasty. And the interesting thing is that Philip is still very, very shy.' An associate from his early BHS days described him as 'a big bully boy who really needs a cuddle', and a former senior member of staff at Topshop said, 'If you see him one-to-one and he's calm, there's a guy in there that's so warm and kind. I've seen him pay people's mortgages and school fees. But the outside world doesn't see it because for him it's some kind of weakness.' Frank Kane, a former business editor of *The Observer*, experienced both sides of Green. After Kane's son survived a vicious attack of meningitis, Green became a charitable supporter of the paediatric intensive-care unit that had looked after him at St Mary's hospital in Paddington. Through Jeff Randall, Green acted as the bidder of last resort at the hospital's black-tie fundraising auctions. It was generous in both the financial and personal senses, but it came with strings attached – as Kane discovered when *The Observer* took a critical stance on the second bid for Marks & Spencer. Green called Kane and shouted, 'Why did I give all that fucking money to your boy?'

It is difficult not to feel torn by the contradictions that have defined this brilliant but flawed human being. In the 1980s and the 1990s, Green became the most talented asset-stripper and trader of his generation. His force of personality, hunger and ability to wiggle himself into the middle of other people's deals made him unique. But his later reputation as a master retailer was based on a mirage. BHS's sales never improved meaningfully. The miraculous take-off in profits during the early years of his ownership was fuelled by cost-cutting and Richard Caring's clever sourcing, and the resulting £1 billion valuation placed on the business by the *Sunday Times* was hyped out of all proportion until Green became more myth than man. It gave him the credibility to buy Arcadia. The runaway success story he acquired through sheer luck in Topshop pulled him into the global premier league. Along the way, Green was lured by the sirens of celebrity, becoming the kind of cartoon character his grittier younger self would have despised. He turned into a grotesque self-parody, a ridiculous projection of the many excesses embraced by the Western world in the years before the financial crisis: greed, fame, self-interest and vanity. He was patronized by the likes of Kate Moss and Rihanna, who sunbathed on his yacht and went to his parties; he revelled in their reflected sparkle in return. His ego carried on expanding, untethered from reality, as the shoppers who bought his clothes shrank under the pinch of recession. Green refused to sell his businesses or even acknowledge that his vaunted retail skills were not working, believing his own PR to the last. Finally, when it was far too late, he offloaded BHS and its £571 million pension deficit to a hopeless chancer, catastrophically gambling that his ability to control every piece on the chess board would protect him from the inevitable fallout. He is in danger of making a similar mistake and leaving it too late to sell Arcadia and Topshop.

Beneath his eternal bravado, the man who once seemed to have it all now carries a jaded air. Old friends find it harder to tempt him out for dinner. Lord Rose, who was made a Conservative peer in 2014, said the bantering dynamic they had kept up since the second M&S bid had become strained. 'For some reason, and it's really probably only happened in the last two or three years, our relationship has deteriorated quite badly,' he said, 'and I don't think that has anything to do so much with me rather than him . . . I went on Radio 4 and I gave a quote to several newspapers saying look, he realizes he's made a mistake, he's paid his dues, leave him alone, I don't believe in the village green lynch mob. It's not as if I haven't defended him. But we hardly speak to each other.' Another old acquaintance thought the tycoon had become isolated and lonely, with many of his confidants having moved on or retired. 'I think he's close to exhausted, and the fun has gone out of it,' he said. Green and his wife complain that Britain is full of people who hate wealth and that Monaco is a 'goldfish bowl'. In his November 2015 email, the HSBC banker David Barraclough told colleagues that he expected Green would eventually move to America, where he 'feels he can shelter his family better'. To borrow Theresa May's infamous phrase, he and Tina have become citizens of nowhere.

Looking back on Green's life, I think again of Sir Charles Clore, his childhood hero, and a particular paragraph from one of Clore's biographers. 'I found to my surprise that, pervading every relationship, there was a peculiar aroma of insecurity,' Charles Gordon wrote. 'An entrepreneur's sudden course of action was almost never inspired by logic but almost always by an emotion brought to the surface erupting from a feeling of anxiety, from a sense of insecurity, from a desire to "show them" – them being a member of the establishment, or a partner or a competitor or a family relation. If there is one common trait in every entrepreneur it is that he is a thoroughly insecure animal whose main drive is vanity and whose main passion is a worship for prestige. His need for money is a need for protection.'

How will history judge Clore's foremost student, whose appetite for money and prestige at its peak made his predecessor look like a bit-part player? Green's CV reads like a tour of the high-street graveyard. Forty-one Conduit Street, Bond Street Bandit, Amber Day, Owen Owen, Owen & Robinson, Olympus, Mark One, Shoe Express, Sears, BHS, Allders: he made huge short-term profits from a career of remarkable deals, yet almost everything he touched crumbled into dust, and the riches accrued by his family stand in stark contrast to the redundancy packages collected by the employees. Desperate to prove himself as a retailer in the tradition of Simon Marks and Israel Sieff, he twice tried to buy M&S, and when that failed he held on to BHS and Arcadia for far too long when he should have traded them on quickly, motivated not by logic but by a deep need to show the industry that he was more than a mere corporate raider.

There is a chance that Green will manage to revive or sell Arcadia and spend the rest of his days relaxing on the deck of *Lionheart*, or at the home he has quietly built outside Tucson in Arizona, near the Canyon Ranch weight-loss facility where he jokes that he sheds the same 9lb twice a year. But in the words of a former Arcadia brand director who left after a falling-out with the boss, 'He's not going to take any counsel from anybody, because when he looks in the mirror every morning, all he sees is success – the billionaire Philip Green.' What remains of Green's scorched reputation will depend on the interlinked fates of Topshop, Arcadia and its pension funds. If he continues to ignore reality, BHS's collapse could turn out to be the opening act in an even greater tragedy. Even then, it is far from certain that he would recognize the face staring back in the mirror. In one of our final conversations, Green said, 'When the dust settles, and the correct story, or the true story, or the facts are written properly, people can make a decision, can't they?' I was silent for a moment. 'Right?' he said. 'Let's hope I can get them written before you can.'

Acknowledgements

With this kind of book, some of the greatest thanks must go to people who cannot be named. They know who they are, and I hope they know I am deeply grateful for their help.

Of those who can be named, I would particularly like to thank the following, in more or less alphabetic order: Mary Abinger, Chris Ball and Mark Barnes at News UK, Brian Basham, Judi Bevan and John Jay, George Bingham, Matthew Engel, Steve Frankham, Maisie Glazebrook and Susan Roccelli at *Private Eye*, Rupert Hambro, Henry Hector, David Hellier at Bloomberg, Brian Hill, Richard Hyman, Madeleine Legwinski, Kiki Loizou, John Lovering, Sir Laurie Magnus, George Malde, Andrew Mitchell at the *Sunday Times*, Eric Musgrave, Dominic Prince, John Ralfe, Toni Rauch, John Richards, Lord Rose, Melissa Tarrant, George Vallossian, and Dick and Virginia Withers.